243511

AF854720

12/21 AL

SPECULATIVE BEHAVIOR AND THE OPERATION OF COMPETITIVE MARKETS UNDER UNCERTAINTY

For my parents, Professor Eugene and Roma Guth.

Speculative Behavior and the Operation of Competitive Markets Under Uncertainty

MICHAEL ANTHONY STEPHEN GUTH
Risk Management International

Avebury
Aldershot · Brookfield USA · Hong Kong · Singapore · Sydney

1474

© M. A. S. Guth 1994

All rights reserved. No part of this publication may be reproduced, stored in a retrieval system, or transmitted in any form or by any means, electronic, mechanical, photocopying, recording or otherwise without the prior permission of the publisher.

Published by
Avebury
Ashgate Publishing Company
Gower House
Croft Road
Aldershot
Hants GU11 3HR
England

Ashgate Publishing Company
Old Post Road
Brookfield
Vermont 05036
USA

British Library Cataloguing in Publication Data

Guth, Michael A. S.
Speculative Behavior and the Operation
of Competitive Markets Under Uncertainty
I. Title
338.52

ISBN 1 85628 985 0

Library of Congress Cataloging-in-Publication Data

Guth, Michael Anthony Stephen, 1962–
Speculative behavior and the operation of competitive markets under uncertainty / Michael Anthony Stephen Guth.
p. cm.
ISBN 1-85628-985-0
1. Speculation 2. Capital assets pricing model. I. Title
HG6015.G87 1994 94-35162
332.64'5--dc20 CIP

The author's correspondence address:
Dr Michael A. S. Guth
116 Oklahoma Ave.
Oak Ridge TN
37830-8604
USA

Printed and bound by Athenaeum Press Ltd.,
Gateshead, Tyne & Wear.

Contents

Figures and tables

Acknowledgements

I would like to thank all those who taught me economics and finance. I am grateful for all I learned from them and the inspiration they gave me. I am particularly indebted to Peter Mieszkowski at Rice University, who first sparked my interest in public and corporate finance. Mieszkowski also taught me that economics theory contains few central ideas, which then keep getting repackaged in different forms. Jack Hirshleifer at UCLA generously gave me numerous appointments to discuss developments in speculation theory even though I was not one of his doctoral students. He also helped shape my thinking on modern versus pre-modern depictions of speculation in the literature. My dissertation advisors at the University of Tennessee encouraged me to change my focus from game and economic theory to the operation of financial markets.

Thanks also go to those who wrote chapter commentaries for this book, some of whom worked under very short deadlines: William J. Baumol, Merton H. Miller, Jay H. Levin, Brendan O'Flaherty, Ronald E. Shrieves, Jack Hirshleifer, Robert F. Nau, as well as my co-author for Chapter 6, Robert A. Jarrow. I would have preferred to include a couple reviewer commentaries after each chapter. However, publication deadlines forced me to submit the book manuscript before I received the additional comments.

About the author

Michael A. S. Guth is private consultant on risk management and risk communications to the public based in Oak Ridge, Tennessee, United States of America. Prior to this he worked as an energy economist at the Jet Propulsion Laboratory and Oak Ridge National Laboratory, 1982 - 1986; as an expert system and approximate reasoning specialist at Oak Ridge National Laboratory, 1986 - 1989; as an investment banker with Deutsche Bank Asset Management, Frankfurt, and Credit Suisse First Boston, London, 1989 - 1992; and as an environmental engineering specialist at Oak Ridge National Laboratory, 1992 - 1994. Dr. Guth received his B.A. in economics (with a minor in space physics) from Rice University, Houston; an M.S. in Social Science (mathematical microeconomics) from Caltech, Pasadena; and a Ph.D. in financial economics from the University of Tennessee, Knoxville. He is currently pursuing a law degree at the University of Tennessee with emphasis on complex litigation and securities. He has published more than fifteen articles in refereed journals on such topics as energy economics; expert system design for robotics, reactor control, and war gaming; econometric modeling of inventories; fault tree analysis and probabilistic risk assessment techniques; and financial economics. His work has appeared in such diverse journals as *Journal of Money, Credit, and Banking*, *IEEE Transactions on Reliability,* and *Nuclear Engineering and Design*. This book contains material from Dr. Guth's doctoral dissertation, which he initially drafted in 1984 at the age of 22.

Introduction

One of the best books I read as a graduate student was James Buchanan's *The Theory of Public Goods*, which uses a two-man inhabited island model to illustrate fundamental and often subtle features of public goods, e.g., externalities in production versus consumption. Even without mathematical models, Buchanan's book is filled with thought-provoking ideas on fundamental issues in public finance. This book aims to identify similar fundamental concepts on speculation theory and the operation of competitive markets under uncertainty.

The book strives to interest both the student of uncertainty economics, information economics, and finance, as well as the seasoned theorist. To accomplish this goal, the book contains about 50% summaries of paradigms in the literature and their extensions and about 50% presentation of new material. This book represents how I would organize material for a graduate course on Applied Microeconomics or Topics in Financial Economics. As a teaching tool, I not only expose the student reader to a range of mathematical techniques used in economic theory, but clarify their use as well: differential equations, difference equations, latttice theory, game theory, and probability spaces.

The literature review sections do not merely describe work done by various authors. Instead they focus on a central issue like 'how is the capital gains motive taken into account in the Modigliani-Miller literature' and critically review works with this narrow focus. As a result, I excluded many articles that were not germane. Rather than offering complete literature reviews, I hope that the reader will find this book intellectually stimulating and that chapters from the book can become bases for subsequent investigations into the impact of speculative behavior on various models.

Most professional books on economics and finance assume the reader is fascinated with the topic and would be happy to read about esoterica.

In contrast, I assume that the reader may have only a slight initial interest in the subject-matter, and consequently, often go to lengths to motivate key insights and dramatize the importance of findings in the literature. My enthusiam stems from my doctoral dissertation research.

For graduate students looking for a research area, I commend this topic. Speculation theory cuts across traditional microeconomic/macro-economic barriers, and articles on speculation can be published in a wide variety of economics and finance journals.

This book presents certain aspects of the operation of competitive economies under uncertainty and explores some implications of speculative behavior (the capital gains motive) for the performance of the economy. Economists' continuing interest in the study of competitive economies derives mainly from the close connection between competitive equilibria and Pareto optimal allocations.

The book focuses on the *ex ante* and *ex post* optimality of the competitive equilibrium under uncertainty, the role of homogeneous beliefs/common knowledge beliefs in asset pricing theories, informational price theory, and the idea of rational expectations in the market for a speculative asset. Problems associated with speculation and the optimality of the competitive equilibrium have received considerable attention, particularly in the writings of Roy Radner. By contrast, almost no attention has been paid to the problems the capital gains motive poses for fair market valuation in most asset pricing theories. Grossman and Stiglitz have pioneered work on the information revealed by prices; however, the speculative impacts of these so-called informational price theory models have only recently been explored in feedback effect purchasing models. Similarly, problems with speculation have been mentioned — though inadequately addressed — in the common knowledge and consensus literature.

Chapter 1 begins by defining speculation and its relevance as a research topic for the mid-1990s. Following the definition, we introduce Milton Friedman's hypothesis that speculators profit by buying low and selling high, and thus tend to dampen or stabilize price fluctuations. I then analyze the literature presenting counterexamples of 'profitable destabilizing speculation' both for substantive points and for the modeling techniques employed. Foreign exchange specialists may be most interested in comments toward the end of the chapter on exchange rate stability in the 1970s compared to the 1980s, after speculators had an opportunity to become more experienced with the free market mechanisms. The chapter concludes that profitable speculation can destabilize markets, but its prevalence is largely an empirical question.

Chapter 2 outlines the Arrow-Debreu contingent claims and securities models, which are the starting points for modern uncertainty economics. Arrow's proof of the *ex ante* optimality is reviewed, as well as extensions and welfare discussions of *ex post* optimality. Then a new research vein is introduced that stems from a brief but salient comment by Nagatani (1975) on Arrow's model. Arrow and Debreu justly won Nobel prizes for their pioneering contributions to general equilibrium theory. Yet as we develop at length, the Arrow-Debreu framework contains a few unresolved inconsistencies.

Nagatani showed that the lack of knowledge about future market prices leads to differing allocations in the contingent claims and securities versions of the Arrow-Debreu model. His objection illustrates one example of a larger class of dimensions of uncertainty upon which traders would optimally wish to hedge. This chapter also reviews work on the constrained optimality of the stock market economy.

Chapter 3 presents the contingent claims model of speculation: the Hirshleifer model. Jack Hirshleifer adapted the Arrow-Debreu economy to an intertemporal model of choice under uncertainty with information events. This chapter distinguishes modern depictions of speculation from some of the *ad hoc* models presented in Chapter 1. This chapter benefits from hindsight. We know that critics have focused on Hirshleifer's zero complementarity assumption. By first presenting his model without this assumption and then later introducing it, we can illustrate the value of the general framework as opposed to specific results within that framework. The key elements of the arrival of new information, multiple trading periods so that speculators can buy and resell, and the objects of probability distributions will be discussed. Tirole's rational expectations, single period approach to speculation will be contrasted with Hirshleifer's model.

Chapter 4 introduces the concept of intrinsic uncertainty, which occurs in the absence of common knowledge, and its relation to the standard homogeneous beliefs assumption of finance theory. When individuals in an informed environment have homogeneous beliefs (common priors), they objectively agree; however, they can agree without knowing they agree. With homogeneous beliefs, individuals still face intrinsic uncertainty over unknown beliefs of others. If two people have homogeneous beliefs and their informed posteriors for an event E are common knowledge, then — contrary to the widely held view — these posteriors may be unequal. The two people can agree to disagree. Similarly, various 'no trading propositions' derived as rational expectations equilibria are shown to be inaccurate as stated. Consensus in these differential information models generally requires an agreed common knowledge priors assumption.

Common knowledge beliefs continues as the central theme of Chapters 5 and 6. Chapter 5 focuses on the celebrated Modigliani-Miller (MM) paradigm, which revolutionized corporate finance theory. MM introduced an 'imputed rationality' assumption into their model in 1961, and only one other work appears to have seriously considered the impact of this assumption or the role of common knowledge in the MM paradigm prior to our work. As a surprise to many finance theorists who have begun invoking common knowledge assumptions, we find that the MM paradigm actually does *not* require investor beliefs to be common knowledge. These results should be of interest to many finance theorists who generally assume that asymmetric information destroys the MM results. Chapter 5 then goes on to examine the need for common knowledge beliefs in two other major assset pricing paradigms: the Capital Asset Pricing Model and Ross's Arbitrage Pricing Theory. We also examine claims that heterogeneous beliefs can be incorporated into these asset pricing paradigms.

Chapter 6 addresses the need for common knowledge prior beliefs in the canonical arbitrage pricing model. This chapter contains the most mathematically challenging material in the book. For a large class of arbitrage pricing models, equilibrium requires only weakly homogeneous priors, not common knowledge priors. This class includes models where assets trade solely to collect cash flows and not for potential capital gains. When any trader knows with certainty that an asset poses limited liability, no positive price will exist for the asset. Since uncertainty over the beliefs/market valuations of others plays an important role in real financial markets, we generalize the model class to include this intrinsic uncertainty as a speculative trading motive. After defining common knowledge based on σ-field measurability, we find assets with zero probability of payoff become common knowledge through prices. If the market range is 'complete,' then prices reveal (make common knowledge) information about other traders' beliefs. Finally, certain formulations of option pricing theory implicitly preclude speculation over intrinsic uncertainty.

Chapter 7 examines feedback effects and speculative bubbles in informational price theory. When uninformed traders buy securities because they have inferred from prices that the informed traders are purchasing, a feedback effect is introduced. One of the puzzling features of informational price theory is that although the uninformed traders are assumed to be smart enough to realize the relationship between prices and informed traders' private information, the informed traders are not smart enough to realize how to capitalize on the uninformed traders' feedback effect. This chapter develops a self-enforcing Bayesian Nash equilibrium solution to a game in which the informed group occasionally tries to fool the uninformed traders into believing that asset returns are better than they actually are. Sometimes this deception succeeds. A bubble results, and after the crash is over and the dust has cleared, the informed group turns out to have gained at the expense of the uninformed. All market participants are fully rational and expected payoff maximizers. A 'negative bubble' is also illustrated. The speculative bubbles result from fully rational and expected payoff maximizing behavior by all market participants. Chapter 7 explains how to construct a game theory model as well as a few subtle points on interpreting parameters of the game that may be new to some students.

1 Profitable destabilizing speculation

Economists have sometimes conjectured that speculators profit from buying low and selling high and thus tend to stabilize market prices. Others contend that speculators can earn profits and simultaneously destabilize markets. The possibility of profitable destabilizing speculation (PDS) affects the operation of competitive markets under uncertainty. For if speculators may profitably destabilize, then clearly real world markets can be unstable. However, if destabilizing speculators always lose money, then in a Darwinian sense they will fail to survive.

Our present knowledge of the relation between speculative profits and stability evolved from studies in international economics, price theory, finance, and modern uncertainty theory. Although PDS represents a sustainable, endogenous source for fluctuations and business cycles, macroeconomic theorists (aside from the Chicago School) have largely overlooked the debate. Yet analyzing this conjecture will provide better understandings of the microfoundations of macroeconomics *under uncertainty*. Indeed many post-Keynesian proponents of active fiscal and monetary policies point out the need to counteract such endogenous, destabilizing market forces.

This chapter reexamines the literature on PDS, integrating various aspects of works into the general theory of speculation. While profitable destabilizing speculation has been theoretically depicted, work in this area appears confusing and contradictory. Many of the early uncertainty

---

A condensed version of this chapter was originally published in the *Rivista Internazionale di Scienze Economiche e Commerciali*, Vol. 35:6, June 1988, pp. 523-538. Permission of the *Rivista Internazionale* to reprint this article is gratefully acknowledged.

theorists employed arbitrary doctrines and primitive models which inadequately portrayed a complex phenomenon like speculation. Utilizing the benefit of hindsight and modern analytic techniques, we aim to clarify and develop more formally some of the main themes of the speculation and stability literature.

The text proceeds as follows. Section 1 restates the basic proposition that profit-earning speculators stabilize markets. Since many theorists adopted different speculation and stability definitions, Section 2 attempts to describe the semantic controversy. Next, Section 3 reviews William Baumol's counterexamples, and the comments and criticisms they elicited. Section 4 continues sorting valid from invalid PDS counterexamples. Section 5 discusses some representative empirical findings, and the final section contains conclusions and a summary. The appendices derive results from Baumol's counterexamples, which provide an excellent review for differential equation modeling in economics, and a class of nonlinear excess demand counterexamples. Readers not interested in differential equations and Hilbert spaces can skip the appendices without losing any economic concepts.

1.1. Speculation and Stability: The Friedman Proposition

A number of economists have argued that profit-earning speculators stabilize markets. The argument dates back at least to the Nineteenth Century, e.g., John Stuart Mill advanced the notion in his *Principles of Political Economy*.[1] Ross (1938) criticized Mill's notion and offered a counter argument based on stock market fluctuations.

The argument resurfaced in the mid-1950s, when economists began debating the merits of flexible exchange rates and the stability of a flexible regime as compared with exchange rates pegged to the gold standard. Milton Friedman's contention that profitable speculation tends to stabilize a market shook the conventional wisdom[2] blaming speculators for exchange rate instabilities during the 1920s and Great Depression era. Supporting flexible exchange regimes and a general free market philosophy, Friedman (1953) asserted

> People who argue that speculation is generally destabilizing seldom realize that this is largely equivalent to saying that speculators lose money, since speculation can be destabilizing in general only if speculators on the average sell when the currency is low in price and buy when it is high....A warning is perhaps in order that this is a simplified generalization on a complex problem. A full

analysis encounters difficulties in separating 'speculative' from other transactions, defining precisely and satisfactorily 'destabilizing speculation' and taking account of the effects of the mere existence of a system of flexible rates as contrasted with the effects of actual speculative transactions under such a system. (Friedman (1953), pp. 175, 175n)

An extensive literature then grew out of the question of whether profit-earning speculators could destabilize markets and whether proposed counterexamples had shortcomings that invalidated them.

1.2. The Semantic Controversy

Originally, theorists, such as Friedman, based their analysis on markets without speculation. The theory asserted profit-earning speculators' entry into such a market would stabilize prices. With the development of the modern uncertainty theory framework, we now know that attempting to model a 'nonspeculative' market is fruitless. Chapter 3 illustrates why in an incomplete market, almost everyone is forced to speculate, because claims are not available for their optimal consumption bundle.

Modern uncertainty theory solves comparative-statics issues for speculation via the general equilibrium contingent claims model and standard economic reasoning. The standard format provides individuals with production functions, preferences, time-distributed endowments, etc., and specifies the available market range. Economists then pose comparative-statics questions: e.g., what happens if preferences change?

Unfortunately, economists have no universally accepted economic *dynamics* framework; therefore, no prescribed methodology exists to address issues such as stability, a dynamic concept. Consequently, what theorists might consider unacceptable modern uncertainty comparative-statics, e.g., arbitrarily specified speculative excess demand functions, have frequently shed light on important dynamic stability concepts. In Sections 3 and 4, counterexamples are illustrated that employ these arbitrary methodologies; the text will thus emphasize substance over technique. By keeping an open mind, one may glean an idea or two from these earlier works that can be transposed into a modern framework.

1.2.A. Definitions of Speculation

The first step in reviewing specific examples of PDS is to define our terminology. The classic speculator definition focuses on the capital gains motive. A *speculator* buys (sells) goods under uncertainty, with the intent to resell (repurchase) them after some anticipated favorable price change. We must emphasize that speculators transact in an uncertain environment. When traders profit from purchasing goods and later reselling them at an *a priori* known price, the traders have engaged in arbitrage not speculation. Moreover, speculators traditionally receive no gain from consuming or using these goods, lest speculation be confused with simple expected utility maximization. Kaldor (1939) characterized speculative sales or purchases as those motivated solely by perceived capital gains.

Some theorists maintain Kaldor's definition excludes 'speculation' involved in dynamic consumption or production plans. For example, does a manufacturer 'speculate' by postponing a required input's purchase to realize an expected capital gain? We can clarify our speculation definition by introducing a legal *per se* distinction. To meet the three criteria for *speculation per se*, a person must (1) purchase (sell) a good, (2) face price/profit uncertainty, and (3) transact primarily with a capital gains motive. The manufacturer above did not sell the desired input with the intent of later repurchasing it; therefore, he did not speculate *per se*. Put another way, he could not be charged with speculation *per se*, since one of the three essential elements (purchase) is missing. He did 'speculate' in the sense of attempting to minimize his input costs over time, but this type of behavior lies outside the definition.

The same distinction holds for consumers who 'speculate' by shopping at a particular grocery store or who consider the potential resale value in their house and automobile purchases. We can distinguish between investors who consider a capital good's salvage value and those primarily concerned with reselling the capital good at a profit. The latter group primarily purchases (sells) to realize a capital gain, while the former group is not speculating *per se*. The more a house purchaser weighs the capital gain potential of his investment, as opposed to wanting to capture the benefits from living in a house, the more he acts like a speculator *per se*.

Consider now an individual who has no intention *ex ante* to speculate, but finds he can realize an *ex post* capital gain. The third essential element of our definition - the capital gains motive - does not influence the individual. An *ex post* transactions focus potentially would include nonspeculative capital gains as well, e.g., a Pigou effect.

Particularly in the stock market, differentiating between *ex ante* and *ex post* speculation would sometimes fail to include investors who speculated but did not realize their *ex post* capital gains or losses. Most importantly, a speculation definition based on *ex post* activity would deemphasize the crucial expectations and motives that economists mean when they discuss speculative behavior.

Rather than proceeding with a common speculation definition, from which theorists might distinguish other market transactions, the profitable destabilizing speculation literature at once began to quarrel over the ongoing problem of defining 'nonspeculators.' As we will now proceed to demonstrate, the old 'nonspeculator' semantic controversy appears avoidable by defining speculation *per se*.

Friedman [(1957) at p.269] suggested that 'perhaps a nonspeculator can only safely be defined (if this is done in terms of his demand curve) as one whose purchases are directly influenced by current prices but not by past prices or price trends.' Telser defended Friedman's notion and added that nonspeculators derive profits from other sources.

> What distinguishes speculators from other traders in the market is that their profits depend only on the price or price change of the commodity they trade. Nonspeculators' profits are determined not only by the price of the commodity traded on the organized exchange but also by the prices of other related commodities. If the nonspeculators are hedgers, they can make their profits almost independent of the price level itself. (Telser (1959), p.295)

Telser illustrated his nonspeculator definition with a textile manufacturer purchasing raw cotton and for whom cotton fabric and textile prices also determine his profit level. To illustrate his 'profit from other sources' criterion, Telser chose an importer who profits from decreases in exchange rates and shipping costs, in addition to the imported commodity's price. Although the textile manufacturer and importer meet Telser's criterion, they would be 'foolish to ignore price trends in their supply and demand decisions.' (Baumol (1959), p.302)

Upon reexamination, we note that if Telser's importer purchases primarily with the intent to resell at a gain, no matter where he may derive additional profits, then he has engaged in speculation *per se*. Telser's 'speculator' definition - an investor who solely profits from exchange rate capital gains - is a convention frequently used in the international economics literature. However, in this chapter we will broadly apply the Friedman Proposition across markets and will not add the *sole profit motive* limitation to the elements of our *per se* definition.

Baumol defined nonspeculators as the speculators' trading partners.

> The practical question which has lain behind the discussion is whether the entry into a market of skillful *professional* speculators, people who have no desire to hedge their holdings, can be stabilizing. Now it is clear the remaining participants in the market, the nonspeculators, the people who would like to hedge, must in their own interests consider price trends. For price changes must also affect the values of nonspeculators' holdings and obligations unless in fact they have succeeded in setting up perfect hedges, which in most markets is out of the question. (Baumol (1959), p.302)

Baumol's comment raises an interesting, though not widely understood, fact about hedging. In futures market jargon, imperfectly hedged contracts sometimes force hedgers to speculate *per se* on the basis, the spread between the cash and futures prices. If the hedgers leave their hedge positions in place and do not unwind them, then they will not speculate *per se*.

Consider an elevator operator who buys W bushels of corn in the period 0 cash market. Let P_0^c and P_0^f denote the period 0 cash and futures prices. For simplicity, assume all futures contracts in period 0 terminate in period 1. The elevator operator short hedges w_h bushels, where $0 \le w_h \le W$. In period 1, the operator sells his corn and cancels his hedge by purchasing w_h futures contracts. Suppose the operator incurs a storage cost of r dollars per bushel. If A_0 denotes his assets in period 0, then his assets in period 1 will be

$$A_1 = (P_1^c - P_0^c)W - rW + (P_0^f - P_1^f)w_h + A_0 .$$

We can rewrite this expression as

$$A_1 = \left[(P_0^f - P_0^c) - (P_1^f - P_1^c) - r\right]w_h + \left[P_1^c - P_0^c - r\right](W - w_h) + A_0.$$

For any value of w_h, an increase in the period 0 basis raises A_1. Similarly, any increase in the period 1 basis reduces A_1. Most hedgers would rationally consider basis changes in formulating their strategies.

Only those hedgers who intend to leave their hedges in place actually refrain from speculating *per se*. In fact, these hedgers are often prepared to accept a small capital loss as the cost of locking in a known price. Clearly, Baumol's comments refer to this type of hedger. Our analysis confirms these hedgers do not speculate *per se*, but they are clearly influenced by spot and futures market prices.

To recap this section, speculation *per se* involves purchases (sales) under uncertainty with the intent to resell (repurchase). This operational definition should not be confused with the layman's use of 'speculate' to refer to simple guessing under uncertainty.

1.2.B. Definitions of Stability

Defining stability and 'destabilizing speculation' is even more complex that the previous effort to define speculation. Unlike speculation, neither 'stability' nor 'instability' have most preferred definitions. This chapter therefore broadly interprets the term 'destabilize' to mean increasing price fluctuations' frequency, volatility (here meaning explosiveness not the standard deviation as in option pricing), or amplitude/variance.

In the speculation and stability literature, economists supporting Friedman most frequently interpreted stability to mean dampening the amplitude of fluctuations; these authors commonly measured stability with the price's mean squared standard deviation (MSSD). This concept corresponds to a random sample's variance without any probability connotation. Kemp (1963) and others loosely term this measure the 'variance' even though prices in their models may contain no random element. Throughout this chapter we call this measure the MSSD, so as not to confuse the reader with the actual price variance in modern uncertainty economics.

Measuring stability with the MSSD required theorists to determine the spread between the MSSD with and without speculation. Alternatively, the MSSD could be compared prior to and following a new speculative group's entry. If the MSSD increased with the new speculators, then theorists concluded the new group destabilized market prices.

The MSSD does not capture increases in the fluctuation's frequency.[3] In criticizing Friedman's model of speculative behavior, Baumol observed 'while the Friedman argument takes account of the levels of the variables it neglects their time derivatives, and the time path is dependent on both.' (Baumol (1957), p.264n) Friedman relied on amplitude, i.e., 'buy high and sell low,' to measure stability. Yet static measures of stability, such as the amplitude, fail to capture destabilizing changes in the time derivative of prices.

Obst (1967) suggested defining stability as dampening the deviations from any trend line rather than exclusively its mean. In Figure 1.1, the dotted lines indicate the impact of some speculative trading on a price over time. These transactions would be regarded as destabilizing, even though they are actually driving prices closer to their mean.

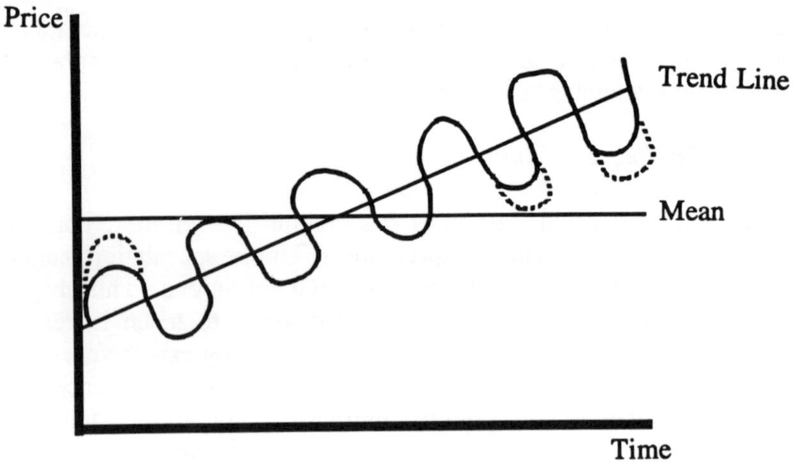

Figure 1.1. Trend Line Instability

Stability can also be defined in terms of an equilibrium's existence or volatility. Kenen (1979) and others examined profitable speculation's impact on the existence of a market-clearing price. A related stability definition examined speculation's impact on generically unstable equilibria, e.g., in a Giffenesque demand.

Finally, within the international economics field, some economists evaluate exchange rate stability based upon the Marshall-Lerner condition. In the short run, a balance of trade deficit, *ceteris paribus*, would tend to increase a country's exchange rate, defined as the units of domestic currency equal to one foreign currency unit. An exchange rate increase would tend, in the short run, to reduce the trade volume's export value and increase its domestic currency import value. However, in the long run, *ceteris paribus*, the increased exchange rate would encourage other countries to import more goods and services from that country, thus tending to raise its total trade volume. The Marshall-Lerner condition is met when long run export volume increases so much that the actual balance of trade increases.

Williamson (1972) restates the Marshall-Lerner stability condition as follows. Let T_t = the trade balance at time t, defined in foreign-exchange terms; and r_t = the units of foreign currency equal to one domestic currency unit. Depreciation of domestic currency implies $\Delta r < 0$. For simplicity if we write the trade balance as a function of the present and preceding exchange rates, then $T_t = T(r_t, r_{t-1})$, with $\partial T_t / \partial r_t > 0$, $\partial T_t / \partial r_{t-1} < 0$, and $\partial T_t / \partial r_t + \partial T_t / \partial r_{t-1} < 0$.

> [T]he immediate effect of a revaluation is to improve the trade balance as a result of price changes preceding volume changes, but the volume change comes through in the next period and is sufficiently powerful to outweigh the price effect (i.e., $\partial T_t / \partial r_t + \partial T_t / \partial r_{t-1} < 0$). (Williamson (1972), p.79)

A Numerical Example. Suppose the dollar-mark exchange rate decreases from \$0.62 to \$0.55 per Deutsche Mark (DM). Having already executed American import contracts, Germany will have an inelastic short-run demand for American dollars. If total German purchases amount to 6 billion dollars, then the short run net effect of the change in the exchange rates will increase the American goods' cost from approximately 9.677 billion DM to 10.909 billion DM. However, Germany has a more elastic long run demand for American dollars. The dollar's appreciation will reduce, *ceteris paribus*, long-run German demand for United States exports. Thus the Marshall-Lerner stability criterion states that the total volume decrease, perhaps down to \$4 billion ≈ DM 7.28 billion, will more than offset the short-run price gain: $(10.909 - 9.677) + (7.28 - 9.677) < 0$.

The Marshall-Lerner stability condition can alternatively be shown to state that the sum of domestic and foreign import demand elasticities must exceed unity. Thus stability requires that appreciation of a given currency reduce world excess demand for that currency.

To close this section on definitions of stability, we have identified at least four separate criteria for judging destabilizing influences: increases in price fluctuations' 1) variance or amplitude; 2) frequency; 3) volatility, explosiveness, or nonequilibriating behavior; and 4) the Marshall-Lerner condition for foreign exchange. The following sections will review the PDS literature assuming each of these four stability definitions are appropriate for applications or counterexamples.

1.3. Speculation and Stability: The Baumol Counterexamples

We begin studying the Friedman Proposition's dynamic aspects by first reviewing William J. Baumol's (1957) counterexamples based on a cyclical time path for prices. He proposed that speculators could profit from buying after the price trough and selling after the price peak. The speculators would in fact purchase on the price upswing and sell on the downswing, thus accelerating price swings and causing other instabilities.

Baumol constructed three counterexamples, each with the same intuitive notion. He attempted to show that speculators can destabilize even while buying low and selling high. Rather than explaining why speculators may behave as he suggests, Baumol only assessed the destabilizing impact of such plausible speculative behavior.

1.3.A. Example 1: Baumol's Difference Equation Model

In his first counterexample, Baumol delineated a cyclical price path using a sinusoidal, second-order difference equation,

$$P_t = 2AP_{t-1} - P_{t-2} + Z, \tag{1.1}$$

where A and Z are constants, with $|A| < 1$. For those readers who would like a brief refresher on differential equations, Appendix A recasts this equation into a more familiar sinusoidal form,

$$P_t = V \cos qt + S \sin qt + R. \tag{1.2}$$

The price path completes a cycle every time qt increases by 360°. The cycle has wavelength $t = 360/q$, and frequency $f = q/360$. The price path without Baumol's speculators follows equation (1.2), where the $\cos q = A$.

When Baumol's speculators enter the market - buying on the upswing and selling on the downswing - they subsequently alter the market price expression to

$$P_t = \frac{K}{W-C} + 2\frac{WA-C}{W-C}P_{t-1} - P_{t-2}. \tag{1.3}$$

Comparing (1.3) with (1.1), we find that with the speculators' transactions, the $\cos q = (WA-C)/(W-C) < A$, since the fraction

$(WA-C)/(W-C) < A$ for $W, C > 0$. This relation implies that Baumol's proposed speculation will increase the frequency of price fluctuations over time.

Second, Baumol demonstrated that, depending on initial conditions, such speculation may increase or decrease the cycle's amplitude. We will focus on an instance where the speculators increase the amplitude. Let $t = 0$ in both the market with and without speculators and assume the same corresponding initial prices. Then the sinusoidal equation (1.2) evaluated at $t = 0$ reads

$$P_0 = V + R.$$

If the initial price rests at the mean price level ($P_0 = R$), then $V = 0$ and

$$P_t = S \sin qt + R,$$

which has amplitude $2S$. For notational convenience, denote the speculative price time path as

$$P_t' = S' \sin q't + R,$$

which has amplitude $2S'$. Suppose the curves also coincide at the peak of the nonspeculative cycle: when $qt = 90$, or $t = 90/q$. Evaluated at this point,

$$S' \sin q'(90/q) = S \sin q(90/q) = S$$

or

$$S/S' = \sin q'(90/q) < 1, \tag{1.4}$$

since $0 < (q'/q) < 1$. Expression (1.4) shows that the amplitude of the commodity's price with Baumol's speculators exceeds the amplitude without these speculators. Intuitively, the two sine curves coincide at an initial value, R, and again at the peak of the nonspeculative curve, which has a longer cycle. Thus the speculative price curve must have already attained its peak and be moving downward: it must have a higher peak than the curve without Baumol's speculators.

1.3.B. Example 2: Baumol's Differential Equation Model

Again proposing the same speculative behavior, Baumol constructed the differential equation model,

$$P = R - A\ddot{P}, \tag{1.5}$$

where A and R are positive constants, and $\ddot{P}$ is the second derivative of price with respect to time. Based on (1.5) the commodity's normal excess demand is

$$E_n = 0 = R - P - A\ddot{P}. \tag{1.6}$$

At the trough when the second derivative is positive, excess demand will be low; similarly, excess demand will be high at the peak. To incorporate the 'buy on the upswing, sell on the downswing' behavior, Baumol defined a speculative excess demand by

$$E_s = U(R - P) + W\dot{P}, \tag{1.7}$$

with $U > 0$, $W > 0$, and $\dot{P} = dP/dt$. These speculators have greatest excess demand with simultaneously low ($P < R$) and rising ($\dot{P} > 0$) prices. In equilibrium, E_n and E_s must sum to zero:

$$R - P - A\ddot{P} + U(R - P) + W\dot{P} = 0,$$

and solving for P

$$P = R + \frac{W}{1+U}\dot{P} - \frac{A}{1+U}\ddot{P}. \tag{1.8}$$

Baumol then demonstrated a different destabilizing impact. Whereas for appropriate values of A the solution of (1.5) has complex roots and therefore a sinusoidal time path, the roots of (1.8) also include a positive real term given by

$$P = Ae^{rt}\cos(qt + B) + R,$$

with A, B constants. Thus the price no longer fluctuates with constant amplitude but will increase at a geometric rate. '[P]rofitable speculation has demonstrated its destabilizing ability by (taking) the system from its position of delicate constant amplitude balance into a time path of explosive fluctuation.' (Baumol (1957), p.269)

1.3.C. Example 3: Baumol's 'Real' Cycle Model

In an effort to construct a counterexample in which past prices or price trends did not affect nonspeculative excess demand, Baumol developed a third model where 'real' factors cause a cyclical price path. In this model a commodity's supply varies sinusoidally, perhaps due to seasonality or other market conditions, expressed by $S = A - B\ddot{S}$, with constants A, B. In keeping with Friedman's criterion, the nonspeculative excess demand depends only on the current price: $D = K - VP$, where K and V are constants.

When speculators then buy on the upswing and sell on the downswing, they transform the price path from its cyclical pattern into an unstable, explosive one. As derived in Appendix *B*, the time path of prices in the economy *cum* speculators has the solution

$$P = A_1 e^{E/W\,t} + A_2 e^{i\sqrt{1/B}\,t} + A_3 e^{-i\sqrt{1/B}\,t} \tag{1.9}$$

where A_1, A_2, A_3 are constants, and E, W, and B are positive constants. The real term creates a problem in Baumol's third model when the speculators try to realize their profits.

> In the short run, the time path may still be cyclical....(but in the long run) the time path of P will eventually approach Ae^{xt} ....In other words, speculators will continue to buy on the rising market and, at least in terms of the value of their assets, this would appear to be profitable. However, it is clear that difficulties can arise if speculators try to cash in these profits or if they run out of funds with which to continue their purchases. (Baumol (1957), p.270)

1.3.D. Comments on Profit Realization and the Underlying Market

1.3.D.1. Speculators Must Realize Their Profits. To derive PDS counterexamples, Baumol had to prove that his speculators could in fact realize positive profits. Lester Telser stated more succinctly the problem with Baumol's third model: '...the latter two terms [in equation (1.9)] are sinusoidal with constant amplitude. Thus the solution is dominated by ($e^{E/W\,t}$ and, since $E/W > 0$), the price rises indefinitely. I must emphasize again that the price necessarily rises indefinitely.' (Telser (1959), p.301) Similarly, if $A_1 < 0$, the price falls indefinitely. In Baumol's third model, if all the speculators attempt to realize their profits the bubble will burst.

Telser also recapitulated Friedman's criticism that Baumol's nonspeculators actually speculated, since past prices influenced their decisions. Current price and recent price trends are shown in the right-hand side of (1.1), thus contradicting Friedman's independence assumption. 'If nonspeculators are not affected by past prices and if speculators have to realize their profits then Baumol's counterexamples are unacceptable.' (Telser (1959), p.301)

Replying to Telser, Baumol conceded that all the speculators could not realize their profits in his third counterexample, or the speculative bubble would burst. 'Hence I must agree that it is unreasonable to cite this as an example of destabilizing *profitable* speculation.' (Baumol (1959), p.301) However, Baumol maintained his first two models had demonstrated PDS, even if price trends influenced the underlying demand in them. More important, Baumol noted that no one had disproved the central idea of buying on an upswing and selling on a downswing.[4]

Kemp (1963) pointed out that Baumol was only constructing a counterexample, not a general theory of speculation. Kemp considered Telser's speculative bubble criticism irrelevant, since economists could view Baumol's counterexample as PDS for a limited time interval before the bubble collapses. Indeed most economists would regard speculative transactions leading to bubble formation and destruction as destabilizing influences. The Friedman Proposition should govern even those speculators who derive profits at the expense of other speculators.

1.3.D.2. Friedman's Criteria Restated. Milton Friedman subsequently remained unconvinced that Baumol, Kemp, and others had validly demonstrated PDS.

> Speculators can make fluctuations wider...only by selling net when prices would otherwise be low and buying net when prices would otherwise be high. But this means that they sell at a lower price than they buy and so make losses. Our model therefore implicitly defines stabilizing speculation as speculation yielding gains...and destabilizing speculation as speculation yielding losses. (Friedman (1969), p.287)

Friedman also restated the criteria necessary to disprove his conjecture.

> Consider any market in operation. Suppose that an additional set of transactions are made in the market by an additional group of people whom we shall call 'speculators' or 'new speculators.' We

> shall then deal only with the question whether this additional set of transactions increases the fluctuations in price ... By dealing this way with a change in the amount of speculation, we can avoid the troublesome intellectual problem of defining zero speculation without any loss in generality. We shall make one further assumption ... that the activities of speculators do not affect the quantities demanded and supplied by other participants in the market at each current price. (Friedman, 1969, pp.286-287)

Superficially, Friedman's assumptions lend support to Baumol's first two counterexamples. In light of Friedman's remarks, we might interpret Baumol's speculators as 'new speculators' in an existing speculative market. However, Friedman maintained in a footnote that Baumol had yet to propose an acceptable counterexample: 'It will be clear that our assumptions rule out the main case (Baumol) considered. Baumol also considers a special case corresponding to our assumptions. His own conclusion is ambiguous but only because in judging the profitability of speculation he does not require it to be carried through to completion.' (Friedman (1969), p.287n)

The price trend terms in Baumol's underlying market excess demand curve continue to be the crux of the objections. Originally, the model was criticized for depicting 'nonspeculators' as speculators. The models fail to meet the restated criteria, because these same price trends show that the 'new group of speculators' have influenced the other market participants' demand, thus violating Friedman's independence assumption.

Friedman's independence assumption has proven to be the most controversial in the literature. Krueger (1969), for example, found the assumption implausible and limiting the Proposition's scope. However, some economists supported Friedman's assumptions.

> The traditional argument is predicated on the assumption that 'real' (by which is meant nonspeculative underlying demand and supply) forces dominate the market and that speculative turnover is only a small part of the traded quantity, which can consequently influence only the magnitude, not the direction, of price changes. (Lipschitz and Otani (1977), p.38)

From the Lipschitz and Otani summary, Baumol's 'nonspeculative' excess demand functions, which Friedman and others consider speculative, cannot drive the cyclical price movements without violating Friedman's criteria. Therefore, even models examining 'new speculative' effects must still distinguish between the speculators and nonspeculators: the models must assure that only real forces predominantly determine price movements.

If we have correctly analyzed Friedman's restated criteria, then we once again face the old conundrum of differentiating between speculators and nonspeculators. We recommend avoiding this difficulty by separating traders using the *per se* distinction. Considering price trends or past prices is not equivalent to buying with the intent to resell.

1.4. Categories of Counterexamples

1.4.A. Pre-Modern Depictions of PDS

Numerous authors have proposed counterexamples to the Friedman Proposition; each author envisions his own market conditions that create opportunities for profitable destabilizing speculation. The interested reader may want to contrast some of the works in this section with the modern contingent claims example in Section 1.4.B.

1.4.A.1. Panic-Stricken Central Bank Counterexample. Stein (1961) proposed a narrative counterexample concerning the vulnerability of a central bank's foreign currency reserves to speculative attacks. Suppose a central bank purchases some speculative group's supply of foreign currency (presumably for balance of trade reasons). After acquiring the foreign currency, the central bank becomes panicked over its depleted home currency reserves and devalues it. Following the devaluation, the speculators buy back the home currency at a profit. The speculators apparently profited at the expense of exchange rate stability.

The difficulty with Stein's counterexample is that when the central bank devalues the home currency, it too speculates. Stein's counterexample depicts a zero-sum game: the private speculative gains equal the central bank's (the public's) losses. The central bank's reaction to the speculative sales, rather than the speculators' activity, creates the opportunity for profits and destabilizes the exchange rates.

Stein's proposed counterexample is important in another respect. His work illustrated how profit-earning speculators may cause government policies to be reshaped in such a way as to destabilize markets more than if the government did not intervene. In private correspondence, Professor Friedman told me that, in retrospect, he perhaps envisioned such misguided intervention when he included the qualifier 'in general' in the Friedman Proposition. Only coordinated and concerted intervention by the G7 central banks has proven successful in fending off speculative attacks on currency reserves.

1.4.A.2. Lagged Trader Responses Counterexample. Williamson (1972) suggested a second counterexample based on traders' lagged responses to exchange rate changes, the so-called 'J-curve' reaction. Recall from the discussion of the Marshall-Lerner condition in Section *1.3.B* that a country's currency appreciation would in the short run raise the value of that country's exports; while in the long run, decreased foreign demand for that country's goods and services would actually reduce its net trade balance.

Suppose a country's period 0 exchange rate rests in equilibrium at r_e. In period 1 a group of speculators begins selling, for whatever reason, domestic currency. The speculative transactions lower the exchange rate to $r_0 < r_e$ and induce a balance of payments deficit. Importers of that country's goods and services have relatively inelastic short-run demand, since many of these orders have been fixed by legal contract. They will attempt to purchase the same quantity of goods and services at the new high exchange rate prices. Thus foreign trading partners must purchase these domestic goods with more units of foreign currency, which tends to depress the value of their own currencies further.

However, in period 2, Williamson's clever speculators realize that long-term forces will eventually raise the country's exchange rate again. When the exchange rate drops to r_0, Williamson's speculators begin buying up the domestic currency's commercial excess supply. The long-term forces combine with the speculators' purchases to raise the exchange rate to $r_2 > r_e$.

If Williamson's proposed speculative behavior recurs, the exchange rate will oscillate about its equilibrium moving from r_0 to r_2. Speculators earn positive profits - buying low at r_0 and selling high at r_2 - yet their actions destabilize the exchange rate. Williamson's speculators exploit profits from traders who determined their volume of exports and imports for nonspeculative reasons, based on advanced legal contracts to trade or based on commitments from experience with the equilibrium rate of r_e.

As Price and Wood (1974) note, this general profit-making opportunity relies on a dichotomy in forecasting ability (or intelligence) among the profit-earning speculators and the other market participants. These other traders cannot forecast when long-term influences will affect the exchange rates as well as Williamson's speculative group. Levin

(1983) extended Williamson's model to a rational expectations framework and obtained results indicating that unanticipated real disturbances can lead to overshooting. Furthermore, Levin found that capital immobility may lead to exchange rate fluctuations around long run equilibrium values due to exchange rate lags behind changes in the balance of trade.

Additional work on the rational expectations theme by Canzoneri (1984) has shown that even for unpegged exchange rates, if a speculator expects 'other market participants' to react to gold price fluctuations, then he too will consider the price of gold in deciding his demand and supply quantities. When enough speculators behave this way, then gold price changes will indeed affect the prevailing exchange rates, thus fulfilling the speculators' destabilizing beliefs.

Under the 'new' macroeconomic approach, Canzoneri's policy prescription occasionally may run counter to the present interventionist philosophy of leaning against the wind.

> If the exchange rate rises above its long run equilibrium value it must be forced down; an appreciation must be engineered. 'Rational' portfolio managers will foresee this appreciation and raise their demand for money; the (real) supply of money must be increased to accommodate this new demand. Put another way, the monetary authority must accommodate the demand for money that is consistent with the expected appreciation or depreciation that moves the exchange rate in the desired direction. (Canzoneri, 1984, p.76)

The correct policy may sometimes call for accommodation: a currency depreciation should be met with an increase in the money supply.

We conclude from the work of Williamson (1972) and Price and Wood (1974) that institutional constraints in the foreign exchange markets can permit profitable destabilizing speculation. Speculators in these works take an exchange rate out of equilibrium by selling their carry-over stock, and then later buy back when the exchange rate has fallen still farther. Their actions cause the exchange rate to oscillate around its long run equilibrium value while the speculators earn profits. Moreover, Canzoneri (1984) has shown that when enough speculators believe gold prices, or other extrinsic factors, influence foreign exchange rates, their behavior leads to a self-fulfilling equilibrium.

1.4.A.3. Giffenesque Good Counterexample. Kemp (1963) proposed a counterexample based on excess demand for a Giffen good. The 'nonspeculative' excess demand is a function of current price 'and to embrace seasonal, trend, and purely random factors, time itself.' (Kemp (1963), p.185). Thus Kemp's nonspeculative demand has the form, *N[P(t),t]*.[5]

Figure 1.2 shows the excess demand for a typical Giffen good. P_1 and P_3 are stable equilibria; P_2 is an unstable equilibrium. Suppose *N(P)* depicts a market's excess demand, and the price rests at the equilibrium value P_1. Speculators enter the market, begin buying up the commodity, and shift the market excess demand from *N(P)* to *N(P)+S*. Eventually, the price would settle at P_4. However, the speculators withdraw from the market when the price exceeds P_2. The excess demand reverts back to *N(P)*, but the price continues to rise until it reaches equilibrium at P_3.

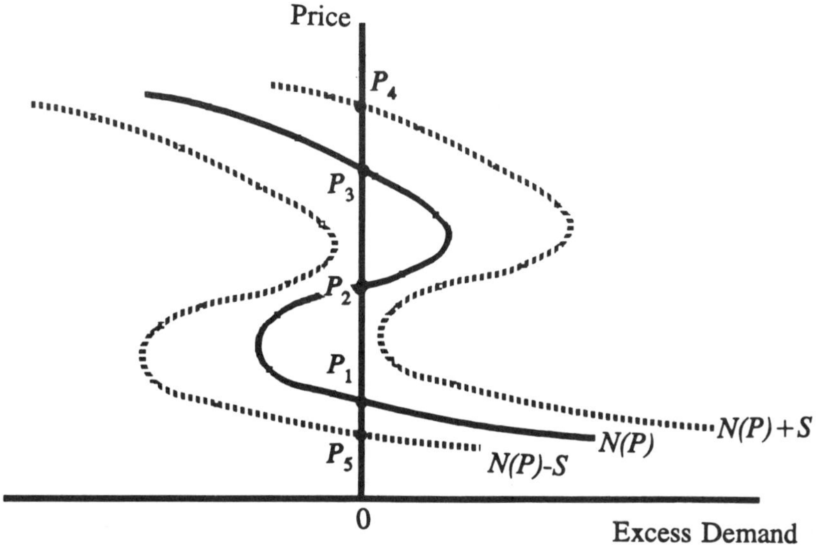

Figure 1.2. Kemp's (1963) Model

At this point, Kemp's speculators now sell their inventory holdings, which they purchased at prices less than or equal to P_2. The speculators enter the market as sellers on curve *N(P)-S*. Again, it appears the price would settle at P_5. However, after the price drops below P_2, the speculators withdraw from the market. The excess demand reverts back to *N(P)*; the price falls to P_1. In fact, the price has now completed a cycle. Kemp's speculators bought the commodities at prices below or equal to P_2 and sold them at prices above or equal to P_2: the speculators profited. By shifting the *N(P)* curve away from its P_2 equilibrium, Kemp's speculators also destabilized the market.

The principal objection to Kemp's counterexample concerns the functioning of a tâtonnement process. In general, traders can only purchase and sell the commodity at the points P_1, P_2, P_3, P_4, and P_5. Kemp's speculators seem to transact outside equilibrium, before the Walrasian auctioneer arrived at a market-clearing price.

1.4.A.4. Multiperiod Buy-Low, Sell-High Counterexample. Consider now a fourth counterexample with changing preferences over time. Let S_i denote an element of a speculative sales vector and P_i^s the corresponding speculative transaction price. Define the speculative profits by $\pi = \sum_{i=1}^{T} S_i P_i^s$. The MSSD for a particular speculative transaction is given by $MSSD_s = 1/T \sum_{i=1}^{T} (P_i^s - \bar{P}^s)^2$, where $\bar{P}^s$ is the average or mean speculative transaction price. Let $MSSD_n$ denote the MSSD without the speculative transaction.

Suppose market excess demand for some good across three periods is given by: $N_1 = P_1 - 30 - 5Q_1$, $N_2 = P_2 - 40 - 5Q_2$, $N_3 = P_3 - 50 - 2Q_3$, where Q_i denotes the equilibrium quantity transacted in period *i*. Market clearing requires zero excess demand. Therefore, the economy has equilibrium prices of $P_1 = 30$, $P_2 = 40$, and $P_3 = 50$. The mean price is 40 and the $MSSD_n$ would equal 200/3.

If a speculator buys 1 unit of the good in period 2 and sells it in period 3, the new equilibrium prices would be $P_1 = 30$, $P_2 = 45$, and $P_3 = 48$. In this case $\pi = (48 - 45) > 0$ and $MSSD_s = 186/3 < MSSD_n$. Therefore, the speculation is both profitable and stabilizing.

If the speculator instead sells 1 unit in period 2 and repurchases it in period 3, the equilibrium price vector will be (30, 35, 52). In this case $MSSD_s > MSSD_n$, but $\pi = (35 - 52) < 0$. Thus the destabilizing speculation has also been unprofitable, just as the Friedman Proposition would predict. Note that the excess demand curves in this illustration exhibit different slope intercepts (if plotted on price-quantity axes) and different slopes, reflecting changes in demand elasticities.

Now consider the following modification. The excess demand for the good across the three periods is $N_1 = P_1 - 30 - 5Q_1$, $N_2 = P_2 - 40 -$

$8Q_2$, $N_3 = P_3 - 50 - 1Q_3$. Only the slopes in time periods 2 and 3 have changed. Therefore, $P_1 = 30$, $P_2 = 40$, and $P_3 = 50$ are still the market clearing prices, 40 is still the mean, and $MSSD_n = 200/3$. If a speculator buys 1 unit in period 2 and sells it in period 3, the new equilibrium prices would be $P_1 = 30$, $P_2 = 48$, and $P_3 = 49$. In this case $\pi = (49 - 48) > 0$, but $MSSD_s \approx 229/3 > MSSD_n$. Thus we have shown a counterexample in which speculation is profitable yet destabilizing.

1.4.A.5. Class of Nonlinear Excess Demand Counterexamples. For some twenty years, a theorem circulated in the speculation and stability literature that models containing linear excess demand curves were sufficient to validate the Friedman Proposition. In contrast, nonlinear excess demand curve models were thought to generate PDS counter-examples. This proposed theoretical limitation began when Kemp suggested if 'the nonspeculative (excess) demand is linear in price and contains a component dependent on time only, profitable speculation cannot fail to be stabilizing....' (Kemp (1963), p.189) Note that our multiperiod counterexample in the preceding section immediately contradicts this assertion.

Farrel (1966) followed Kemp's lead and emphasized Friedman's independence assumption.

> In the absence of transactions costs linearity (in price) of the nonspeculative excess demand function is a sufficient condition for the validity of the basic proposition...In markets where the *independence assumption* holds and where transaction costs are large enough to cover actual departures from linearity of the nonspeculative excess demand function, the basic proposition holds. (Farrel (1966), p.192)

Since these assumptions - independence from past speculative activity and price linearity - severely restricted his model, Farrel concluded that his analysis had limited value. 'But ... this paper will not have been wasted if it has persuaded economists that our basic proposition is too strong to hold with any great generality and that they should therefore seek to establish weaker propositions concerning the properties of speculative markets.' (Farrel (1966), p.192)

Schimmler (1967) simplified and unified Kemp's and Farrel's proofs using a Hilbert space. Lien (1984) found an error in these proofs that permitted us to generate the counterexample in Section 1.4.A.4. Lien showed that the linear excess demand curve theorem is valid only when the slopes of the excess demand curves do not change.

Schimmler (1967) went on to develop an entire class of counterexamples based on nonlinear excess demands. Unfortunately, his class of models lack intuitive appeal, such as 'buy on the upswing, sell on the downswing.' Given the nonlinear excess demand curves in Baumol's and Kemp's counterexamples, it is not too difficult to imagine problems that these curves might create for the Friedman Proposition. The derivation would also distract the reader for several pages just to establish the Hilbert space framework. Therefore, we have placed the derivation of this class of counterexamples and the proof of the linear excess demand curve theorem in Appendix *C*.

1.4.B. Modern Uncertainty Theory Counterexample

Salant (1974) proposed a counterexample incorporating speculative carry-overs in economies with stochastic endowments. Only the speculator has carry-over facilities. Consider a consumer's planning problem in a two good, two period economy. The individual has known current endowments of the two goods (X, B) and random future endowments $(X^r, B^r; X^s, B^s)$ depending on whether it rains, r, or shines, s. If the consumer had carry-over facilities, he might store part of his current endowment, K_x and K_b, for consumption in the next period. The consumer's present and future consumption would then be $(X - K_x, B - K_b; [X^r + K_x, B^r + K_b; X^s + K_x, B^s + K_b])$.

Suppose the consumer expects rain with probability π and has a separable utility function which permits us to write his expected utility as

$$EU(K_x) = f(X-K_x) + \alpha(B-K_b) + \pi[g(X^r+K_x) + \alpha(B^r+K_b)]$$
$$+ (1-\pi)[g(X^s+K_x) + \alpha(B^2+K_s)],$$

where $f(\cdot)$ and $g(\cdot)$ are concave, increasing functions, and α is a constant. The first order condition that emerges from maximizing expected utility with respect to K_x is:

$$f'(X - K_x) = \pi\, g'(X^r + K_x) + (1 - \pi)\, g'(X^s + K_x),$$

This expression describes the optimal quantity of good X to carry-over and the second expression shows the consumer's indifference to good B

carry-overs. Therefore, treat good B as a numeraire and set its price equal to one. The consumer would then desire to equate his marginal utilities from present and future consumption.

However, suppose the consumer cannot carry-over either good. Instead of treating consumption as a dynamic programming problem, the consumer simply maximizes utility separately in each period. In period 1 the consumer maximizes utility subject to an income constraint:

$$\underset{X,\,B}{MAX}\ f(X) + \alpha(B) + \lambda(Y - P_{x1}X - P_b B),$$

where λ is the associated Lagrange multiplier and Y is his income. The emerging optimality condition equates the marginal rate of substitution with the price ratio, $f'(X)/\alpha = P_{x1}/P_b = P_{x1}$.

In period 2 the individual again maximizes utility subject to an income constraint:

$$\underset{X,B}{MAX}\ g(X) + \alpha(B) + \lambda(Y - P_{x2} - P_b B),$$

with corresponding optimality condition $g'(X)/\alpha = P_{x2}/P_b = P_{x2}$. If the speculator transports K_x of good X into the next period and sells it, then in period 1 the price of X will be $P_{x1} = f'(X - K_x)/\alpha$. Similarly, in period 2 the good X price conditional on each state, rain or shine, will be $P^r_{x2} = g'(X^r+K_x)/\alpha$ and $P^s_{x2} = g'(X^s+K_x)/\alpha$ with probabilities π and $(1-\pi)$, respectively. The speculator expects to receive profits $R(K_x)$ given by

$$R(K_x) = [\pi P^r_{x2} + (1-\pi)\, P^s_{x2} - P_{x1}]K_x\,.$$

How does speculative carry-over affect the random period 2 price? If $g'''(\cdot) < 0$, the consumer's inverse demand curve, $g'(x)/\alpha$, is concave. Any speculative carry-over will *always* increase the price variance.[6] With concave and therefore increasingly steep demand, speculative carry-over, K_x, widens the spread between good X's conditional prices for each state of the world. See Figure 1.3. Thus for any set of prices for which $R(K_x) > 0$, speculative carry-over can increase some good's price variance.

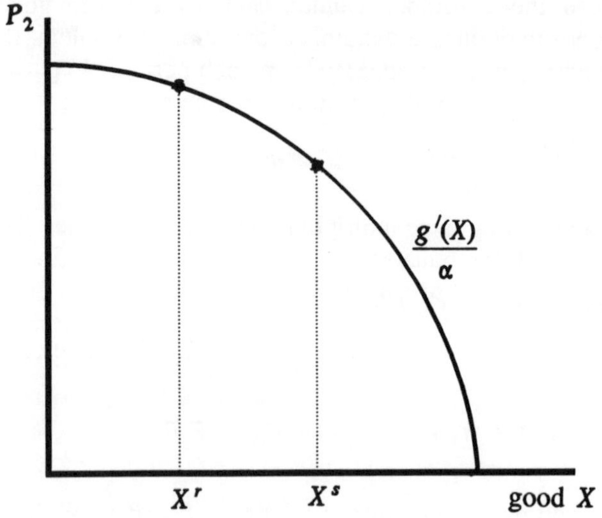

Figure 1.3. Concave Market Demand Curve.

1.5. Brief Empirical Overview on Destabilizing Speculation

1.5.A. Econometric Tests

One of the first theoretical PDS counterexamples contained the warning: 'The effects of profitable speculation on stability is in part an empirical question and ... attempts to settle it by *a priori* arguments must somewhere resort to fallacy.' (Baumol (1959), p.302) Although one might have expected the empirical tests of Friedman's Proposition to employ data on stock market speculation, the empirical work in this area has primarily used exchange rate data. The empirical tests have yielded inconclusive results. Frequently the research confirms that a speculative group earned profits and simultaneously stabilized prices. However, these findings fail to disprove any of the counterexamples or theoretical limitations to the Friedman Proposition. Representative works on both sides of the Proposition include Arndt (1968) and Kenen (1975).

Arndt's study indicated that speculators in his sample from the Canadian foreign exchange probably follow the logic in Friedman's Proposition. Arndt concludes, "In a stable environment ... our theory predicts - and the data tentatively support this conclusion - that speculators' expectations will be a slowly changing variable with considerable inertia, and that speculative sales and purchases will have a dampening effect on movements in the exchange rate." (Arndt, 1968, p.69)

On a more ambiguous note, Kenen (1975), in examining speculation under different exchange regimes, found no uniform data to support the conclusion that profit-earning speculators generally stabilize prices. 'Although long lags and high elasticities appear to amplify instability, we cannot conclude from (its profitability) that speculation is indeed stabilizing.' (Kenen, 1975, p.134)

The empirical work as a whole - as might be expected from the theoretical difficulty in isolating when a speculative group has transacted - has not provided conclusive evidence one way or the other for the validity of the Friedman Proposition. Overall, one senses a reluctance among the econometricians who examined this relationship to categorize professional (and presumably profitable) speculation as a stabilizing influence.

1.5.B. General Comments on Foreign Exchange Rate Stability

In the opening paragraphs of this chapter we pointed out that speculation must be profitable over time, or the losses from speculative activity would be a self-correcting problem: the destabilizing speculators would fail to survive in a Darwinian sense. It is of some interest then to examine how speculation has generally been perceived to influence the stability of foreign exchange markets. Exchange rate forecasters were initially optimistic that free market speculation would attenuate exchange rate fluctuations.

In the early 1970s when countries first adopted flexible exchange regimes, the initial swings in exchange rate values were thought to be "what one might expect during a learning period, when speculators' views regarding long-run equilibrium values are weakly held and substantial stimulus is therefore required to make them act on them." (Whitman, 1975, p.138)

After many years experience with flexible regimes, the prevalent view shifted to some disillusionment that the exchange rate mechanism may have inherent instabilities spawned by professional speculation.

> The focus of attention then shifted to market imperfections, including insufficiency of stabilizing speculation, as the cause of the volatility that characterized real world exchange rates. But, with

> the passage of time, an explanation of these imperfections as temporary phenomena characteristic of a transition period became less and less credible. (Whitman, 1984, p.300)

Economists have thus recognized that professional (profit-earning) speculation does not necessarily stabilize foreign exchange markets, and at least some have attributed enhanced volatility to this same speculation.

1.6. Conclusions and Future Research

We have reexamined the proposition that speculators buy low and sell high, and thus tend to stabilize market prices. Although this proposition dates back to the Nineteenth Century, the proposition was given new life in the 1950s when Milton Friedman endorsed it to support the adoption of flexible exchange rates. However, Friedman carefully restated the proposition in terms of 'new speculators' and the reaction of 'other market participants.' This restatement seemed more closely tailored to real world conditions.

Baumol challenged Friedman's assertion by proposing counter-examples that depict an early portrayal of 'overshooting.' The gist of Baumol's counterexample is that (some fraction of) speculators wait until after the trough and peak of a cycle, so that they wind up buying on the upswing and selling on the downswing of the cycle.

Comments on the technical features of Baumol's model raised questions about the restrictions under which the Friedman Proposition would be valid. These criteria include minimal, if any, effect on other market participants by the speculative group under consideration. Baumol's work illustrates one group of speculators profiting at the expense of another speculative group, not unlike everyday transactions in capital and foreign exchange markets.

The international exchange markets have particular institutions that may yield theoretical possibilities for profitable destabilizing speculation: intervention by monetary authorities, 'J-curve' time-delayed reactions, and overshooting. The empirical literature has found evidence of both stabilizing and destabilizing speculation without providing conclusive evidence of speculation which is simultaneously destabilizing and profitable. Indeed some of the initial optimism for flexible exchange regimes voiced by economic theorists and forecasters in the 1960s and early 1970s gave way to disillusionment in the wake of foreign exchange instabilities under flexible rates.

The 30% crash in the Dow Jones Industrial Average over October 16 - 19, 1987, has shown that endogenous influences can cause greater instabilities in the market than even external factors. Panic buying and selling can lead to further panic, or trigger computer-driven program trading. If such speculative behavior were on the whole unprofitable, then it would not be expected to recur. Those speculators who panic and lose capital would be part of a self-correcting problem. Yet new constraints imposed to limit program trading, such as the New York Stock Exchange's "uptick rule," show concern for this ongoing form of destabilizing speculation. So we are left with a proposition that has engendered valid theoretical counterexamples and some anecdotal evidence to the contrary on inherent foreign exchange instability and program trading.

Appendix A: Outline of Baumol's Difference Equation Model

In his first counterexample, Baumol proposed that some 'nonspeculative' group creates a cyclical path for a commodity's price over time. To represent the time path, Baumol constructed a sinusoidal second-order difference equation,

$$P_t = 2AP_{t-1} - P_{t-2} + Z, \qquad \textbf{(A.1)}$$

where A and Z are constants, with $|A| < 1$. Applying the quadratic formula permits us to recast this equation in a more familiar sinusoidal form. In the homogeneous equation,

$$P_t - 2AP_{t-1} + P_{t-2} = 0,$$

let $a = 1$, $b = -2A$, and $c = 1$. Substituting these values into the formula for the solution of a quadratic equation yields

$$P = \left[2A \pm \sqrt{4A^2-4}\,\right] / 2 = A \pm i\sqrt{1 - A^2},$$

and note $A^2 < 1$. Let q be some angle such that $\cos q = A$, then

$$P = \cos q \pm i\sqrt{1-\cos^2 q} = \cos q \pm i \sin q.$$

The general solution for P_t from this equation is

$$\begin{aligned} P_t &= C_1 (\cos q + i \sin q)^t + C_2 (\cos q - i \sin q)^t \\ &= C_1 (e^{iq})^t + C_2 (e^{-iq})^t \\ &= C_1 e^{i(qt)} + C_2 e^{-i(qt)} \\ &= C_1 (\cos qt + i \sin qt) + C_2 (\cos qt - i \sin qt) \\ &= (C_1 + C_2) \cos qt + i (C_1 - C_2) \sin qt. \end{aligned}$$

Let $V = C_1 + C_2$, $S = i(C_1 - C_2)$, and R denote the mean price level. To derive the value of R in terms of Z and A from equation (A.1), set $P_t = R$, a constant, for all t. Substituting this value into (A.1) yields $R = 2AR - R + Z$, and solving for R leads to $R = Z / 2(1-A)$. Therefore P_t in equation (A.1) can be expressed as

$$P_t = V \cos qt + S \sin qt + R. \qquad \textbf{(A.2)}$$

This result clearly illustrates equation (A.1)'s sinusoidal characteristics. We can verify that R is the mean price level by evaluating (A.2) at its peak, $P_t = V\sqrt{2}/2 + S\sqrt{2}/2 + R$, and at its trough, $P_t = -V\sqrt{2}/2 - S\sqrt{2}/2 + R$. These two prices sum to $2R$, and the mean price is therefore R.

Baumol then constructs a 'nonspeculative' or underlying excess demand from (A.1):

$$E_{nt} = K - WP_t + 2WAP_{t-1} - WP_{t-2} \qquad \textbf{(A.3)}$$

where K is a constant, and W is a positive constant. Current price and recent price trends, as evinced by the lagged prices in (A.3), influence Baumol's nonspeculative excess demand.

Baumol next specified a speculative excess demand function given by

$$\begin{aligned} E_{st+1} &= C\,[(P_{t+1} - P_t) - (P_t - P_{t-1})] \\ &= C\,(P_{t+1} - 2P_t + P_{t-1}), \end{aligned} \qquad \textbf{(A.4)}$$

where C is a positive constant. If P_{t+1} is the price immediately following a trough, then these speculators have positive excess demand. Similarly, the speculators wish to sell immediately after a peak.

In equilibrium the speculative and nonspeculative excess demand functions must sum to zero: $E_{nt} + E_{st} = 0$. Summing equations (A.3) and (A.4), expressed in period t, yields

$$0 = K - WP_t + 2WAP_{t-1} - WP_{t-2} + C\,(P_t - 2P_{t-1} + P_{t-2}).$$

And the solution for P_t is

$$P_t = \frac{K}{(W-C)} + \frac{2(WA-C)}{(W-C)} P_{t-1} - P_{t-2}. \qquad \textbf{(A.5)}$$

Since equations (A.5) and (A.1) have the same form, (A.5) is also sinusoidal. Furthermore, the price expression in (A.1) must also solve (A.4), the speculative excess demand function. With this basic construction, Baumol then illustrated that maximum speculative purchases immediately follow the trough, while maximum sales immediately follow the peak. Consider (A.1) evaluated at period $t+1$: $P_{t+1} = 2AP_t - P_{t-1} + Z$. Substituting this value of P_{t+1} into equation

(A.4) produces

$$E_{st+1} = C\,(2AP_t - P_{t-1} + K - 2P_t + P_{t-1}) = C\,[\,2(A-1)P_t + K\,].$$

Since A is a constant with $|A| < 1$, we may rewrite the equation as $E_{st+1} = -D(P_t - L)$, where L is a constant, and D is a positive constant.

This latter equation incorporates speculative sales after a peak and purchases immediately following the trough 'since it states essentially that speculative excess demands fluctuate inversely with prices *one period earlier* (note the time subscripts of E and P).' (Baumol (1957), p.266). Baumol's speculators profit from this activity, since the prices at which they sell exceed those at which they purchase.

Appendix B: Derivation of Baumol's 'Real' Model's Solution

In equilibrium supply equals demand ($S = D$), so that $S = K - VP$, and $\ddot{S} = -V\ddot{P}$, where $\ddot{S} = d^2S/d^2t$. The equilibrium *cum* speculation is the same as before, but nonspeculative excess demand is represented by the difference between demand and supply: $D - S + E_s = 0$, where E_s is expressed in equation (1.8) from the second counterexample. Substituting for D and E_s in the latter equation yields,

$$K - VP - S + U(R - P) + W\dot{P} = 0,$$

and solving for S,

$$S = K - VP + U\,(R - P) + W\dot{P},$$

which can be rewritten as

$$S = C - EP + W\dot{P}$$

where C, E are constants. This solution for S and the corresponding value for $\ddot{S}$ can again be substituted into equation (1.10) to obtain the following third-order differential equation:

$$C - A = EP - W\dot{P} + BE\ddot{P} - BW\dddot{P}. \qquad \textbf{(B.1)}$$

Based on this result Baumol asserts that the preceding equation has at least one real root, which must be positive since the terms in equation (B.1) alternate in sign. 'It follows that the time path of prices is changed by speculation from a cyclical pattern of constant amplitude into an unstable, explosive movement.' (Baumol (1957), pp. 269-270)

We will first derive the homogeneous solution for equation (B.1):

$$EP - W\dot{P} + BE\ddot{P} - BW\dddot{P} = 0.$$

Let $P = e^{xt}$, and substituting in the latter equation yields,

$$Ee^{xt} - Wxe^{xt} + BEx^2e^{xt} - BWx^3e^{xt} = 0.$$

Next, by dividing through by e^{xt} and simplifying the equation becomes

$$\begin{aligned} E - Wx + BEx^2 - BWx^3 &= 0 \\ (E - Wx) + Bx^2(E - Wx) &= 0 \\ (Bx^2 + 1)(E - Wx) &= 0 \\ (x^2 + 1/B)(x - E/W) &= 0, \end{aligned}$$

with solutions $x = E/W$, and $x = \pm i\sqrt{1/B}$. Therefore, the third-order differential equation has a solution

$$P = A_1 e^{E/W\,t} + A_2 e^{i\sqrt{1/B}\,t} + A_3 e^{-i\sqrt{1/B}\,t}, \qquad \textbf{(B.2)}$$

where A_1, A_2, and A_3 are constants.

Appendix C: Schimmler's Hilbert Space Model

Let $S = (s_1, s_2, \ldots, s_T)$ denote a speculative excess demand vector and N the 'nonspeculative' or existing excess demand. Equilibrium price vectors with and without this speculation are denoted by P_s and P_w, respectively. Requiring the speculators to realize their profits implies that the speculative transactions must sum to zero, or more formally, $S \cdot U = 0$, where U is a vector of unity elements.[7] By convention, speculative profits, $\pi = -P_s \cdot S$, have a negative sign to indicate that net sales are negative while purchases are positive.

The MSSD for price vector P is denoted $MSSD(P) = (1/T)(P - \bar{p}U)^2$, where $\bar{p} = (1/T)P \cdot U$. To measure stability, define $c = MSSD(P_w) - MSSD(P_s)$. When c is positive, the speculative activity has stabilized prices. Friedman proposed that $\pi > 0$ implies $c > 0$.

Farrel (1966) made the nonspeculative excess demand independent of the speculative activity by assuming that the price spread, $p_{s_t} - p_{w_t}$, is a function of s_t alone: $p_{s_t} - p_{w_t} = h(s_t)\ \forall\ t$. Schimmler (1967) extended Farrel's results to temporal independence:

$$P_s - P_w = H(S). \tag{C.1}$$

This seemingly innocuous assumption turns out to be pivotal to the analysis that follows. It turns out that only linear excess demand schedules follow condition (C.1).[8]

Schimmler denoted centralized vectors with an asterisk, e.g., $X^* = X - \bar{x}U$, where $\bar{x}$ is the mean element of X. Thus $H^*(S) = H(S) - \overline{h(s)} \cdot U$. Consider now the inner product of $H^*(S)$ and U:

$$\begin{aligned} H^*(S) \cdot U &= [H(S) - \overline{h(s)} \cdot U] \cdot U \\ &= H(S) \cdot U - \overline{h(s)} \cdot [U \cdot U] \\ &= \textstyle\sum_{t=1}^{T} h_t(s) - T \cdot \overline{h(s)} \\ &= 0. \end{aligned}$$

Since $S \cdot U = 0$, Schimmler maintained

$$H^*(S) = f(s)\ S, \tag{C.2}$$

where $f(s)$ is some real valued function. When $f(s) > 0$, speculative purchases increase the spread between P_s and P_w. As Schimmler noted, equation (C.2) 'shows the difference between p_{s_t} and p_{w_t} is a linear function of s_t with temporally independent slope and temporally independent constant term.' (Schimmler (1967), p.113).

Schimmler's work also defined an entire class of counterexamples based on excess demand curves that are nonlinear in price. We begin by defining the product of T and c:

$$\begin{aligned} Tc &= T\,[MSSD(P_s) - MSSD(P_s)] \\ &= T\,[(1/T)(P_w - \bar{p}_w U)^2 - (1/T)(P_s - \bar{p}_s U)^2] \\ &= (P_w^*)^2 - (P_s^*)^2 \\ &= -\,[(P_s^*)^2 - (P_w^*)^2] \end{aligned}$$

$$= -(P_s^* - P_w^*) \cdot (P_s^* + P_w^*)$$

$$= -H^*(S) \cdot (P_s^* + P_w^*) \tag{C.3}$$

$$= -H^*(S) \cdot [2P_s^* - H^*(S)] \tag{C.4}$$

If $H^*(S)$ does not follow the linear relationship in (C.2), then there exist two vectors P_w and S, such that $\pi > 0$ and $c < 0$. Let S' denote a vector linearly independent from $H^*(S)$. In the plane spanned by $H^*(S')$ and S', the two half-planes

$$A = \{X^*: \ X^* \cdot H^*(S') > 0\} \tag{C.5}$$

and

$$B = \{X^*: \ X^* \cdot S' < 0\} \tag{C.6}$$

have a nonempty intersection. A vector X^* can be selected from $A \cap B$ so that

$$X^* + H^*(S') \in A \cap B.$$

From the definition of $H(S)$ in (C.1), it follows that

$$P_{s'}^* - P_w^* = H^*(S').$$

Let $P_w^* = (1/2)[X^* - H^*(S')]$, then $P_{s'}^* = (1/2)[X^* + H^*(S')]$. X^* can then be defined by

$$P_{s'}^* + P_w^* = X^*.$$

Recall from (C.3) that

$$Tc = -H^*(S') \cdot (P_{s'}^* + P_w^*)$$

$$= -[H^*(S') \cdot X^*] < 0,$$

from the definition of the half-plane A in (C.5). The speculative profits are

$$\pi = -P_{s'}^* \cdot S'$$

$$= -(1/2) \ [(P_{s'}^* + P_w^*) + (P^* - P_w^*)] \cdot S'$$

$$= -(1/2) \ [X^* + H^*(S')] \cdot S' > 0.$$

This latter expression is positive since $X^* + H^*(S') \in A \cap B$, and thus the properties of the half-plane B in (C.6) hold as well. Thus the speculation has been profitable and destabilizing, or more succinctly $\pi > 0$ while $Tc < 0$.

Notes

1. Mill (reprinted 1921, at pp. 707-708) stated, 'When a speculation in a commodity proves profitable to the speculators as a body... their purchases make the price begin to rise sooner than it otherwise would do, thus spreading the privation of the consumers over a longer period, but mitigating it at the time of its greatest height...[I]t often happens that speculative purchases are made in the expectation of some increase of demand, or deficiency in supply, which after all does not occur, or not to the extent which the speculators expected. In that case the speculation, instead of moderating fluctuations, has caused a fluctuation of price which otherwise would not have happened, or aggravated one which would. But in that case the speculation is a losing one...[A]nd though (speculative transactions) are sometimes injurious to the public, by heightening the fluctuations which their more usual office is to alleviate, yet whenever this happens the speculators are the greatest losers.'

2. See, e.g., Dulles (1929).

3. Kemp illustrates this point more rigorously as follows. If the price follows a regular sine path, $P(t) = \sin Bt,$ the cycle has period $2\pi/B$ and frequency $B/2\pi$. The price has MSSD equal to $B/2\pi \int_0^{2\pi/B} \sin^2 Bt \, dt = 1/2,$ and note $\partial[MSSD(P)]/\partial B = 0$. Thus a change in the amplitude B has no impact on the MSSD.

4. The literature has more frequently noted Baumol's concession than his defense of this general theme of buying on the upswing and selling on the downswing. Compare Logue (1975), Glahe (1966), Krueger (1969), Farrel (1966), Johnson (1976), and Telser (1981); with Kemp (1963), Baumol (1965, pp.17-31), and Eichengreen (1982).

5. Speculation, as differentiated from arbitrage, only occurs under uncertainty. Modern uncertainty theorists would explicitly define the variable adding randomness to a model, e.g., the state of the world, not merely append uncertainty to the passage of time.

6. The only instance where carry-over would not increase the price

variance is if $X^r = X^s$.

7. Schimmler's model incorporates time-dependent variables expressed as vectors in the T-dimensional Euclidean space, $\Re^T$. Alternatively, his model could be formulated with functions of time, such as Kemp (1963), using measurable and Lebesgue square-integrable functions in the Hilbert Space $L^2_{[0,T]}$. The scalar or inner product $S \cdot U$ of the vectors S and U would thus be defined by $\sum_{t=1}^{T} s_t u_t$ in the $\Re^T$ and by $\int_0^T s(t)u(t)$ in the $L^2_{[0,T]}$.

8. This point is due to Lien (1984).

References

Arndt, Sven W., (1968), 'International Short Term Capital Movements: A Distributed Lag Model of Speculation in the Foreign Exchange,' *Econometrica*, Vol. 36, pp. 59-69.

Baumol, William J., (1957), 'Speculation, Profitability, and Stability,' *Review of Economics and Statistics*, Vol. 39, pp. 263-71.

-----, (1959), 'Reply,' *Review of Economics and Statistics*, Vol. 41, pp. 301-302.

-----, (1965), *The Stock Market and Economic Efficiency*, New York: Fordham University Press.

Canzoneri, Matthew B., (1984), 'Rational Destabilizing Speculation and Foreign Intervention Policy,' *Journal of Macroeconomics*, Vol. 36, pp. 59-89.

Dulles, Eleanor Lansing, (1929), *The French Franc 1914-1928*, New York: MacMillan Company.

Eichengreen, Barry J., (1982), 'Did Speculation Destabilize the French Franc in the 1920s?,' *Explorations in Economic History*, Vol. 19, pp. 71-100.

Farrel, M. J., (1966), 'Profitable Speculation,' *Econometrica*, Vol. 33, pp. 183-93.

Friedman, Milton, (1953), 'The Case for Flexible Exchange Rates,' in *Essays on Positive Economics*, Chicago: University of Chicago Press.

-----, (1969), 'In Defense of Destabilizing Speculation,' reprinted in *The Optimum Quantity of Money and Other Essays*, Chicago: Aldine Publishing Company.

-----, (1971), 'The Need for Futures Markets in Currencies,' in *The Futures Market in Foreign Currencies*, Chicago: Chicago Mercantile Exchange.

Glahe, Fred R., (1966), 'Professional and Nonprofessional Speculation, Profitability, and Stability,' *Southern Economics Journal*, Vol. 33, pp. 43-48.

Hart, Oliver D., (1984), 'Price Destabilizing Speculation,' Working Paper 84/92, International Center for Economics and Related Disciplines, London School of Economics and Political Science.

Jesse, Richard R., Jr., and Radcliffe, Robert C., (1981), 'On Speculation and Price Stability Under Uncertainty,' *Review of Economics and Statistics*, Vol. 63:1, pp. 129-32.

Johnson, Harry, (1976), 'Destabilizing Speculation: A General Equilibrium Approach,' *Journal of Political Economy*, Vol. 84, pp. 101-108.

Kaldor, Nicholas, (1963), 'Speculation and Economic Stability,' *Review of Economic Studies*, Vol. 40, pp. 1-27.

Kemp, Murray C., (1963), 'Speculation, Profitability, and Price Stability,' *Review of Economics and Statistics*, Vol. 45, pp. 185-189.

Kenen, Peter B., (1975), 'Floats, Glides, and Indicators,' *Journal of International Economics*, Vol. 5, pp. 107-51.

Kohlhagen, Steven W., (1979), 'The Identification of Destabilizing Foreign Exchange Speculation,' *Journal of International Economics*, Vol. 9, pp. 321-40.

Krueger, Anne O., (1969), 'Balance of Payments Theory,' *Journal of Economic Literature*, Vol. 7, pp. 1-26.

Levin, Jay H., (1983), 'The J-Curve, Rational Expectations, and the Stability of the Flexible Exchange Rate System,' *Journal of International Economics*, Vol. 15, pp. 239-251.

Lien, Donald, (1984), 'A Note on the Nonspeculative Excess Demand Theorem,' Social Science working paper series, California Institute of Technology.

Lipschitz, Leslie and Otani, Ichiro, (1977), 'A Simple Model of the Private Gold Market, 1968-1974: An Exploratory Econometric Exercise,' *International Monetary Fund*, Vol. 24, pp. 36-63.

Logue, Dennis E., (1975), 'Market-making and the Assessment of Market Efficiency,' *Journal of Finance*, Vol. 30, pp. 115-23.

Mill, John Stuart, (1921, reprinted) *Principles of Political Economy*, Book IV, Chap. 2, Sec. 5, London: Longmans, Green, and Co.

Obst, Norman P., (1967), 'A Connection Between Speculation and Stability in the Foreign Exchange Market,' *Southern Economic Journal*, Vol. 34, pp. 146-49.

Price, Lionel D. D., and Wood, Geoffrey E., (1974), 'Another Case of Profitable Destabilizing Speculation - A Note,' *Journal of International Economics*, Vol. 4, pp. 217-20.

Ross, James A., Jr., (1938), *Speculation, Stock Prices, and Industrial Fluctuations*, New York: Harcourt, Brace, and Jovanovich.

Schimmler, Jorg, (1967), 'Speculation, Profitability, and Price Stability - A Formal Approach,' *Review of Economics and Statistics*, Vol. 49, pp. 110-114.

Stein, Jerome L., (1961), 'Destabilizing Speculative Activity Can Be Profitable,' *Review of Economics and Statistics*, Vol. 43, pp. 301-02.

Salant, Stephen, (1974), 'Profitable Destabilizing Speculation,' unpublished manuscript, Board of Governors of the Federal Reserve, Washington, D.C.

Telser, Lester G., (1959), 'A Theory of Speculation Relating Profitability and Stability,' *Review of Economics and Statistics*, Vol. 41, pp. 295-301.

-----, (1981), 'Why There Are Organized Futures Markets,' *Journal of Law and Economics*, Vol. 24, pp. 1-22.

Whitman, Marina v.N., (1975), 'The Payments Adjustment Process and the Exchange Rate Regime: What Have We Learned,' *American Economic Review*, Vol. 65, pp. 133-46.

-----, (1984), 'Assessing Greater Variability of Exchange Rates: A Private Sector Perspective,' *American Economic Review*, Vol. 74:2, pp. 298-304.

Williamson, John, (1977), 'Another Case of Profitable Destabilizing Speculation,' *Journal of International Economics*, Vol. 2, pp. 77-84.

Comment

I am grateful to Michael Guth for his useful summary of the discussion, and for providing me the opportunity to add a few words. More than thirty years have elapsed since I left the controversy over the possibility that profitable speculation can be destabilizing. The length of that interval certainly suggests obsolescence and reduces my qualifications for reentry into the fray. Nevertheless, I remain convinced that speculation need not always be stabilizing to be profitable, and that the counterexamples I have supplied are perfectly legitimate.

Two comments may perhaps help the reader to see why I am not moved by my critics. The first deals primarily with the behavior of nonspeculators. Let me suggest that the critics struggled to escape their trap through resort to semantics, but that, of course, will never do. They argued that my 'nonspeculators' were really speculators, because they were (subconsciously?) taking more than one period's prices into account. This is surely an odd requirement for someone to qualify as a nonspeculator. Is there any mentally competent adult buyer or seller of anything who has never compared past and present prices? Yet, let me show that even with such a tortured use of the word it is easy to reinterpret my models to contain only two groups, one unambiguously composed of speculators and the other of persons absolutely free of that taint.

For this purpose, assume that the second group is made up entirely of persons who simply put cash into the market when they happen to receive it, and withdraw it whenever they happen to need it for exogenously-determined transactions purposes. They put it into the market to avoid the expected interest or dividend opportunity costs that would be incurred by keeping the money idle in the form of cash between the date of its receipt and the day it will be spent. These totally passive investors-disinvestors are surely not 'speculators' by any definition remotely related to standard use of language, and their purchases and sales of securities are determined fully from outside the model, with absolutely no consideration of any security prices, past, future or even present. Now suppose that the exogenous forces happen to lead to investments and withdrawals whose time path would entail cyclical security-price behavior in the absence of speculator activity. There you have my models, and my conclusions surely follow, exactly as before.

Second, let me turn to a question that has been raised about the postulated behavior of my speculators. Why do I assume that speculators sell just after the downturn and buy just after the upturn? How can this assumption constitute a *plausible* element in my counterexamples? Two reasons. First, in an uncertain world, if prices have been rising monotonically, how else can a speculator (who, like the rest of us, cannot really foresee the future) be guided systematically to select dates at which he has some confidence that the expansion phase of the price cycle is coming to an end? How else can that person hope to judge when the market has hit bottom? Surely, it is not unreasonable to wait until prices actually *show* some manifestation of the beginnings of a downturn or the start of an upturn.

There is another reason why this is not an implausible story. For I have spoken to some speculators, and they have told me that this *is* how they actually behave. That is not to claim that all speculators do so, or even that a substantial proportion do so always, but only that the assumption seems to me far more plausible than the one implying that speculators regularly manage to sell exactly at the top and buy just at the bottom. In any case, since as Kemp noted, my goal is just to provide counterexamples, it is hardly necessary for me to offer a universally-accurate depiction of speculator behavior.

W. J. Baumol
C.V. Starr Center for Applied Economics
New York University

Comment

This chapter shows that controversy still remains about whether speculation under the floating exchange rate system is stabilizing or destabilizing. My own work on the subject (*Journal of International Economics*, November 1983) dealt with the implications of the J-curve for the stability of floating exchange rates. The J-curve is the empirical phenomenon in which a depreciation of the home currency initially causes a trade deficit to widen because of the immediate upward pressure on import prices with no initial impact on trade volumes. The latter respond only with a lag to the exchange rate movement. Consequently, over time import volume declines and export volume expands, and the trade deficit eventually begins to move in a desirable direction. Ultimately, the depreciation will cause the trade deficit to shrink, but the dynamic response of the trade deficit resembles the letter *J* tilted sideways.

The implication of the J-curve for floating exchange rates should now be obvious. A depreciation of the home currency initially causes the trade deficit to expand, and one might then expect the currency to depreciate even further in response. In turn, the J-curve reaction would produce an even larger trade deficit and therefore a downward spiral of the currency. In this scenario, the floating exchange rate system becomes completely unstable. In my work on this subject, I introduced speculators with perfect foresight into the system but allowed them to be risk averse. Three conclusions emerged from the analysis. First, speculators would stabilize the floating exchange rate system, provided capital mobility is sufficiently high (i.e., speculators are not too risk averse); second, unless the degree of capital mobility exceeds an even higher critical level, exchange rates will oscillate around their long-run equilibrium values; and third, a real unanticipated disturbance will cause the exchange rate to overshoot its long-run equilibrium level.

The first conclusion is the most important one for this discussion, because it suggests that the J-curve will not be a source of instability for floating exchange rates provided speculation is sufficiently sensitive to prospective exchange rate movements. In the limiting case, if speculators were risk neutral, the exchange rate would be completely stabilized by speculation. No cycles would occur. Real disturbances would cause the exchange rate to move immediately to its new long run equilibrium level.

These conclusions are very sanguine for the stability of floating exchange rates in the presence of speculation. They suggest that the more speculation the better and that the imposition of capital controls is likely to be a disruptive element to a well functioning floating exchange rate system. Moreover, although this chapter shows that a number of counterexamples have been developed in the literature suggesting that destabilizing speculation can be profitable, many of them rest on collusive behavior on the part of speculators or other unrealistic assumptions. This suggests to me that the Friedman proposition that speculation will be stabilizing in the long run is a very plausible one, although the argument that professionals could feed off of a revolving group of amateurs and that the group as a whole could be destabilizing is also a plausible one to me. Nor do these arguments tell us much about the possibility of speculative bubbles. These questions can be resolved only by considering empirical tests on speculation.

My own view is that we know very little about the stabilizing or destabilizing nature of speculation from the current body of empirical work. There is some evidence [Froot and Frankel (1989) and Takagi (1991)] that speculators in the major currencies may be very close to being risk neutral but that their expectations may not be rational. To the extent that speculators make systematic errors in their forecasts of future exchange rates, this could have a destabilizing effect on exchange rates. The counter-argument is that if speculators form their expectations adaptively or regressively or with distributed lags, as some evidence suggests [Frankel and Froot (1987)], these types of mechanisms are stabilizing. Moreover, some evidence suggests that speculators with short-term horizons may be destabilizing and those with long-term horizons may be stabilizing [Frankel and Froot (1990)]. Finally, there is little empirical evidence on the existence of speculative bubbles. These conclusions, however, are tentative and require further empirical confirmation.

Jay H. Levin
Department of Economics
Wayne State University

References

Frankel, Jeffrey A., and Kenneth A. Froot, (1987), 'Using Survey Data to Test Standard Propositions Regarding Exchange Rate Expectations,' *American Economic Review*, March 1987.

Frankel, Jeffrey A., and Kenneth A. Froot, (1990), 'Chartists, Fundamentalists, and Trading in the Foreign Exchange Market,' *American Economic Review*, May 1990.

Froot, Kenneth A., and Jeffrey A. Frankel, 'Forward Discount Bias: Is It an Exchange Risk Premium?,' *Quarterly Journal of Economics*, February 1989.

Takagi, Shinji, (1991), 'Exchange Rate Expectations: A Survey of Survey Studies,' International Monetary Fund Staff Papers, March 1981.

2 Arrow-Debreu theory

Throughout the discussion of speculation and stability in Chapter 1, we emphasized that uncertainty theorists now have a generally accepted framework for modeling choice under uncertainty. Economic theorists have chosen to model uncertainty as the revelation of a state of the world. Individuals in these models face investment and consumption decisions based on payoffs that vary across different states of the world.

This chapter examines the state-preference framework (Arrow-Debreu Theory) in detail. The Arrow-Debreu world has two versions: a state-contingent claims model and a securities version. After 1975, revised general equilibrium models began to incorporate future spot market prices into the definition of the state space. This change was brought about to remove speculative considerations identified in the literature. Yet the revised state definition introduces new problems of its own.

2.1 Review of Arrow's (1964) Contingent Claims and Securities Models

Any introduction to modern uncertainty theory in economics must begin by recalling two fundamental theorems from welfare economics. The first states that assuming no externalities or non-convexities in production or consumption, then every competitive equilibrium is a Pareto optimum. The second theorem holds that given an appropriate redistribution of resources, then, roughly speaking, every Pareto optimal allocation can be achieved as a competitive equilibrium.[1] These theorems applied to an economy with no randomness or uncertainty.

The contingent claims model enabled economists to extend the relationship between competitive equilibria and Pareto optimality to an economy operating under *uncertainty*. So powerful a modeling tool was this conception that it provided the general framework for uncertainty theorists for the next forty years, spawned a new field of study known as contingent claims analysis in finance, and contributed to the award of Nobel prizes to two of its creators.[2]

Arrow (1953, reprinted 1964) introduced uncertainty into the standard pure-exchange economy via a random variable designating the 'state of nature.' The Arrow-Debreu literature alternatively refers to this variable as a 'state of the world.' The first part of Arrow's article proposed a market with I individuals, C commodities, and S possible states of nature. Prior to the realization of a state, individuals could buy and sell contingent claims, denoted X_{sc}, which entitled the owner to one unit of commodity c if state of nature s occurred. In the earliest formulations of the model, the states represented physical conditions of the environment, e.g., rain or shine. But the state variable soon became broadly interpreted to represent other exogenous forms of uncertainty a trader might face.[3]

The basic feasibility constraint for the economy requires that the sum of the contingent claims equals the total stock of a commodity in that state of the world:

$$\sum_{i=1}^{I} X_{isc} = \bar{X}_{sc}, \quad \forall\ s,c. \tag{2.1}$$

With a complete set of contingent claims, i.e., one claim for each commodity in each possible state of nature, Arrow noted that the competitive economy operating under uncertainty was isomorphic to the standard pure exchange economy, with a couple exceptions.

First, the total number of trading instruments had increased by a factor of S. Whereas the standard pure exchange economy had C goods being traded, the contingent claims economy had $S \times C$ instruments.[4] This point was relatively innocuous. The second difference was that instead of maximizing utility from consumption across the range of C commodities, each individual i would maximize *expected utility* given by the product of his utility from consuming each commodity c and his subjective probability (ρ_{is}) for state s. Arrow assumed each individual had preferences represented by the following utility function:

$$V_i\,(X_{i11}, \ldots, X_{iSC}) \equiv \sum_{s} \rho_{is}\; U_i(X_{is1}, \ldots, X_{iSC}),$$

where U_i is assumed to be a non-decreasing, concave function. This assumption in turn implies that V_i is non-decreasing and quasi-concave.

Expected utility maximization *seemed* like an innocuous change. However, the change led to some controversy over what objects of uncertainty agents should have subjective probabilities. This controversy continues to the present day.

The sequence of events in Arrow's model begins with trading in the X_{sc} contingent claims. Then a competitive equilibrium is achieved, trading stops, the state of nature is subsequently revealed, and only those contingent claims for the realized state s^* are executed. Given the quasi-concavity of V_i and a set of positive weights $(w_1, \ldots, w_I)$, a central planner could maximize $\sum_i w_i V_i$ subject to (2.1) and arrive at the optimal allocation X^*_{isc}. With a set of money incomes Y_i for individual i and taking prices $\bar{P}_{sc}$ for a claim to one unit of commodity c in state s as given, if the individual chooses the quantities X_{isc} that maximize V_i subject to

$$\sum_s \sum_c \bar{P}_{sc} X_{isc} = Y_i,$$

then the chosen quantities X_{isc} would be the optimal allocation X^*_{isc}. Thus, the competitive equilibrium in the contingent claims market achieves a Pareto optimal allocation. This result is Arrow's (1964) Theorem 1.

In the second part of his article, Arrow formulated a securities market version of the contingent claims model, which introduced paper claims to money. Each security s pays one dollar if state s occurs and zero otherwise. Arrow assumes that there exist precisely S securities, whose S-dimensional payoff vectors are thus linearly independent.

In the securities version of Arrow's model, individuals first purchase securities before the state has been revealed. After the realization of a state, the individuals cash in their money claims and purchase commodities in a spot market. With a complete market, individuals would allegedly need access to only $S + C$ markets (down from $S \times C$ contingent claims in the first part of Arrow's article) to achieve the same Pareto optimal competitive equilibrium.

To prove the equivalence of the contingent claims and securities market allocations, we shall follow the steps restated by Nagatani (1975), which are more fully developed than those in the original article. The feasibility constraint in the securities model imposes a double condition on the income, Y_i, available to individual i. Let q_s denote the price for security s, P_{sc} the future spot market price for commodity c in state s, and X_{isc} the quantity of commodity c purchased by individual i in state s. Then technical feasibility requires

$$\sum_s q_s Y_{is} = Y_i, \tag{2.2}$$

and

$$\sum_s \sum_c P_{sc} X_{isc} = Y_i. \tag{2.3}$$

The question is how are the prices q_s and P_{sc} determined.

Arrow chose the security prices to meet the condition

$$q_s P_{sc} = \bar{P}_{sc}. \tag{2.4}$$

The values of $\bar{P}_{sc}$ are precisely the contingent claims prices from the first part of Arrow's model. Thus Arrow asserts that individuals facing these prices have the same range of alternatives in the market and, consequently, will acquire the same claims as in the first part of his article. Each individual i will purchase the quantity

$$Y_{is}^* = \sum_c P_{sc} X_{isc}^* \tag{2.5}$$

of security s. The Y_{is}^* must satisfy (2.2) and (2.3) above. Furthermore, the total income in the economy must equal the sum of the individuals' income: $Y \equiv \sum_i Y_{is}$ for all s. After substituting this expression into (2.3), summing across individuals i, and combining it with (2.4); the security prices can be expressed as

$$q_s = \frac{\sum_i \sum_c \bar{P}_{sc} X_{isc}^*}{Y}. \tag{2.6}$$

Arrow uses (2.6) and (2.4) to define q_s and P_{sc}, respectively. As Nagatani (1975) and Radner (1970) pointed out, if the $\bar{P}_{sc}$ were known to individuals in the Arrow-Debreu economy, then indeed there would exist a set of prices (q_s, P_{sc}) such that the sequential securities trading followed by spot market trading would yield the same allocation X_{isc}^*. This equivalent allocation result is Arrow's (1964) Theorem 2, perhaps the more important of the two theorems in his article.[5]

2.2 The 'Early' Arrow-Debreu Literature, 1955 - 1975

Following the publication of Arrow's seminal work, a large and complex literature on general equilibrium theory and contingent claims analysis evolved. The literature contains many optimality and non-optimality results spanning various extensions of the Arrow-Debreu model; it would be infeasible to attempt to review all of the works here. Fortunately, Radner (1982) summarized the key findings of the early literature.

Although some of the works discussed in this section were published after 1975, they all commonly assume that the state of the world described one or more joint events about the external environment. This early literature also accepted the equivalence of the contingent claims and securities version of Arrow's model without objection.

Theorists interpreted Arrow's results in different ways. A lemma circulated in the literature that with a complete set of contingent claim markets, all desired trading would take place in the prior trading round. In the absence of new information or a change in preferences or budget constraints, no one would want to retrade from their prior round position even if given the opportunity in sequential trading rounds. The subsequent trading rounds would be pointless.

In an earlier article, Radner (1968) indicated that this widely-circulating lemma only worked in one direction. If everyone believes future spot prices are inessential, they will be. However, if some individuals believe something new will change expected spot market prices, they can take positions in intermediate and sequential trading rounds that will force prices to depart from the prior trading round equilibrium. Ultimately, these individual positions may have to be reversed, but in the intermediate trading periods, the terms of trade may adversely affect the value of the prior trading round positions. In short, the traders can adopt paradoxical strategies that become self-fulfilling equilibria.

Radner (1968) extended the Arrow-Debreu model to include agents with differing information about the economy. He found that when information was restricted to the environment, the Arrow-Debreu contingent claims equilibrium can achieve an optimum (relative to a given structure of information). However, if agents receive information about the trading behavior of other market participants, then externalities arise. These externalities often distort preferences or otherwise diminish the optimality of the competitive equilibrium. In particular, the 'set-up cost' of gathering information, which may be independent of the scale of production, introduces non-convexity into the production possibility set. And non-convexities, of course, violate the basic assumptions of the optimality theorems.

Radner's (1968) formal model dealt only with the case in which agents had fixed information structures. His informal remarks in that article, some of which are quoted in this chapter, went beyond that to suggest what might happen (and how Arrow-Debreu theory would have to be changed) if agents learned from prices and the actions of others.

Radner (1970) noted that the original Arrow-Debreu model assumes that all individuals have equal access to and the same information. Concerning information needed by market participants in the prior trading round(s) of the securities version of the Arrow-Debreu model, Radner observed

> Although the second part of the price system might be interpreted as spot prices, it would be a mistake to think of the determination of the equilibrium values of these prices as being deferred in real time to the dates to which they refer. The definition of equilibrium requires that the agents have access to the complete system of prices when choosing their plans. In effect, this requires that at the beginning of time, all agents have available a (common) forecast of the equilibrium spot price that will prevail at every future date and event. Radner (1970), p.456.

Radner's point about implied knowledge of spot market prices became the focus of the post-1975 Arrow-Debreu literature.

Radner (1982) identified a second line of criticism of Arrow-Debreu theory as inadequate treatment of money, the stock market, and active markets at every date. To correct these deficiencies Radner recommended that future extensions of the Arrow-Debreu model include 1) uncertainty about future prices as well as uncertainty about the environment; 2) a method for producers to compare net revenues at different dates and across states of the world; 3) consumers facing a sequence of budget constraints over time, rather than the single present net worth budget constraint of the Arrow-Debreu model; 4) speculation in future markets by storage, hedging, etc.; and 5) agents' attempts to forecast future prices based on information about both the environment and other market participants' behavior up to that point in time.

Radner's own work addressed some of these issues. Radner (1968) assumed that markets were complete but argued that some of these markets would be redundant and have no trading if agents' information structures were sufficiently different. Four years later, Radner (1972) provided a formal treatment of multiperiod incomplete markets, but agents were restricted from learning about the environment through prices. Finally, Radner (1979) studied what happens when agents are allowed to learn from prices, although he worked with a two-period model. These different information structures and corresponding equilibrium notions are clarified in Radner (1982).[6]

Another branch of the Arrow-Debreu literature questioned whether *ex ante* optimality or *ex post* optimality was the appropriate measure of efficiency.

> As a practical matter, the achievement of an Arrow optimum is a normative dead end. After all, we are not so much interested in expectations as in results. Given an Arrow optimal distribution of contingent claims and supposing the occurrence of some event, we can then ask whether in that event the distribution of real goods resulting from the given distribution of contingent claims is a Pareto optimal distribution of real goods. If the answer is 'no,' then it is comparatively small comfort to know that the economy had achieved an optimal allocation of risk bearing....the appropriate quality to seek is that there be no redistribution that will increase some trader's realized utility while decreasing no trader's realized utility. Such a situation will be termed an *ex post* Pareto optimum. Starr (1973), p.82.

For the pure exchange economy, Starr (1973) finds that Arrow's contingent claims equilibrium will be *ex post* Pareto optimal if and only if all of the market participants assign the same probability value to a given state *s* occurring. Starr refers to this property as 'universally similar' beliefs.

For the case of production, Starr finds the Arrow-Debreu equilibrium will be *ex post* Pareto optimal under even more restrictive conditions. Market participants must have 'universally similar' beliefs, and the prevailing contingent claim prices must be consistent with both universal similarity and profit-maximizing production. For both the pure exchange and the production economy, information about what state will occur is not particularly important for achieving *ex post* Pareto optimality in Starr's model. Pareto optimality results from the unanimity of traders' beliefs rather than their accuracy.[7]

Harris (1978) addressed the issues of (1) whether a decentralized resource allocation mechanism could be found such that *ex ante* choices result in an *ex post* optimal equilibrium, and (2) given an *ex post* efficient allocation, can an *ex ante* resource allocation mechanism be found to achieve that equilibrium solution? Recall that a Lindahl equilibrium achieves an efficient allocation of a public good by providing each individual with a specific price corresponding to the utility he receives from consuming that public good. Harris (1978) borrowed this concept to introduce a 'Personalized Price Mechanism,' which turns out to be the product of the contingent claims market price times the individual's subjective probability for that state to occur. Thus, the personalized price of commodity c in state s for individual i is $P_{sci} = \rho_{is} P_{sc}$, using the notation of Section 2.1. 'Compared to Lindahl prices, these 'personal prices' are very special, since the relative prices of two goods to be delivered in the same state of the world are the same for all persons.' Harris (1978), p.430.

Harris starts by assuming (1) all states of nature are assigned positive probability by all consumers, (2) non-satiated consumers in all states of nature (follows from assumptions on concave, continuous, and strictly monotone utility functions), (3) additively-separable utility functions, and (4) a pure exchange economy. He then shows that his Personalized Price Mechanism will yield an *ex post* efficient allocation for a given state s, a 'universally *ex post* efficient' allocation across every state, and an *ex ante* optimal allocation for each consumer's endowed probability beliefs. Conversely, by further assuming strictly positive consumption of goods and that all consumer utility functions are continuously differentiable, Harris shows a universally *ex post* efficient allocation can be achieved as the outcome of market trading with a Personalized Price Mechanism.

Grossman (1981) examined the nature of a rational expectations equilibrium (REE) in an Arrow-Debreu contingent claims economy with diverse information. A Walrasian equilibrium, in such an economy, will generally allocate resources differently than if each trader had access to all the information available in the market. Furthermore, traders will learn over time how market clearing prices relate to changes in underlying demand. Individuals will use this information to revise their demand schedules and want to retrade.

In the long run, prices will clear at a level at which no one desires to retrade. Grossman calls this latter solution a REE. In an economy with asymmetric information, the REE may yield an allocation that is identical to one in which all traders had full access to the information, but there is no guarantee. Grossman demonstrates that if the Arrow-Debreu markets are complete in the sense of spanning the entire range of the commodity-state space, and if traders have (1) additively separable, (2) non-satiable, (3) strictly concave, and (4) differentiable utility functions, then there exists a REE that is *ex post* Pareto optimal. Grossman (1981) characterized this finding as 'a powerful extension of the fundamental theorem of welfare economics to economies with diverse information....However, the reader is cautioned that there may be multiple REE.' (p.555)

Coutinho (1986) provided the complementary analysis to Grossman (1981): he illustrated a REE under the same assumptions as Grossman (1981) that reflects only a portion of the available information and another REE that could be *ex post* Pareto dominated. Since the REE plays an important role in subsequent chapters of this book and since Coutinho employs a particularly straight-forward Arrow-Debreu contingent claims model, we will retrace the key features of his examples.

Consider a two-period contingent claims model with two possible states of the world, s_1 and s_2. The market contains two consumers with identical preferences, which can be described by a von Neumann-Morgenstern utility function. The endowments for consumers 1 and 2 across the two states of the world are $e_1 = (0,1)$ and $e_2 = (1,0)$, respectively. Thus, if the state turns out to be s_1, consumer 1 has 0 units of the good and consumer 2 has 1 unit.

Each consumer is informed about the result of one of two coin tosses. Consumers know that if both coins come up heads or both come up tails, then the state will be s_1. If one coin comes up heads and the other tails, then the state will be s_2; however, each consumer only knows the value of his own coin toss, not the other's toss. After receiving this information, the consumers trade in a complete set of Arrow-Debreu contingent claims markets. Let y_i denote the information signal received by consumer i.

Coutinho (1986) defines a REE for this economy as a triple of vectors $p = [p^1(y), p^2(y)]$; $x_1 = [x_1^1(y_1,p), x_1^2(y_1,p)]$; $x_2 = [x_2^1(y_2,p), x_2^2(y_2,p)]$ such that

$$x_i = arg \max U(x_i^1)\, Pr(s_1 | y_i, p) + U(x_i^2)\, Pr(s_2 | y_i, p)$$

with $U' > 0$, $U'' < 0$, and subject to $p \cdot x_i \le p \cdot e_i$, and $x_1^J + x_2^J \le e_1^J + e_2^J$, for $i = 1, 2$, and $J = 1, 2$. To prove the existence of an equilibrium, Coutinho sets $U(x_i^J) = \ln x_i^J$, which implies the consumers have Cobb-Douglas utility functions. 'It is a well-known result that an Arrow-Debreu economy where consumers have Cobb-Douglas utility functions has a unique equilibrium.' (Coutinho (1986), p.884)

The price vector $p(y) = (1,1)$, for all y, coupled with demand functions $x_1 = (1/2, 1/2)$ and $x_2 = (1/2, 1/2)$, constitute an REE. The price vector conveys no additional information about which of the two states is more likely, hence each consumer will continue to assign probability $Pr[s_J|y_i, p=(1,1)] = 1/2$ for $J, i = 1, 2$. In this equilibrium, each consumer insures against the uncertain outcome by allocating half of his endowment to each state of nature. The equilibrium price vector reveals no information even though the economy as a whole has a conclusive signal about the state. Given the price vector $p(y) = (1,1)$, no consumer has any incentive to retrade if subsequent contingent claims trading markets were opened to him. Thus Coutinho has illustrated a REE that imperfectly reveals information in the economy.

> According to Grossman (1977), this economy must have also a fully revealing equilibrium. Indeed, consider now the following case: $p = (1,0)$ if $y_1 = y_2$, and $p = (0,1)$ if $y_1 \neq y_2$. This is a fully revealing equilibrium price system since $Pr(s_J|y_i, p) = Pr(s_J|y_1,y_2)$ and demand equals supply at each state of nature. Coutinho (1986), p.884.

Next, Coutinho illustrates a REE that is *ex post* Pareto dominated by another equilibrium. First, let us assume the same structure in the economy as in the previous example, but with one exception. Consumers can now chose a production technology that will allow them to select their endowment vector from the convex hull of (0,1), (1,0), and (1/2, 1/2).

Facing the price vector (1,1), each consumer will chose an endowment that splits his income and risk across the two possible states: (1/2, 1/2). This strategy maximizes expected utility and yields an equilibrium. However, a central planner could choose the production technology more efficiently. If both coin tosses yielded the same result, the central planner could choose the production technology that leads to endowment vector $e_i = (1,0)$ for $i = 1, 2$. Similarly, if the coin tosses yield opposite results, the central planner could select technology leading to endowments $e_i = (0,1)$ for both consumers. In both instances, the central planner's allocation clearly dominates the competitive equilibrium allocation (1/2, 1/2).

Coutinho has this to say about the optimality of these equilibria:

> It is interesting to note that while the non-revealing REE is *ex post* Pareto inferior to the fully revealing REE, it is *ex ante* Pareto superior to the fully revealing REE (in fact the non-revealing REE is *ex ante* Pareto optimal). This is because *ex ante* (with) the realization of information, the non-revealing REE price vector $p =$ (1,1) allocates income in a way that consumers fully insure each other. Coutinho (1986), p.884.

The appropriateness of either the *ex ante* or *ex post* optimality concept remains an open issue for discussion. In addition to the works surveyed here, others who have contributed to this discussion include Dreze (1970) and Hammond (1976), who introduced the notion of *ex post* social welfare optimality.

Articles in this literature that employed additively-separable utility functions follow the Arrow tradition of the Arrow-Debreu literature. Debreu (1959), by contrast, specifies only the preference preorder of the ith consumer, not his utility function. 'This preference preordering, reflects the tastes of the consumer for goods and services (including, in particular, their spatial and temporal specifications), his personal appraisal of the likelihoods of the various events, and his attitudes toward risk.' Debreu (1959, p.101). Endowed with this preference preordering and his wealth, an individual takes prices as given and chooses consumption bundles that optimize his preferences.

As we shall see in Chapter 3, critics have focused upon the additively-separable utility function, which implies zero complementarity between the commodities, as a major objection to the contingent claims models of speculation. Yet this assumption has significantly simplified the resulting first-order conditions. Although it has yet to be explored in the speculation theory models, the preference preordering adopted by Debreu (1959) may yield a solution to the current modeling handicap.

2.3 The Revised Arrow-Debreu State Space

Extensions and comments on Arrow and Debreu's work in the early literature left the basic equilibrium solution and the equivalence theorem intact. However, the situation changed when Nagatani (1975) raised a fundamental question about how individual traders could know future spot market prices in the securities version of the Arrow-Debreu model.

Recall that Arrow chose the security prices to meet the condition

$$q_s P_{sc} = \bar{P}_{sc}. \quad \textbf{(2.4)}$$

As outside observers, we know that the $\bar{P}_{sc}$ should equal the contingent claims market prices in the first part of Arrow's article. Yet individuals trading in the securities version cannot be expected to know prices in a market that does not even exist.

No mechanism in the securities version of Arrow's model transmits information about the value of $\bar{P}_{sc}$ to these individuals trading securities in the prior round. The lack of knowledge about $\bar{P}_{sc}$ in turn means that individuals face uncertainty over what prices will prevail in the future spot markets once a given state of the world has been realized; without knowing $\bar{P}_{sc}$, the individuals cannot compute P_{sc} from (2.4). This dimension of uncertainty creates risk and a source for speculation. Absent securities that payoff according to the price in a given state of the world, individuals might seek inefficient allocations to offset real or perceived risks from price uncertainty.

As Nagatani (1975) noted, individuals trading in the commodity claims version of Arrow's model reveal more information than they do in the securities market version. In the former case each individual *i* reveals the whole *SC* vector X_{isc}, whereas in the securities version, he reveals only the *S* vector Y_{is}. It is not surprising then that the securities market in turn contains less information to be inferred by any individual. An agent will know how much income he will have in any state *s*, but he will not know at the time he purchases securities how much of commodity *c* he can afford to purchase in that state.

Thus individual *i* would try to solve the following decision problem:

$$\underset{Y_{is}}{MAX} \sum_{s} \rho_{is} \, E\,[U_i(X_{ics}(P_{cs}, Y_{is}) \,|\, s] \quad \textbf{(2.7)}$$

subject to income constraint $\sum_{s} q_s Y_{is} = Y_i$. In expression (2.7), *E* is an expectation operator taken over the subjective probability distribution of prices, P_{sc}, given state *s*, and X_{isc} is individual *i*'s demand as a function of the spot market prices he faces and his income. Let Y_{is}^{**} denote the solution to (2.7). Nagatani stated the crux of the problem succinctly:

For the given social endowments X_{sc}, these individual solutions would generally lead to the same allocation X^*_{isc} if and only if $Y^{**}_{is} = Y^*_{is}$ for all i, s. But generally $Y^{**}_{is} \neq Y^*_{is}$...(and) some individuals will have more money and others less relative to the allocation under perfect information. Nagatani (1975), pp. 484-485.

In a footnote Nagatani pointed out that for a Cobb-Douglas utility function, the proportion of income spent on any good is independent of prices. For this one special case, $Y^{**}_{is} = Y^*_{is}$. But, in general, speculative considerations about future spot market prices will lead to sub-optimal trading allocations in the Arrow-Debreu securities market.

Arrow's (1975) response offered two possible solutions to this dilemma. First, the Arrow-Debreu world could be considered a succession of identical lotteries. After a sufficiently long period of time, individuals would become familiar with what commodity prices prevail in a particular state of the world. The mechanics of this identical lottery process appear cumbersome. Every state of the world would have to be randomly selected multiple times so that the individuals could compare what prices had previously prevailed when that state occurred. Even then individuals might face uncertainty over whether preferences or other features of the market have changed over time.

Arrow's second, alternative response became the norm in the post-1975 Arrow-Debreu literature: prices were defined as part of the state of the world.[8] In fact, the state of the world evolved to a complete description of every conceivable dimension of uncertainty in the market. But redefining the state space represented a major departure in the original formulation of the model. As Radner observed

> The distinction between (1) uncertainty and information about the environment, and (2) uncertainty and information about others' behavior or the outcome of as yet unperformed computations appears to be fundamental. The analyses of Arrow and Debreu deal with uncertainty about the environment. Radner (1968), p.32.

In the early Arrow-Debreu literature, the state of the world had only described the physical environment.

2.4 Problems with the Revised Version of Arrow's Model

The revised state space incorporating future spot market prices creates new objections:

> [T]here can be no uncertainty about prices that will prevail in a given state if those prices are made part of the very definition of the state. But it must be admitted that there are some difficulties with this interpretation. Implicitly, at least, the uncertainties in the model are exogenous to the economic system; but prices are endogenous to it, and this might complicate our understanding of the model. Arrow (1975), p.487.

The first objection is that treating prices as exogenous undermines the general equilibrium character of the Arrow-Debreu framework. If shocks to prices - rather than shifts in underlying demand and supply - are the focus of attention, then we are back in the realm of pre-modern partial equilibrium analysis. We should also note that Debreu's (1959) extension defined futures prices in terms of events, not *vice versa*.

Next, the problem identified by Nagatani, namely uncertainty over future spot market prices, is actually just one example of a class of potential dimensions of uncertainty affecting the Arrow-Debreu model. We call this class of problems 'intrinsic uncertainty' in Chapter 4. Individuals in the Arrow-Debreu economy might reasonably also face uncertainty over possible (1) changes in preferences over time, (2) changes in beliefs stemming from new information, (3) the effects of 'sunspots' on the equilibrium,[9] and (4) virtually any other object of uncertainty that individuals feel might influence other market participants. Complete contingent claims markets under such circumstances are impossible to create,[10] and all the individuals would likely never agree on how many relevant factors or variables must be accounted for in the contingent claims contracts. Anyone could dream up a new factor and say it is relevant.

Harris (1978) previously noted the problem with changing preferences in connection with the *ex post* optimality literature.

> The conflict between *ex post* and *ex ante* Pareto efficiency of intertemporal resource allocation under uncertainty is an example of the problems caused by changing tastes. The problem has serious implications for making welfare judgments, as there may well be a divergence between *ex ante* choice and *ex post* preference. This (problem) casts doubt on the validity of the

principle of consumer sovereignty as a means of evaluating resource allocations. Harris (1978), p.427.

A third problem relates to expanding the state space to eliminate uncertainty about changing preferences. Suppose *arguendo* that the state space also depicted consumer preferences as well. A moral hazard problem would then likely arise in that individuals would recognize their payoffs from alternative securities depend in part on their own preferences. Individuals who own securities paying off for a given value of their preferences would clearly benefit by changing their preferences to match that value. Similarly, they could cancel their liabilities by modifying preferences from those values of the state space that match the contingent securities they had sold.

> Radner (1970) gives lack of information and moral hazard as two distinct reasons for the failure of some markets for contingent claims to exist. But in fact the latter is a special case of the former; if an insurance company could distinguish whether a fire was due to arson or not, it could pay in the latter case but not in the former. Thus moral hazard arises only because the insurance company cannot distinguish between two states of nature. Arrow (1970), p.463.

A fourth problem for the revised Arrow-Debreu economy is that individuals trading claims in a sequence of markets, and Debreu extended Arrow's word into a multiperiod model, would not know what state has been revealed until they witnessed the unfolding strategies of the other market participants. Prices in these sequential markets could follow any number of transient paths before arriving at the same final equilibrium value. Radner expressed this point as follows:

> (Spot market prices) would depend, at a given date, on the evolution of the economy up to that date, including the evolution of the environment, both through direct observations of the environment...and indirectly through the decisions made up to that date...Unfortunately, in order correctly to infer something about the state of nature from the value of the new prices, an agent must in principle know the strategies used by other agents up to that date....In particular, an agent will no longer be able to assign a definite value to a strategy for given prices in the futures market. Radner (1968), p.35.

Other authors expressed this point somewhat differently:

> A state of the world in this model is a complete specification of the physical environment and of spot market equilibrium prices as well, for all dates from the present to the end of the history of the economic system....[I]ndividuals will not know what state of the world has actually occurred until the history of the economic system is completed, hence there is no way that securities paying off on the basis of states of the world can be cashed in prior to that time, and hence no way that consumption plans can be implemented in the spot markets. It appears that incorporating spot market prices into the specification of states of the world leads to a restriction of the model to a two-period framework, today's security markets and tomorrow's spot markets and consumption. Burness, Cummings, and Quirk (1980), p.15.

Finally, from a theoretical viewpoint, the construction of the revised Arrow-Debreu economy - with subjective probabilities over possible spot market prices - drives an inappropriate nexus between Pareto optimality (a welfare concept) and particular institutions (that generate prices).

> By including subjective probabilities as to equilibrium prices in the objective functions of consumers, and by using these objective functions in defining an *ex ante* optimum for the economy, the idea of an optimum has now become tied directly to a specific institution for allocating resources. How would one go about making a comparison between, say, a centrally planned allocation of resources and a competitive allocation with such a criterion? It seems clear that this is just an incorrect mixing of categories; from a descriptive or predictive point of view, beliefs of consumers as to equilibrium prices should be included in their objective functions, but from the point of view of welfare economics, they don't belong in the picture. Thus it seems that to the extent that future spot markets are to be active, the welfare results of the Arrow-Debreu model generally hold only because a flawed notion of *ex ante* optimality - one incorporating beliefs of consumers as to future spot prices - is employed. Burness, Cummings, and Quirk (1980), p.13.

2.5 Price Uncertainty in the Contingent Claims Economy

George Feiger examined the impact of the scope of markets on speculative behavior in the contingent claims economy. Commenting on Radner's (1968) paradoxical trading hypothesis, Feiger (1976) essentially restated Nagatani's objection to the Arrow-Debreu securities economy.

> The resolution of the paradox represents both the strength and the weakness of the concept of complete markets. For its arises only when the markets are incomplete in that *one cannot insure against future spot market prices*. Thus, logical incompleteness makes it necessary to suppose that the contingencies allowed in the prior trading include all future spot prices. If this is acceptable, then speculation will never take place under complete markets. Feiger (1976), p.680.

Hirshleifer's (1976) analysis of Feiger's point with respect to a multiperiod contingent claims model of speculation led him to conclude the following:

> My contention was that price uncertainty was an endogenous, not an exogenous consideration, that the probability distribution of prices was the resultant of an underlying stochastic variability of the quantity magnitudes. But my contention, to be strictly valid, rested upon the *computability* of price conditional upon the requisite beliefs or information about quantity. I emphasized certain special cases (e.g., concordant beliefs) where computability was clearly possible....[W]ith less special and more 'realistic' assumptions, computability is attenuated. In the extreme we can imagine computability entirely replaced by free-floating beliefs; more or less 'wild fancies' about prices then indeed become autonomous determinants of behavior and equilibrium. Feiger (1976) suggests that the remedy, in principle, would be to provide prior contingent contracts for any commodity conditional not only upon state and message but also upon posterior price. This would grotesquely enlarge dimensionality of the decision problem, unfortunately. Hirshleifer (1976), pp. 695-696.

So a contemporaneous exchange between Feiger and Hirshleifer - on the contingent claims model - parallels the conclusions of the exchange between Nagatani and Arrow on the securities model. Yet look how the definition of 'complete markets' has expanded.

In the original Arrow article, a complete market would require $S \times C$ contingent claims. With Feiger's comment, the revised complete market would contain $S \times C \times \tilde{P}$ markets, where $\tilde{P}$ depicts a continuum of possible spot market prices in a given state of nature. Finally, for an intertemporal investment economy with information events, a complete market must contain $S \times C \times \tilde{P} \times M$ markets, where M represents the set of possible messages that could be received. Even for the case of conclusive information, so that $M \equiv S$, market completeness we would still require $S \times C \times \tilde{P}$ contingent claims markets in advance of the information. The previous problems identified in the last section - reduction to partial equilibrium analysis, uncertainty over changing preferences, moral hazard, collapse to two period model - resurface in the revised state space definition in the contingent claims setting as well.

2.6 The Stock Market Efficiency Literature

In demonstrating the *ex ante* optimality of the competitive equilibrium with production, Debreu introduced the notion of maximizing the value of a firm's shares and explained its equivalence to profit maximization for a world of complete markets:

> Given a price system p and a production y_j, the *profit* of the jth producer is $p \cdot y_j$. Considering the price system as a datum, the jth producer tries to maximize his profit in his production set. For this he needs neither an appraisal (conscious or unconscious) of the likelihoods of the various events, nor an attitude toward risk. His behavior amounts to maximizing the value of the stock outstanding of the jth corporation. In other words, the jth corporation announces a production plan y_j; as a result, its share has a determined value on the stock market; it chooses its plan so as to maximize the value of its share. Debreu (1959), p.100.

Real financial markets obviously contain incomplete contingent claim markets. A share in a firm entitles the owner to receive a proportion of the firm's earnings across every state of the world. A share of a firm is a so-called 'unconditional' contingent claims contract. Incomplete markets imply potential risks cannot be effectively hedged with prevailing financial instruments; and consequently, the competitive equilibrium allocation would be expected to be sub-optimal. To accommodate this shortfall, Diamond (1967) introduced the notion of 'constrained optimality': Pareto optimality relative to the set of allocations that can be achieved through existing market structures. In a one-good, two-period economy, Diamond showed that a competitive equilibrium will be a constrained Pareto optimum.

Diamond contrasted the competitive allocation resulting from firms maximizing their market value with the allocation by the government under restricted conditions: any taxes, subsidies, or other form of redistribution could not be state-dependent. Each individual received a payoff from the profits of the firm according to the number of shares he owned. Assuming constant returns to scale (so that the ratio of output in any two states is independent of scale) and each firm believes that its market value is proportional to its production scale, then firms operating to maximize their market values achieved a constrained Pareto optimum.

However, Hart (1975) showed that Diamond's result holds with little generality; with two or more goods, or three or more periods, the stock market economy fails to achieve even constrained optimality. Furthermore, an equilibrium need not exist. For particular values of the exogenous parameters, Hart's generalized stock market model contained multiple equilibria, so that a given equilibrium could be Pareto dominated by another. Starrett (1973) also found that transactions costs in Diamond's model could prevent efficient allocations.

Hart's multiple equilibria result might be called a 'structural inefficiency' in the stock market. Stiglitz (1972) had also found structural inefficiencies in stock market allocations using the Capital Asset Pricing Model. In Stiglitz (1982), he focused on 'marginal inefficiencies': the private market incorrectly decides how to invest at the margin and would do so even if there were a unique equilibrium. Hart (1975) coined the phrase 'strong optimality' to define an allocation with no marginal inefficiencies. Like Stiglitz, Hart found an equilibrium may be strongly sub-optimal even if it is unique.

Stiglitz summarizes his marginal inefficiency argument as follows:

> With a complete set of risks markets, we know we wish to equalize the marginal rates of substitution between any two states for all individuals. With an incomplete set of markets, we cannot do this, but we may be able to have a more 'efficient' distribution of risks (come closer to equalizing, on average, the marginal rates of substitution) if we change the price distribution (and thus the 'profit distribution') associated with the risky asset. The government

> recognizes that it can change this price distribution by altering the allocation of investment and the ownership of shares in the different assets. The market ignores this effect. Stiglitz (1982), p.242.

In essence, Stiglitz argues that while individual firms exhibit price taking behavior and perceive that their profits remain constant across any two states of nature even if they increase output, profits and prices for industries as a whole do change. A central planner can take advantage of this 'price distribution effect' to rearrange ownership of shares and the productive capital available to firms for expansion and thus create a Pareto superior allocation.

In Stiglitz's (1982) model, individuals attempt to maximize the payoff from holding a portfolio of stocks; he shows the portfolio holdings will generally be inefficient. All of the firms in his model produce a single good, and all have constant returns to scale. A related model by Loong and Zeckhauser (1983) examined the effects of pecuniary externalities in incomplete contingent claims markets.

> Since the firms in (Stiglitz's (1982) model) have constant returns to scale, his example can be interpreted to refer to individuals who decide what to produce themselves, rather than individuals who invest in stock. This makes Stiglitz's example directly comparable to ours. The essential remaining difference is that we are explicitly concerned with individuals who have a choice of alternative technologies for producing the same good, and we show that under conditions of uncertainty they will often make inefficient choices. Loong and Zeckhauser (1983), p.173.

Using a two-period, two-good model with two representative classes of individuals, Loong and Zeckhauser show that individuals will generally undertake inefficient and sometimes overly risky production decisions - even when compared against the constrained Pareto optimum concept of Diamond. The source of the inefficiency rests with (1) technological externalities in the production of goods and (2) differences in marginal rates of substitution for the two goods between the two classes of individuals. Bankruptcy introduces another form of non-convexity in production that can create optimality problems for a stock market economy.

2.7 Conclusions

The pioneering contributions of Arrow and Debreu have forever changed the way economic theorists formulate uncertainty models. After more than forty years of scrutiny and extensions, their general equilibrium framework and approach continues to be the starting point for new theories on the operation of competitive markets under uncertainty.

While the general approach has been widely endorsed, the substantive results of the Arrow-Debreu have been sharply restricted. Following the exchange between Arrow and Nagatani, the optimality results may be restated as follows. The competitive equilibrium of the two-period contingent claims economy achieves an *ex ante* Pareto optimum, and every contingent claims competitive equilibrium can be achieved, roughly speaking, with an appropriate redistribution of resources. The two-period securities model and multiperiod versions of either the contingent claims or the securities models achieve optimality only in the flawed sense identified in Section 2.4.

The optimality results of the original models were derived under certain idealizing assumptions about individual preferences, production, the information available to all market participants, and the scope of markets. Grossman, Starr, Harris, and others, relaxed some of these simplifying assumptions and developed alternative optimality results based on variations of the original model. Other authors such as Radner, Nagatani, and Feiger raised fundamental questions about the validity of the optimality results even under the restrictive conditions of the Arrow-Debreu world. These authors uncovered various internal inconsistencies in the treatment of uncertainty faced by individual agents in these models.

It is surprising how little the economics profession has understood these latter set of inconsistency results. In university after university, Arrow-Debreu theory continues to be taught as a perfectly consistent paradigm for uncertainty economics. We also find continued erroneous assertions about no trading in multiperiod contingent claims models, when these assertions apply to a two-period Arrow-Debreu model.

For example, economists will assert that if contracts contingent on *each* state of nature were allowed for each commodity, speculation would not occur. They will argue Arrow, among others, has shown that no one could gain from spot market trading if all traders had been previously able to trade in complete markets. Moreover, they would boast that no one would trade even if inconclusive information arrived in the economy.[11] The Milgrom and Stokey (1982) No Trading Theorem is a rational expectations variant of this same complete markets concept.

Yet we know from Radner's work on sequential equilibria where traders do not have the same information that 'complete' markets will not necessarily preclude subsequent rounds of trading.

> Suppose, however, that new markets were introduced at later dates; would there be any incentive to trade in these new markets? In general there would, because the equilibrium prices in such markets would convey additional information beyond that contemplated in the original structure of information....The introduction of the spot markets brings with it the need for economic agents to be concerned not only with uncertainty about the environment, but also with uncertainty about other agents' strategies....Therefore the announcement of (spot prices) at the beginning of date *T* would typically provide each agent with (additional) information....to the extent that he could guess the strategies (or acts) of the other agents. Radner (1968), p.35, p.55.

At present an open question remains as to the extent of speculation in a fully complete and perfect contingent claims regime. Many economic theorists would argue that no speculation will take place. It is unclear how many of these theorists are aware of the dimensions of uncertainty (future spot market prices, changing preferences, changing beliefs) inherent in the Arrow-Debreu model with the passage of time.[12] Aside from these risks, individuals may still attempt to capture capital gains from others who do not share their probability beliefs over states of nature. From the work of Harris (1978) and Starr (1973), we would expect that only multiperiod models where traders share the same beliefs would exhibit no subsequent trading rounds, but even these possible results would have to be limited by a *ceteris paribus* argument (e.g., holding preferences constant). We will explore these issues in Chapter 3.

This discussion of trader information, objects of speculation, and the scope of markets leads naturally to the development of the Hirshleifer contingent claims model of speculation. This general equilibrium model is the focus of the next chapter.

Notes

1. Arrow (1951) provided a rigorous proof of the connection between competitive equilibria and Pareto optima. Gerard Debreu, independently of K. J. Arrow (1951), introduced convex analysis methods into welfare theory. See Gerard Debreu (1951), in particular Section 6, and W. Hildenbrand (1983), in particular Section 2.

2. Gerard Debreu (1959) extended Arrow's pure exchange model in several important ways, hence the name 'Arrow-Debreu' to describe the contingent claims and securities economies. Debreu added production and multiple periods, and his proofs demonstrated the importance of convexity, preordering or ranking of the consumption set, and other key assumptions of the model. The complete citation for the 1972 Nobel Memorial Prize in Economics to J. R. Hicks and K. J. Arrow is 'for their pioneering contributions to general economic equilibrium theory and welfare theory.' The complete citation for the 1983 Nobel award to G. Debreu is 'for having incorporated new analytical methods into economic theory and for his rigorous reformulation of the theory of general equilibrium.'

3. Aumann (1987) expresses the position that *every* object of uncertainty should be defined as part of the state space.

   The term 'state of the world' implies a definite specification of all parameters that may be the object of uncertainty on the part of any player...Conditional on a given ω, everybody knows everything; but in general, nobody knows which is really the true ω. Taking the 'atoms' of Ω to represent *all* aspects of uncertainty on the part of any player - including uncertainty about the uncertainty of other players - by means of the partitions. Aumann (1987), p.6.

4. Debreu (1959) subsumes the $S \times C$ contingent claims into his definition of a commodity under uncertainty:

   One is thus led to define a *commodity* in this new context by its physical characteristics, its location, and its event (or vertex of the event tree; this vertex defining implicitly the date of the commodity). A contract for delivery of wheat between two agents takes, for example, the form: the first agent shall deliver to the second agent, who shall accept delivery, five thousand bushels of what of a specified type at location *s*, at event e_t. If e_t does not obtain, no delivery takes place....Therefore the definition of an uncertain commodity may require here several events (and several locations)....An agent who buys a bushel of No. 2 Red Winter Wheat in Chicago at date *t in any event* buys in facts as many commodities as there are events at *t*. Debreu (1959), pp.99-100.

5. Arrow's (1964) article is entitled 'The Role of Securities in the Optimal Allocation of Risk-Bearing,' and emphasis seems to have been placed on the securities version of his model.

6. Most of these ideas are contained in Radner's (1967) French article.

7. Starr (1973), p.94.

8. Many authors subsequently developed revised general equilibrium models, in which prices are defined as part of the state of the world, without citing Nagatani's (1975) comment as the impetus for this salient change in the established Arrow-Debreu framework.

9. See Cass and Shell (1983).

10. Loong and Zeckhauser (1982) note the nonexistence problem for contingent claims markets as follows:

    If there were some measure of performance for market failures that was in some way equivalent to a batting average, contingent claims markets might well lead the league. That is, the ratio of non-established contingent claims markets to all desirable contingent claims markets is high in relation to, say, the ratio of public goods relative to all goods, or goods generating nontrivial externalities relative to private goods. (p.171).

    Chapter 6 contains several nonexistence propositions for fully 'complete' markets.

11. Salant (1976), p.674.

12. In private correspondence with me in 1994, Radner emphasized that

in a multiperiod model if (1) all traders have the same information at each date and in each event, (2) traders observe all 'payoff relevant' events when they occur, and (3) markets completely span the elementary events that traders observe, then in an equilibrium of the prior round of Arrow-Debreu contingent claims economy, no one will want to reopen trading at subsequent dates. Radner's carefully worded assumptions eliminate future spot market price uncertainty as well as uncertainty over changing beliefs or preferences, which are 'payoff relevant.' Radner's Assumption (2) also implies that no firm has uncertainty about the profitability of any given production plan.

References

Arrow, Kenneth J., (1951), 'An Extension of the Basic Theorem of Classical Welfare Economics,' in Neyman, J., editor, *Proceedings of the Second Berkeley Symposium on Mathematical Statistics and Probability*, (Berkeley: University of California Press), pp. 507-532.

Arrow, Kenneth J., (1964), 'The Role of Securities in the Optimal Allocation of Risk-Bearing,' *Review of Economic Studies*, Vol. 31, pp. 91-96.

Arrow, Kenneth J., (1970), untitled comment, *American Economic Review*, Vol. 60, pp. 462-463.

Arrow, Kenneth J., (1975), 'On a Theorem of Arrow: Comment,' *Review of Economic Studies*, Vol. 42, pp. 487-488.

Aumann, Robert J., (1987), 'Correlated Equilibrium as an Expression of Bayesian Rationality,' *Econometrica*, Vol. 55:1, pp. 1-18.

Burness, Stuart, Ronald Cummings, and James Quirk, (1980), 'Speculative Behavior and the Operation of Competitive Markets Under Uncertainty,' Staff Paper 80-11, Department of Economics, Montana State University, Bozeman, Montana.

Cass, David and Karl Shell, (1983), 'Do Sunspots Matter?,' *Journal of Political Economy*, Vol. 91:2, pp. 193-227.

Coutinho, Paulo C., (1986), 'Non-Optimality of Rational Expectations Equilibrium: the Complete Markets Case,' *Review of Economic Studies*, 53, pp. 883-884.

Debreu, Gerard, (1951), *Econometrica*, Vol. 19, pp. 273-292.

Debreu, Gerard, (1959), *Theory of Value*, (New York: John Wiley & Sons, Inc.), Chapter 7.

Dreze, J., (1970), 'Market Allocation Under Uncertainty,' *European Economic Review*, Vol. 2, pp. 133-165.

Diamond, Peter A., (1967), 'The Role of a Stock Market in a General Equilibrium Model with Technological Uncertainty,' *American*

Economic Review, Vol. 57, pp. 759-776.

Feiger, George, (1976), 'What is Speculation?,' *Quarterly Journal of Economics*, Vol. 90, pp. 677-687.

Grossman, Sanford J., (1977), 'The Existence of Futures Markets, Noisy Rational Expectations, and Informational Externalities,' *Review of Economic Studies*, Vol. 64, pp. 431-449.

Grossman, Sanford J., (1981), 'An Introduction to the Theory of Rational Expectations Under Asymmetric Information,' *Review of Economic Studies*, Vol. 48, pp. 541-559.

Hammond, Peter J., (1976) '*Ex Ante* and *Ex Post* Welfare Optimality Under Uncertainty,' Essex University Discussion Paper No. 83.

Harris, Richard, (1978), 'Ex-Post Efficiency and Resource Allocation Under Uncertainty,' *Review of Economic Studies*, Vol. 45, pp. 427-436.

Hart, Oliver D., (1975), 'On the Optimality of Equilibrium When the Market Structure Is Incomplete,' *Journal of Economic Theory*, Vol. 11, pp. 418-443.

Hildenbrand, Werner, (1983), 'Introduction,' in Gerard Debreu, *Mathematical Economics*, Cambridge University Press, pp. 1 -29.

Hirshleifer, Jack, (1976), 'Reply to Comments,' *Quarterly Journal of Economics*, Vol. 90, pp. 689-96.

Loong, Lee Hsien, and Richard Zeckhauser, (1982), 'Pecuniary Externalities Do Matter When Contingent Claims Markets Are Incomplete,' *Quarterly Journal of Economics*, Vol. 97, pp. 171-180.

Milgrom, Paul, and Nancy Stokey, (1982), 'Information, Trade, and Common Knowledge,' *Journal of Economic Theory*, Vol. 26, pp. 17-27.

Nagatani, Keizo, (1975), 'On a Theorem of Arrow,' *Review of Economic Studies*, Vol. 42, pp. 483-485.

Radner, Roy, (1967), 'Equilibre des Marchés à Terme et au Comptant en Cas d'Incertitude,' *Cahiers d'Econometrie*, Vol. 9, pp. 30-47.

Radner, Roy, (1968), 'Competitive Equilibrium Under Uncertainty,' *Econometrica*, Vol. 36, pp. 31-58.

Radner, Roy, (1970), 'Problems in the Theory of Markets Under Uncertainty,' *American Economic Review*, Vol. 60, pp. 454-460.

Radner, Roy, (1972), 'Existence of Equilibrium in Plans, Prices, and Price Expectations in a Sequence of Markets,' *Econometrica*, Vol. 40:2, pp. 289-303.

Radner, Roy, (1979), 'Rational Expectations Equilibrium: Generic Existence and the Information Revealed by Price,' *Econometrica*, Vol. 47:3, pp. 655-678.

Radner, Roy, (1982), 'Equilibrium Under Uncertainty,' in Arrow, K. J., and M. D. Intrilligator, eds., *Handbook of Mathematical Economics*, Vol. II, Chapter 20, (North Holland, Inc.).

Salant, S., (1976), 'Hirshleifer on Speculation,' *Quarterly Journal of Economics*, Vol. 90, pp. 667-675.

Starr, Ross M., (1973), 'Optimal Production and Allocation Under Uncertainty,' *Quarterly Journal of Economics*, Vol. 87, pp. 81-95.

Starrett, David, (1973), 'Inefficiency and the Demand for Money in a Sequence Economy,' *Review of Economic Studies*, Vol. 40, pp. 437-448.

Stiglitz, Joseph E., (1972), 'On the Optimality of the Stock Market Allocation of Investment,' *Quarterly Journal of Economics*, Vol. 86, pp.25-60.

Stiglitz, Joseph E., (1982), 'The Inefficiency of the Stock Market Equilibrium,' *Review of Economic Studies*, Vol. 49, pp. 241-261.

Comment

I am happy to take up Michael Guth's invitation to comment on this chapter, a beautifully clear survey of state-preference theory.

As background for the issue to be addressed, let me point to an informational paradox in standard micro theory. Individuals supposedly optimize their consumption choices in the light of known commodity prices. Yet these prices are themselves endogenous variables determined by the aggregate of such individual decisions, hence unknowable to traders at the time the decisions are made. *So prices are known, yet unknown!*

In our textbooks we deal with the seeming contradiction on two levels. *First*, we say the traditional intersection of supply and demand generates a 'static' equilibrium — or, in another terminology, a Nash solution. Such an equilibrium is non-constructive, meaning we do not attempt to examine the process by which it is achieved. It is an equilibrium in the sense that everyone is making a best response to circumstances; given objective conditions and other traders' choices, no one wants to modify his/her choices. *Second*, if a constructive solution is wanted, we have to concern ourselves with 'dynamics.' In various versions we talk about auctioneers, recontract assumptions, cobwebs, optimal search theorems, etc. For certain problems it is absolutely necessary to deal with dynamics. Yet on the whole we have a well-justified confidence that the simpler static analysis very often successfully predicts economic behavior. I will only add that the exciting field of experimental economics has shed considerable light upon the market institutions and dynamic protocols needed to support our textbook static solutions.

Turning now to state-preference theory, I shall deal separately with Arrow's two models: (1) the 'state-claim markets' version, and (2) the 'security markets' version.

State-claim markets: As pointed out in the chapter, Arrow's first version is a straightforward generalization of standard theory. Instead of individuals choosing over C commodities subject to prices P_c, they now choose over a space of $S \times C$ contingent commodities subject to prices P_{cs}. Lurking within this generalization is the same paradox as before: prices are assumed known, yet unknown. But, I would claim, if we are looking only for 'static' solutions, there is no more paradox than in standard micro theory. The only issue is how successful this extension of standard static theory will be in describing the real world.

Some theorists have, however, been disturbed by the following question. Suppose markets were to *re-open* after determination of the state. There would be $S \times C$ markets in the first round and C in the second. But then beliefs about prices in the second round — let us denote these prices $P_{c,s}$ — would affect first-round choices. Hence, it has been suggested the possible second-round prices should themselves be among the contingencies priced in the opening round. Thus, first-round markets would generate price-quantity solutions over a space of $S \times C \times P_{c,s}$ tradable entities.

I have been unsympathetic to this extension. No so much because of unrealism, though I'm unaware of any real-world phenomenon that even approximates such tradable entities. My main objection is to the discordant mixture of static and dynamic considerations. Static analysis provides only a best response equilibrium. Subjective preferences and beliefs, about re-opening of markets or whatever, are already incorporated into individuals' supply-demand offers in the original market. At equilibrium no one is motivated to change his position, and nothing more needs to be said so long as we remain in the domain of statics. To go further we must explicitly model the dynamics: how are prior expectations formed, how are they modified by one's own experience, how does one go about making optimal inferences from the observed behavior of others, and so forth. Expanding the space of tradable entities is not needed for statics, and provides no aid for dealing with dynamics.

Securities markets: Arrow's second version allows for two stages. In the first round, S prices for claims to income in each state are determined; in the second round, after everyone knows which state has come about, C commodity prices are determined. In this model only $S + C$ rather than the previous $S \times C$ markets are required.

Since second-round trading is essential to the model here, beliefs about posterior prices seemingly pose a more serious problem. In the prior round when the state-prices P_s are determined, the second round commodity prices $P_{c,s}$ are strictly unknown — rather than 'known-yet-unknown' as in our familiar paradox. In fact, not only are these $P_{c,s}$ prices invisible in the first round, but only the one subset of them conditional upon the actually realized state s will *ever* become visible.

Nevertheless, so long as we remain within the context of static equilibrium, a slight modification resolves the problem. If a *2-round set of prices* — P_s in the initial round and $P_{c,s}$ in the succeeding round — is proposed *ex ante* to all individuals, and an associated set of allocations is arrived at such that no one wishes to make further changes, we have an equilibrium. (Subject to a number of technical conditions not essentially different from those needed even for standard micro theory.) These 2-round prices are known-yet-unknown in exactly the same sense as before. And in particular, the posterior prices are nothing but the 'rational expectations' prices arrived at in another branch of economic literature. (There may be more than one such equilibrium, but that also is a possibility in standard micro theory.) So once again, expansion of the space of tradable entities to include second-round prices as contingencies is not needed for a static equilibrium, and is unhelpful if we need to deal with dynamics.

Returning to the static equilibrium, the important question is: 'What real world inferences can be drawn from it, and are those inferences actually observed?' And indeed, until convincing evidence is obtained we are entitled to remain somewhat skeptical about rational expectations predictions.

The only additional point I want to emphasize here is that, to *apply* the theory, we do not need to solve it in full generality. More or less rough approximations are all that can ever be achieved. In standard theory the argument against protective tariffs, with which the vast majority of economists certainly concur, rests upon such a rough-approximation theoretical development. In a similar spirit we can use approximate solutions from state-preference theory to cast light upon many issues of practical concern. For example: (1) Under what circumstances are futures markets for a particular good likely to come into existence, and when not? (Note that a regime of futures and spot markets for commodities corresponds to a $C + C$ rather than to Arrow's $S + C$ pattern. Thus, state-beliefs have to somehow be translated into unconditional supply-demand offers for particular goods.) (2) As a related question, given such a $C + C$ regime, to what extent do individuals' speculative/hedging choices depend upon factors like differential risk aversion versus differential beliefs? (This question is to be addressed in the chapter following.) And finally, going somewhat farther afield, various rough-approximation versions of state-preference theory have been shown to cast light upon broader topics like (3) security prices (the CAPM model), (4) firms' balance sheet choices between debt versus equity, and (5) the demand for financial liquidity.

Jack Hirshleifer
Department of Economics
University of California, Los Angeles

3 The contingent claims model of speculation

3.1. Introduction

For the modern reader, the literature on profitable destabilizing speculation as a whole appears confusing and contradictory. Many of the early works in the 1950s and 1960s employed models which simply failed to come to grips adequately with a complex phenomenon like speculation. For example, speculation can only occur under uncertainty. Yet many of the early works contained models with no randomness. In a world of certainty, profits from purchases and sales at a known price illustrate *arbitrage* not speculation.

Financial economists now have a general equilibrium, contingent claims model to illustrate speculation. This model solves comparative static issues via standard economic reasoning. The standard format provides individuals with production functions, preferences, time-distributed endowments, etc., and specifies the available market range. Economists then solve for the general equilibrium and pose comparative static questions, e.g., what happens if preferences change?

In the Hirshleifer (1975, 1976, 1977) model, investors buy Arrow-Debreu contingent claims knowing that they will have the opportunity to revise their portfolio after new information arrives and before the state of the world is revealed. In presenting Hirshleifer's model, we benefit from hindsight. A zero complementarity assumption in the original model led to several objections. We will introduce the model without the assumption, show the first-order conditions, and then impose the assumption to simplify the expressions.

Circa 1975 speculation theorists included, but were not limited to, two competing groups. The first group maintained in the Keynes-Hicks tradition that different tolerances for risk largely explained who would hedge and who would speculate. In the Keynes-Hicks view, futures markets serve the beneficial social role of transferring price risks from those more risk averse (hedgers) to those less risk averse (speculators). The opposing group, led by the empirical writings of Holbrook Working, contended that different beliefs (subjective probability values) primarily determined who chose to speculate. Working regarded speculation as the means by which market prices come to reflect the best information among market participants.

Jack Hirshleifer (1975) initially slanted his work toward providing evidence for the Working view of speculation: differences in beliefs account for speculation. For example, his article illustrates how prices would change if unexpected information arrives and causes beliefs to change. He also attempted to show that only a 'belief deviant' individual would speculate. But Hirshleifer's (1976, 1989) subsequent replies to comments expanded on the impact of other significant factors including the regime/completeness of markets; risk preferences; the nature of information and endowments; and, due to subsequent work by his son David Hirshleifer (1989a, 1989b, 1990, 1991), demand elasticities and transaction costs.

Hirshleifer's valuable framework reflects the importance of (1) planning based on the arrival of new information, (2) multiple trading periods — so that traders have time to buy (sell) and resell (repurchase), (3) subjective probability distributions over shifts in underlying demand or supply;[1] and (4) market incompleteness. As we describe in Sections 3.4 and 3.5, Hirshleifer's model represents a philosophy about looking at speculative activity: identifying the factors most important to speculation, some of which are missing even from recent attempts to portray speculation. Perhaps this chapter will rekindle interest his contingent claims model of speculation. If so, the general theory of speculation will benefit.

3.2 Hirshleifer's (1975) Model Specification

Consider a two-commodity pure exchange economy with a risky commodity, Z, and a riskless commodity, N. The total quantity of 'riskless' commodity N is fixed and consequently does not depend on the state of the world. The economy begins in period *0* and ends in period *2*, at which time either state A or state B is revealed. The total quantity of commodity Z will depend on the state of the world; states A and B can be thought of as a 'good crop' and 'bad crop' scenario, respectively. Let some individual believe state A will occur with probability p and thus state B with probability $1\text{-}p$. This individual's endowment vector can then be represented as

$$E = [(N^e,Z_a^e),(N^e,Z_B^e);\ p,1-p] \equiv (N^e;Z_A^e,Z_B^e)\,, \tag{3.1}$$

and his expected utility as

$$U(N;Z_A,Z_B) = p\ u(N,Z_A) + (1-p)\ u(N,Z_b)\,. \tag{3.2}$$

We can treat the riskless commodity, N, as a numeraire and set its price equal to 1: $P_N \equiv 1$. The market regime is 'semicomplete' in that state-contingent claims are available on asset Z but not on asset N. Hence, the available contingent claims have prices P_N, P_{ZA}, P_{ZB}. If state-contingent claims N_A and N_B were available on N as well, the market regime would be fully complete.

3.2.1. The Noninformed Equilibrium

Consider now the following sequence of events. First, the individual trades from his endowment, E, to a consumptive optimum, C^*, based on his preferences, beliefs, and budget constraint. After the trading has been completed, state A or state B is revealed. The state contingent claims pay off according to which state of the world occurs. Graphically, the sequence of events appears as

Endowment Gamble E → Trading (period *0*) → Consumptive Gamble C^* →

Nature's Choice of state A or state B (period *1*) → Consumption (period 2)

In this pure exchange economy, the individual faces the budget constraint

$$N^e + P_{ZA}Z_A^e + P_{ZB}Z_B^e = N + P_{ZA}Z_A + P_{ZB}Z_B\,. \tag{3.3}$$

When the expected utility function (3.2) is maximized with respect to N, Z_A, and Z_B and subject to (3.3), the consumptive optimality conditions are

$$P_{ZA} = \frac{p\,\dfrac{\partial u(N,Z_A)}{\partial Z_A}}{\mathscr{E}\left(\dfrac{\partial u}{\partial N}\right)} \quad \text{and} \quad P_{ZB} = \frac{(1-p)\,\dfrac{\partial u(N,Z_B)}{\partial Z_B}}{\mathscr{E}\left(\dfrac{\partial u}{\partial N}\right)}. \tag{3.4}$$

where $\mathscr{E}\left(\dfrac{\partial u}{\partial N}\right) \equiv p\,\dfrac{\partial u(N,Z_A)}{\partial N} + (1-p)\,\dfrac{\partial u(N,Z_B)}{\partial N}$. We can eliminate the $\mathscr{E}$ term from (3.4) by assuming the individual's utility function is additively-separable: $u(N,Z) = u(N) + u(Z)$. Recall this assumption appeared in numerous extensions of the Arrow-Debreu model reviewed in Chapter 2. Additive separability implies the individual derives no complementarity from consuming the two goods. If the two goods are food and gold, the zero complementarity assumption seems reasonable. If the two goods are different kinds of food, then some complementarity effects would be expected.

With zero complementarity, conditions (3.4) reduce to

$$p\frac{\partial u/\partial Z_A}{\partial u/\partial N} = P_{ZA} \quad \text{and} \quad (1-p)\frac{\partial u/\partial Z_B}{\partial u/\partial N} = P_{ZB}. \tag{3.5}$$

Conditions (3.5) together with the budget constraint (3.3) determine what quantity of commodities N and Z the individual will purchase. But the right-hand side of the equations in (3.5) still contain the market prices, which any individual will take as given under the competitive assumptions of this model.

The prevailing market prices cannot be determined from (3.5), because we do not know how many other market participants share this individual's endowments, preferences (utility function), and beliefs (probability assignments). We have arrived at the fundamental issue confronting all asset pricing theory and the central theme of Chapter 5: how can individual equilibrium conditions be translated into an aggregate, market-clearing equilibrium model? Hirshleifer (1975) used the heuristic device of a 'representative individual,' i.e., all the people in the market are so similar that any one individual's beliefs and preferences could be assumed to reflect the market's as well. As Hirshleifer noted,

> In a world of pure exchange the equilibrium prices are then governed by the necessity of 'sustaining' the representative

> endowment vector; since a representative individual can find no one to trade with in a closed economy, his endowment vector must be his consumptive optimum....Without a representative individual, equilibrium prices would of course reflect some *average* measure of the various individuals' differing probability beliefs and some *average* measure of their respective marginal utilities. Hirshleifer (1975), p. 527.

If π denotes the market's probability assigned to state A occurring and μ denotes the market's collective utility function, then market clearing prices can be determined from the optimality conditions

$$\pi \frac{\partial\mu/\partial Z_A}{\partial\mu/\partial N} = P_{ZA} \text{ and } (1-\pi)\frac{\partial\mu/\partial Z_B}{\partial\mu/\partial N} = P_{ZB}. \qquad \textbf{(3.6)}$$

Assuming zero complementarity and the arrival of unexpected information that changes the representative probability beliefs from $(\pi, 1-\pi)$ to $(\pi^*, 1-\pi^*)$, the new market clearing prices P^*_{ZA} and P^*_{ZB} will adjust according to the following ratios:

$$P^*_{ZA}/P_{ZA} = \pi^*/\pi \text{ and } P^*_{ZB}/P_{ZB} = (1-\pi^*)/(1-\pi). \qquad \textbf{(3.7)}$$

Note that (3.7) contains no marginal utility functions. Hirshleifer observed that condition (3.7) will hold even if the 'representative individual' assumption is relaxed. In its place, he assumes individuals have homogeneous or 'concordant beliefs.' His logic then holds that if all of the individual probability assignments, p, equaled π before the new information and now equal π^*, then condition (3.7) still holds. Of course, while beliefs change, we must assume that preferences and endowments are held constant.

3.2.2 The Informed Equilibrium

Suppose the following sequence of events now occurs. Individuals trade from their endowment position to a consumptive optimum, knowing that new information will arrive that will change probability beliefs. After the information event, individuals can retrade their contingent claims. Following the second round of trading, the state of the world will be revealed as either state A or state B. Traders will then consume their commodities. Graphically, the new sequence of events prior to the state of the world being revealed is

Endowment Gamble E	→	Prior Trading Round (period 0)	→	Speculative Gamble T^* →
Arrival of Information (period 1)	→	Posterior Trading Round (period 2)	→	Consumptive Gamble C^{**}

The complexity of the individual's decision problem has now increased substantially, because in selecting his prior trading consumptive optimum, he must not only take into account the prices that prevail in the market at that time, but also the prices he anticipates will prevail in the posterior trading round as well. To simplify the analysis further, Hirshleifer assumes that the information that arrives will be decisive, so that every individual will know with certainty what the state of the world will be. Thus in the posterior trading round, the probability assigned to either state A or state B will drop to zero. Consequently, the prices of contingent claims for that state will drop to zero as well. Thus the budget constraint in the prior trading round will contain both state A and state B contingent prices, whereas the posterior trading round budget constraint will only contain the actual state's prices.

In the prior trading round, the individual faces the following dynamic optimization problem:

$$\underset{N^t,\, Z_A^t,\, Z_B^t}{MAX} \quad p\; u(N',Z_A') + (1-p)\; u(N'',Z_B'') \tag{3.8}$$

subject to

$$\begin{aligned} N' + P_{ZA}'Z_A' &= N^t + P_{ZA}'Z_A^t \equiv W' \\ N'' + P_{ZB}''Z_B'' &= N^t + P_{ZB}''Z_B^t \equiv W'' \\ N^t + P_{ZA}^0 Z_A^t + P_{ZB}^0 Z_B^t &= N^e + P_{ZA}^0 Z_A^e + P_{ZB}^0 Z_B^e \equiv W^e. \end{aligned} \tag{3.9}$$

The single primed notation reflects the information that the state of the world will be A, and the double primed notation applies to state B. The first two budget constraints indicate that the individual's wealth in period 2 (when the state is revealed to be either state A or B) must equal the value of his prior round trading position. The third budget constraint shows that the value of the prior trading round (with superscript t) must equal the value of the individual's endowed wealth (with superscript e).

One prominent feature emerging from this informed environment relates to prices in the uninformed environment: $P^0_{ZA} = P_{ZA}$ and $P^0_{ZB} = P_{ZB}$. The prior round prices in the informed environment match the prevailing prices in the uninformed environment. Hirshleifer (1976) shows that this key result does not depend on the zero complementarity assumption. However, individuals must be able to compute future prices, a subject we will return to in Section 3.2.4.

3.2.3 Speculation Defined

Hirshleifer defined 'speculation' as any portfolio position T^* in the informed environment that differed from the consumptive optimum C^* in the noninformed environment. However, in a regime of incomplete markets, essentially everyone would speculate once the zero complementarity assumption is relaxed.

In earlier work, Hirshleifer and Rubinstein (1973) examined the operation of a single commodity market with a state-complete regime as well as for information event-state-complete markets. Obviously, with a single commodity, no complementarity effects will complicate the first-order conditions. For this model, Hirshleifer and Rubinstein defined a speculator as someone who plans for differential contingent consumptions *over information events*.

Speculation in this earlier model does not depend on portfolio revision but does require a capital gains motive or plan. If information unexpectedly arrived in the market, prices would normally adjust and some traders would revise their portfolios. However, these transactions would not amount to speculation, since potential capital gains did not motivate any *prior* behavior. The only individuals who met the nonspeculator definition had ratios of conditional posterior probabilities equal to the corresponding ratio of conditional posterior prices. The nonspeculator definition in this earlier model thus depends only on beliefs and prices, not on resources or preferences.

Similarly, Rubinstein (1975) found if all individuals have homogeneous beliefs in a single commodity contingent claims economy, then all would have 'nonspeculative' beliefs. In a heterogeneous beliefs version of the same economy, those individuals who happened to match the consensus beliefs would be 'nonspeculators.' These consensus beliefs are more complicated than just the average of individual beliefs, because additional information is imparted in computing the average. Joseph Stiglitz has similarly encountered problems in defining speculation.

> Stiglitz (1970) also identifies speculation with portfolio revision.... Stiglitz introduces uncertainty by assuming the date t=1 price of long-term bonds is uncertain at date t=0. Unfortunately, since Stiglitz admits no purely risky securities into his model, in an equilibrium context his economy is riskless and the injected uncertainty disappears together with the purpose of his model. Rubinstein (1975), p.815n.

Recall from Chapter 1 that a semantic controversy arose over how to define a 'nonspeculator' in the speculation and stability literature. If 'nonspeculators' could be defined, then everyone else left in the model would presumably be a speculator. Friedman and Telser maintained that 'nonspeculators' could not base their investment decisions on past prices or price trends. Baumol and others countered that people would be irrational to ignore past prices.

Against this backdrop, Hirshleifer (1975) introduced his contingent claims model of speculation, and the resolution appeared clear and simple. Traders who utilize the informed environment to alter their choice of a consumption lottery from what it would have been in a noninformed environment are speculators. Those who choose the same lottery in the two environments are nonspeculators. Yet this result depended on the particular regime of incomplete markets selected and the zero complementarity assumption. When the latter assumption was relaxed, then utility-deviant traders as well as belief-deviant traders were found to be speculators. The only nonspeculators in the semicomplete market regime were those who exhibited zero complementarity in their preferences for goods. As a result, the current generation of speculation theorists seem disillusioned with the general equilibrium contingent claims framework and favor instead noise trader, partial equilibrium, and so-called rational expectations models of speculation.

Returning now to the Keynes-Hicks tradition that risk preferring individuals speculate, the Hirshleifer (1977) model offers some support for this position. '[G]iven differences of belief so that speculation occurs, the extent of an individual's speculative commitments will vary with his risk-tolerance.' But without trading rounds before and after the known arrival of information, traders will have no capital gains motive. The new information can certainly change equilibrium beliefs. Preferences and degrees of risk aversion normally will not change in a model just with the arrival of information; the theorist afterall has fixed the utility functions as a specification of the model. These facts suggest that differences in beliefs have a greater impact than differences in risk aversion in defining who will speculate.

Ironically, we have come full circle. The extent to which speculators profitably destabilize markets remains as an empirical question. The same can be said for whether differences in beliefs or risk aversion are more important determinants of speculation.

3.2.4. Common Knowledge Beliefs and Price Computability

Even under the zero complementarity assumption, the relationship between prices and probability assignments will not be valid with merely a 'concordant beliefs' assumption. Although individual market traders may agree in their probability beliefs, they have no way of knowing *a priori* they agree. Chapter 4 is devoted entirely to this topic, and Chapter 5 applies this topic to asset pricing theories. Unless the traders' beliefs are both agreed and common knowledge, equation (3.7) will not hold once the representative individual assumption is relaxed.[2] To say that traders' beliefs are common knowledge means that all the traders know their own and everyone else's beliefs, know everyone knows everyone else's beliefs, knows everyone knows everyone knows everyone else's beliefs, and so on.

Hirshleifer (1976) was aware of this point when he stated 'If all have concordant beliefs as to the likelihood of the possible states of the world, *and all know this*, there will be no problem in assigning probability weights.' (p.693, emphasis added) However, we face an additional difficulty, which is precisely the same problem Nagatani (1975) identified for the Arrow-Debreu securities market in Chapter 2. The future spot market prices to which probability measures are to be assigned cannot be computed from the information available in the prior trading round.[3]

Hirshleifer avoided this difficulty by establishing a martingale process on prices:

> If everyone believes that the martingale proposition is valid, and acts accordingly, then (in a zero-complementarity world of concordant beliefs) the proposition will be valid! But...equation (3.7) does not in general hold true if the zero-complementarity assumption is relaxed. Absent independence in demand, if everyone believes in martingales, and acts accordingly, then everyone will then be wrong! So without zero complementarity, the conditional posterior prices that are necessary to form a correct probability distribution for guiding decisions in the prior round of trading cannot simply be computed from publicly available data (the agreed probabilities) available in the prior round. In general, detailed information as to endowments and utility functions would

be needed to compute the conditional posterior prices properly, knowledge of which is needed to guide prior-round decisions properly. (Hirshleifer 1976, p.693)

The other alternative is to assume that future spot market prices are common knowledge. This assumption would limit the robustness of the martingale results, but it would enable individuals to solve the maximization problem set forth in (3.8) and (3.9).

3.2.5. Zero Complementarity Revisited

Two of Hirshleifer's results in one application of his framework — speculation only by a belief-deviant individual and the martingale property of prices ($P^0_{ZA} = \pi\ P^{/}_{ZA}$ and $P^0_{ZB} = (1 - \pi)P^{//}_{ZB}$) — hinge on the zero complementarity assumption. One critic complained that zero complementarity was unrealistic for a consumptive lottery between a left and a right shoe or for different grades of wheat. But clearly Hirshleifer's (1975) Semicomplete Market model intended to portray consumption among more varied commodities.

Readers may be left with the unfortunate impression that most economists find the zero complementarity assumption objectionable. Any theoretical model abstracts from reality. Useful models include the most important elements of reality and exclude the rest. For many commodities, zero complementarity is not only a close but a perfect approximation to reality.

David Hirshleifer (1991) uses the zero complementarity assumption to establish futures prices follow a martingale, i.e., the futures price exhibits no upward or downward bias. However, futures prices do reflect seasonal variations with harvesting. David Hirshleifer (1990) also shows that with positive (negative) complementarity, the futures prices is a downward (upward) biased predictor of the future spot price. Furthermore when transactions costs are introduced, if demand is inelastic/elastic, the futures price is a downward/upward biased predictor of the future spot price. However, David Hirshleifer's results on the effect of demand elasticity depend on the extent of consumer participation. David Hirshleifer (1990) finds that nonparticipation by consumers causes the direction of the bias to correlate to the hedging positions of producers. If consumers more actively trade futures, then the bias results could be reversed. Zero complementarity tends to support the martingale property and offset bias effects in contingent claims or futures prices.

3.3 Market Incompleteness and Speculation

Commenting on Hirshleifer's article, Feiger (1976) noted that with complete contingent claims markets, no one has any desire to speculate. With incomplete markets, everyone will form contracts with the intent of revising them.[4] A reader may question why only belief-deviant individuals were found to speculate in Hirshleifer (1975), and whether the zero complementarity assumption is so strong that it negates the general proposition that everyone will speculate. We will therefore employ another variant of Hirshleifer's (1977) framework to explore how speculation and incomplete markets relate.

This section will show that in a general equilibrium contingent claims model, utility maximizing individuals will generally speculate even if zero complementarity is assumed. The particular form of the contingent claims model we employ resembles a stock market economy. It turns out that the zero complementarity assumption only eliminated speculation for a so-called Semicomplete Market (with claims for N, Z_A and Z_B), which is the application covered in Section 3.2. First we will define a Fully Complete Market, an Unconditional (incomplete) Market, and speculation.

Again we have a pure exchange economy with riskless good N, risky good Z, and states A and B. All individuals receive the same endowment for good N, but society's total endowment for good Z differs across states: $N_A \equiv N \equiv N_B$ and $Z_A \neq Z_B$.

Definition 1: A *Fully Complete Market* contains separate contingent claims for N_A, N_B, Z_A, and Z_B.

A fully complete regime only requires enough contingent claims to span the space of potential consumption vectors; separate state-commodity contracts shown in Definition 1 are sufficient but not necessary.

Definition 2 (Hirshleifer 1977): An *Unconditional Market* contains claims to N and ζ, where ζ represents a 1:1 entitlement package of $Z_A : Z_B$.

The unconditional market regime corresponds to a claim for a numeraire, such as money, and a stock market security that entitles the purchaser of ζ to one share of Z for every possible state of the world.

Definition 3: *Speculation* occurs in any market regime when individuals trade to intermediate consumption lotteries in an informed environment that differ from their consumption lotteries in a non-informed situation.

Proposition: Assuming zero complementarity between N and Z, a utility-maximizing individual will speculate in an Unconditional Market regime.

Proof: *The Noninformed Environment.* Let some individual assign probability ρ to state A occurring and $(1-\rho)$ to state B. The individual receives the same endowment for the riskless asset N in either state; moreover, the individual cannot trade claims for N conditioned on each state of the world so that $N_A = N_B = N$. The individual maximizes expected utility

$$\underset{N, Z_A, Z_B, \zeta}{MAX} \ \rho \ U(N, Z_A) + (1 - \rho) \ U(N, Z_B)$$

subject to the budget constraints

$$N = N^e - P_\zeta \zeta, \qquad Z_A = Z_A^e + \zeta, \qquad Z_B = Z_B^e + \zeta,$$

where $P_\zeta \equiv P_z$ represents the 1:1 sandwich price for Z_A, Z_B, and the superscripts e denote the individual's endowment.

Let $U_{Z_A} = \partial U(N, Z_A)/\partial Z_A$, $U_{Z_B} = \partial U(N, Z_B)/\partial Z_B$, $U_N = \partial U/\partial N$. Feasibility in the pure exchange economy requires $\Sigma N = \Sigma N^e$ and $\Sigma \zeta = 0$. Because $U_{NZ} = 0$ by the zero complementarity assumption, the optimality conditions emerging from this expected utility maximizing problem reduce to

$$\rho \frac{U_{Z_A}}{U_N} + (1 - \rho) \frac{U_{Z_e}}{U_N} = P_\zeta \equiv P_Z \, .$$

As a further consequence of zero complementarity, the individual's marginal rate of substitution for N across states will equal unity:

$$U_{N_A} \, / \, U_{N_B} = 1. \qquad \textbf{(3.10)}$$

The Informed Environment. The individual trades first to an intermediate contingent claim bundle, denoted with superscript t. In period *1*, conclusive information on the state emerges. In period 2, the contingent claim market reopens, and the individual retrades to his final period 2 consumptive optimum. The conclusive information collapses the 1:1 sandwich across states to simply a claim for Z in the known state.

The individual now maximizes expected utility

$$\underset{N^t, Z_A^t, Z_B^t, N', N'', Z_A', Z_B''}{MAX} \quad \rho\, U(N', Z_A') + (1 - \rho)\, U(N'', Z_B'') \tag{3.11}$$

subject to the budget constraints

$$N' + P_{ZA}' Z_A' = N^t + P_\zeta' Z_A^t, \tag{3.12}$$

$$N'' + P_{ZB}'' Z_B'' = N^t + P_\zeta'' Z_B^t, \tag{3.13}$$

$$N^t + P_{ZA}^0 Z_A^t + P_{ZB}^0 Z_B^t = N^e + P_{ZA}^0 Z_A^e + P_{ZB}^0 Z_B^e. \tag{3.14}$$

P_{ZA}^0 and P_{ZB}^0 represent the implicit prices for good Z in states A and B, had such claims existed. In particular, since ζ represents a 1:1 package of Z, $P_\zeta^0 = P_{ZA}^0 + P_{ZB}^0$. The primes denote the conditional prices and quantities that would prevail in each state: one prime denotes state A, two primes denote state B. Furthermore $P_{ZA}' \equiv P_\zeta'$, $P_{ZB}'' \equiv P_\zeta''$.

Let λ_1, λ_2, λ_3 denote the Lagrange multipliers associated with constraints (3.12), (3.13), and (3.14) respectively. Then the individual's marginal rate of substitution across states is

$$\frac{U_{N'}}{U_{N''}} = \frac{\lambda_1}{\lambda_2} \frac{1 - \rho}{\rho}. \tag{3.15}$$

Comparing expressions (3.15) and (3.11), we see they equate only when

$$\frac{\lambda_1}{\lambda_2} \equiv \frac{\rho}{1 - \rho}. \tag{3.16}$$

Individuals whose shadow prices (λ_1, λ_2) differ from the ratio defined in (3.16) will purchase contingent claim lotteries in informed environments that differ from their lottery in the noninformed environment. (End of Proof)

This proof employs the Unconditional Market regime; however, analogous steps would apply to other incomplete market regimes. Transactions costs may also prohibit traders from speculating in an incomplete market regime. With complementarity between the goods, expressions (3.1) and (3.5) would become functions of N_A, N_B, Z_A, Z_B. The generalized proof would then show that the two functional relationships (involving both probabilities and marginal utilities) differ. We conclude that even with a zero complementarity assumption, virtually everyone will speculate in an Unconditional Market regime.

3.4. A Contrast with Tirole's Model of Speculation

A market achieves exchange efficiency if participants have no desire to create markets not already provided in the economy. Perhaps the two most frequently cited articles examining the efficiency of a speculative equilibrium are Kyle (1985) and Tirole (1982). We will discuss Kyle's model further in Chapter 7 and focus our attention in this section on Tirole's work.

In the early 1980s, Tirole (1982) and Hirshleifer (1984, published 1989) had an insightful exchange over whether differences in beliefs could predominantly account for speculative trading.[5] Hirshleifer's general equilibrium approach to speculation features these key elements: optimizing individual behavior coupled with market equilibrium conditions, individuals facing both price and quantity risks, changes in prices relating to changes in underlying demand or supply, and trading prior to and after the known arrival of information.

Tirole (1982) presents a static model of transient price paths and concludes no speculation or trading can occur. In Tirole's model, no one consumes or produces anything. The sequence of events begins with traders sharing a common prior probability over possible states of the world. Traders then receive heterogeneous signals about the price vector. After the information event, the market opens, but no trading takes place. The mere willingness to trade by one party causes his potential trading partner to recoil in expectation of concluding a disadvantageous transaction.

Groucho Marx once said that he would never join a club that would have him as a member.[6] Tirole's model expands on this theme with zeal. No one is willing to trade with anyone who wants to trade with him or her. If someone wants to trade, he must be trying to sell a 'lemon.' Tirole's model belongs to the common knowledge literature, which failed to recognize that individuals in a market who have common priors may not know they agree. As a result, Chapter 4 shows that these traders can rationally 'agree to disagree' and execute a trade. But as a general observation, given our preceding analysis that incomplete markets force everyone to speculate, a model that implies no speculation at all will occur would seem to be flawed.

Tirole attempted to use his model (1) to invalidate what he called the 'Working-Hirshleifer-Feiger' view that investor beliefs primarily determine speculative behavior, and (2) to reestablish the preeminence of the Keynes-Hicks risk transfer theory of speculation. Tirole in fact focuses upon intraperiod trading in a zero-sum game. His model contains no production, no growth, and essentially no randomness. Traders receive signals about prices, but Tirole's model has no trading prior to the arrival of that information. Thus no one could stake out a position with a capital gains motive of retrading.

Furthermore, his model relates risk solely to prices, rather than shifts in underlying demand and supply. This feature led Hirshleifer (1989) to describe Tirole's model as an 'extreme partial equilibrium.' At one point, Tirole mentioned that the contingent claims model of speculation contained an inconsistency. Hirshleifer responded that he had better information about the consistency of his model than Tirole and offered a friendly bet on that point.

> Thus, by his own logic, and following his 'seminar speaker' tale, Tirole must now concede that I am correct! My unconditional willingness to bet (a year's subscription to *Econometrica*), according to his theory, must make him recoil — leaving me in sole command of the field, like Napoleon at Austerlitz. (Hirshleifer 1989, Note 4, p.299)

Tirole's model helps clarify that in certain idealized situations, people will not just trade because they believe they are getting a good deal. They will rationally consider their trading partner's motives and in all modesty concede that he or she may have better information about the object's value. If traders engage in strategic play and attempt to induce a feedback effect or stubbornly refuse to concede that others might have better information than they have, then speculation will occur. Tirole also introduces risk-preferring traders into his model, and the consequences are predictable.

In a multiperiod extension of his original model, Tirole allows for changes in underlying demand and supply. Not surprisingly, speculation does occur in this setting. Tirole concludes that the market can provide 'price insurance' thereby vindicating the Keynes-Hicks view. All of his focus is on price risks; signals are about market prices, subjective probability distributions are over prices. Yet individuals face quantity risks too. Tirole describes his multiperiod model as 'dynamic,' which could lead to some confusion:

> Tirole unfortunately employs the terms 'statics' and 'dynamics' in a non-standard way. His 'dynamics' refers to multi-date analysis, his 'statics' to single-date analysis. This provides no terminology for the needed distinction between the analysis of equilibrium states and the analysis of transient paths or oscillations. In the standard terminology, we use 'comparative statics' to analyze how a change in parametric underlying conditions modifies the equilibrium attained; we use 'dynamics' if we are concerned with the specifics of the transition path. This distinction is quite crucial for the current discussion. For, in comparative static analysis, a price change can *only* occur in consequence of underlying changes in supply or demand conditions — a key point in the (contingent claims) model. But Tirole is basically concerned with the possibility of 'pure' price fluctuations (such as might emerge in 'bubbles'), where mutually interacting anticipations about the prospective movement of prices of themselves (i.e. *without* any exogenous change in supply-demand determinants) feed back into the very price path thus generated. (Hirshleifer 1989, Note 3, p.299)

Finally, toward the end of his article, Tirole acknowledges that if his common prior beliefs assumption is relaxed, then trading will occur. One might say, paraphrasing Tirole's own words, that speculation due to differences in (prior) beliefs in his model thereby 'vindicates' the position of Holbrook Working et al. If Tirole's model had contained a closer link to fundamental changes in the economy, it would have contributed more to the general theory of speculation.

3.5 Conclusions

The contingent claims model of speculation combines intertemporal investment with choice under uncertainty and has all the desirable properties to look for in a theory of speculation. The value of a general framework should not be confused with the robustness of particular results (definition of a speculator or the martingale property of prices) in one application of that framework. The Hirshleifer framework is more than the (1975) Semicomplete Market regime with claims to N, Z_A and Z_B. It is the Unconditional Market regime model of Section 3.3, and the Equity Market, Numeraire Contingent Market, and other regimes identified in Hirshleifer (1977).

Which is more important for determining speculation — differences in attitudes toward risk or differences in beliefs? We cannot answer that question definitively at this time. We can say that in work to date in the general equilibrium contingent claims model, differences in belief have played a more important role, although differences in degrees of risk aversion certainly do account for some speculative trading. Differences in risk preferences were never directly addressed in the contingent claims model of speculation. The exchange between Hirshleifer and his critics focused on whether utility-deviant individuals, i.e., those with complementarity in their preferences, would speculate. The Hirshleifer model proved that they would. However, someone with complementarity in preferences may not be risk averse. Presumably, other forms of utility variation, i.e., risk aversion, would lead to speculation in the contingent claims model.

The more important step would then be to write a trader's objective function to include both probability beliefs and risk aversion. We could then pose the question of whether a proportionate change in beliefs had a bigger impact than a proportionate change in the degree of risk aversion. This topic should be the focus of future research with this valuable framework.

In Section 3.2.3, we noted that preferences and degrees of risk aversion normally will not change in a model due to the arrival of new information; these parameters were fixed by the theorist in his or her initial model specification. But preferences and attitudes toward risk do frequently change in reality over time. We need to portray dynamic changes in preferences over time and incorporate these changes into the general equilibrium model. This addition will pose significant modeling challenges, but the benefits are worth the effort.

Notes

1. Even to the present day, some articles on speculation continue to model prices as the objects of uncertainty, rather than underlying supply and demand. Instead of having probability distributions over prices (an endogenous variable), traders in these models should have subjective probability distributions over exogenous variables, which might lead to shifts in demand or supply.

2. A similar problem crops up in the single commodity contingent claims model employed by Hirhsleifer and Rubinstein (1973). In that work they observe '[b]ut this requires that he already know, in the prior round, the posterior equilibrium prices ... that will not be determined until the posterior round!' p.800.

3. As explained in Chapter 2, for the Arrow-Debreu securities market, Nagatani's (1975) comment on price computability is even more salient. Computing future spot market prices requires traders in the securities version to know what prices would have prevailed in the contingent claims version, i.e., in markets that do not even exist!

4. 'Where markets in contingent claims are not complete, all agents will speculate except in exceptional circumstances. This does not mean that everyone will be found trading gold futures. Rather, in a world of incomplete contingent markets, all agents possess endowed assets (such as health and ability to work), which cannot be completely traded away at some initial time. Therefore, they will be forced to make initial commitments that will be revised after nature has determined the random event that occurs (such as the state of their health).' (Feiger 1976, p.677)

5. Hirshleifer submitted his witty article, which included numerous French expressions and military quotations and was a pleasure to read in that regard alone, to *Econometrica*. That journal would not accept his reply article, even though it published Tirole's original comment. We have half-seriously discussed that this experience confirms the existence of a 'common knowledge mafia,' who have succeeded in keeping several articles that criticize the consensus results from appearing in certain economics theory journals. Members of this mafia have written articles in the esoteric common knowledge literature and invariably serve as reviewers on articles pertaining to common knowledge. They have a vested interest in

protecting the no trading and 'the posteriors must be equal' results. Members of this common knowledge mafia refuse to concede that assuming common priors is not equivalent to assuming priors are common knowledge.

6. Milgrom and Stokey (1982) refer to their no-trading theorem in a footnote as the Groucho Marx Theorem.

References

Feiger, George, (1976), 'What is Speculation?,' *Quarterly Journal of Economics*, Vol. 90, pp. 677-687.

Hirshleifer, David, (1989a), 'Determinants of Hedging and Risk Premia in Commodity Futures Markets,' *Journal of Financial and Quantitative Analysis*, Vol. 24:3, pp. 313-331.

(1989b), 'Futures Trading, Storage and the Division of Risk: A Multiperiod Analysis,' *The Economic Journal*, Vol. 99, pp. 700-719.

(1990), 'Hedging Pressure and Futures Price Movements in a General Equilibrium Model,' *Econometrica*, Vol. 58:2, pp. 411-428.

(1991), 'Seasonal Patterns of Futures Hedging and the Resolution of Output Uncertainty,' *Journal of Economic Theory*, Vol. 53:2, pp. 304-327.

Hirshleifer, Jack, (1975), 'Speculation and Equilibrium: Information, Risk, and Markets,' *Quarterly Journal of Economics*, Vol. 89, pp. 519-42.

(1976), 'Reply to Comments,' *Quarterly Journal of Economics*, Vol. 90, pp. 689-96.

(1977), 'Theory of Speculation Under Alternative Regimes of Markets,' *Journal of Finance*, Vol. 32.

(1989), 'Two Models of Speculation and Information,' in J. Hirshleifer, *Time, Uncertainty, and Information* (Cambridge, Mass: Basil Blackwell).

Hirshleifer, Jack, and Mark E. Rubinstein, (1973), 'Speculation and Information in Securities Markets,' *Proceedings of the Institute for Management Science*, Tel-Aviv, Vol. 2, pp. 799-802.

Kyle, Albert S., (1985), 'Continuous Auctions and Insider Trading,' *Econometrica*, Vol. 53, pp. 1315-1335.

Milgrom, Paul, and Nancy Stokey, (1982), 'Information, Trade, and Common Knowledge,' *Journal of Economic Theory*, Vol. 26, pp. 17-27.

Nagatani, Keizo, (1975), 'On a Theorem of Arrow,' *Review of Economic Studies*, Vol. 42, pp. 483-485.

Rubinstein, Mark, (1975), 'Securities Market Efficiency in an Arrow-Debreu Economy,' *American Economic Review*, Vol. 65:5, pp. 812-824.

Stiglitz, Joseph E., (1970), 'A Consumption-Oriented Theory of the Demand for Financial Assets and Term Structure of Interest Rates,' *Review of Economic Studies*, Vol. 37, pp. 321-351.

Tirole, Jean, (1982), 'On the Possibility of Speculation Under Rational Expectations,' *Econometrica*, Vol. 50, pp. 1163-1181.

4 Intrinsic uncertainty in financial economics

'I saw you take his kiss!' "Tis true.'
'Oh, modesty!' "Twas strictly kept:
He thought me asleep; at least, I knew
He thought I thought he thought I slept.'

——Coventry Patmore

4.1 Introduction[1]

Individuals in financial markets typically do not know the beliefs, preferences, income constraints, and other exogenous parameters of the rest of the market. This form of uncertainty is intrinsic to the market participants and arises in the absence of common knowledge. 'Intrinsic uncertainty' and higher-order beliefs — i.e., beliefs about other people's beliefs — are important in financial economics, game theory, and any field where the beliefs and actions of others determine payoffs. Indeed, intrinsic uncertainty may be the single most important determinant of stock market volatility.

A theorist can impose common knowledge in a model to eliminate this intrinsic uncertainty. When the value of some parameter θ is common knowledge among agents, it means that each agent knows the value of θ, knows everyone knows the value, knows everyone knows everyone knows the value, *ad infinitum*.

The finance literature often assumes individuals have 'homogeneous beliefs' to circumvent the aggregation problems associated with heterogeneous probability beliefs. Yet a homogeneous beliefs assumption can still permit disagreement and intrinsic uncertainty over state-contingent variables. Some models may actually require a stronger 'agreed common knowledge beliefs' assumption.

This article proves that if two people have the same priors, receive private signals, and have posteriors for an event that are common knowledge, then — contrary to the widely held view — these posteriors may be unequal. The two people can agree to disagree. We have obtained the opposite conclusion of the common knowledge literature,[2] even under that literature's rigid assumptions. Furthermore, this state of disagreement arises even under the homogeneous beliefs assumption prevalent throughout finance theory.

In financial markets, investors' collective behavior determines equilibrium prices. Investors concerned with capital gains must therefore consider the beliefs and trading positions of other market participants. They need to know if others intend to buy more or sell their holdings. Consequently, assumptions about investor beliefs will determine the existence and nature of the market equilibrium. By showing the possibility of multiple equilibria under a homogeneous beliefs regime, we clarify the fundamental assumptions that underpin the existence and uniqueness of an equilibrium in financial economics theory.

Financial agents can also have differing priors that are common knowledge: they can disagree and know they disagree (on the correct prior distribution). Section 4.5 covers heterogeneous common knowledge beliefs.

4.2 Intuition Distinguishing Common and Common Knowledge Priors

People with common priors[3] agree on the likelihood of some outcome by assigning it the same probability *a priori*. However, they can agree without knowing they agree. With agreed common knowledge priors, individuals not only have the same priors but know they have the same priors. Suppose an individual has homogeneous beliefs, receives a private signal, and hears someone call out a (posterior) probability for a subset of states of the world that differs from his own posterior for that subset. He can attribute the difference between the posteriors to either different information contained in the private signals, different priors, or a combination of both. In short, market traders could not distinguish between (1) someone who has the same prior beliefs but different information and (2) someone with different prior beliefs.

If prior beliefs for all market traders were the same and were common knowledge, then, in theory, market traders could attribute any difference in posterior beliefs to informational asymmetries. This deduction would enable market traders to achieve a pooling equilibrium. Thus, in contingent claims analysis, market participants who have the same and common knowledge prior beliefs cannot 'agree to disagree' over the probability that individual states will be revealed.[4]

An event is common knowledge between traders i and j when both traders know that event has occurred, i knows that j knows the event has occurred, j knows that i knows that j knows the event has occurred, *ad infinitum.* Beliefs are common knowledge among market traders when everyone knows everyone knows .... everyone's beliefs; however, assuming beliefs are common knowledge need not imply they also agree.

Consider an economy operating under uncertainty with n people. Define the state of the world for each individual i on the probability space $(\Omega, \mathscr{F}, \rho_i^1)$. The subjective probability distributions $\rho_1^1, \ldots, \rho_n^1$, over Ω represent the prior beliefs of the n individuals as to the likelihood of each possible state. We refer to the distribution ρ_i^1 as the *first-order beliefs* of i, and hence, write the probability distribution with '1' as a superscript. Let $\psi \subset \Omega$ denote an event or subset of possible states of the world. Then $\rho_i^1(\psi)$ denotes the (prior) probability i assigns to the outcome that the true state $\omega \in \psi$.

Definition 1: The individuals have *common* (same) *first-order beliefs* when $\rho_i^1(\psi) = \rho_j^1(\psi)$, for all individuals $i, j,$ over events $\psi \subset \Omega$.

The 'homogeneous beliefs' assumption of finance theory refers to Definition 1. Let Φ_i denote the information partition of individual i that separates the elements of Ω into disjoint subsets and completely spans the space. In game theoretic terms, the information partitions correspond to information sets comprising indistinguishable nodes for a given player.

When the actual state of nature is ω, individual i receives a private signal that the true state belongs to a particular *class of his partition*, $\Phi_i(\omega)$, where $\Phi_i(\omega) \subset \Phi_i$. For example, suppose $\Omega = \{\alpha,\beta,\gamma,\delta\}$, $\Phi_i = \{\alpha\beta,\gamma\delta\}$, $\Phi_j = \{\alpha\gamma,\beta\delta\}$, $E = \alpha\delta$, and $\omega = \alpha$.[5] Let both i and j have the same prior probability distribution over the four events in Ω: $\rho(\alpha) = 0.4$, $\rho(\beta) = 0.1$, $\rho(\gamma) = 0.2$, $\rho(\delta) = 0.3$. These priors may be based on a history of ten trials, where the state α was revealed four times, β was revealed once, and so on. Then

$\rho_i^1[E \mid \Phi_i(\omega)] \equiv \rho_i^1(\alpha\delta \mid \alpha\beta) = .4/.5 = 4/5$, and $\rho_j^1(\alpha\delta \mid \alpha\gamma) = 4/6$.

At this point some theorists have erroneously inferred that by hearing trader i call out the posterior 4/5 for the event E, trader j can somehow tell that trader i received the signal $\alpha\beta$. Yet, unless trader j knows something about trader i's prior beliefs, he has no way of knowing whether the posterior 4/5 applies to i's conditional event $\alpha\beta$ or $\gamma\delta$.

Individual i knows the event E occurs with probability 1 only if $\Phi_i(\omega) \subseteq E$. Depending on his prior probability distribution and how he updates his prior beliefs, i can potentially assign any probability in the interval [0,1] to E when $E \subset \Phi_i(\omega)$.

The first-order beliefs of the other n-1 traders are typically unknown to a trader, and standard Bayesian reasoning encourages the treatment of any unknown by assigning a subjective probability distribution to it. Therefore, in addition to his own distribution ρ_i^1 for Ω, each trader i must also have a subjective probability distribution for the unknown first-order beliefs $(\rho_i^1, \ldots, \rho_{i-1}^1, \rho_{i+1}^1, \ldots, \rho_n^1)$ of the other n-1 market participants. Let ρ_i^2 denote this subjective probability distribution over the first-order beliefs of the other n-1 traders.[6]

Definition 2: The *second-order beliefs* of individual i, ρ_i^2, are a probability distribution for individual i over the possible values of $(\rho_i^1, \ldots, \rho_{i-1}^1, \rho_{i+1}^1, \ldots, \rho_n^1)$.

Returning to the example, if trader j assigns positive probability (in his second-order belief) to trader i employing any of the following priors: (.2, .3, .1, .4); (.1, .4, .1, .4); (.4, .1, .1, .4); (.35, .6, .01, .04), then the posterior $\rho_i^1[E \mid \Phi_i(\omega)] = 4/5$ could mean i received the signal $\Phi_i(\omega) = \gamma\delta$, rather than $\Phi_i(\omega) = \alpha\beta$.

The same intrinsic uncertainty holds for trader i. Upon hearing the posterior $\rho_j^1[E \mid \Phi_j(\omega)] = 4/6$, trader i might conclude that trader j received the signal $\Phi_j(\omega) = \alpha\gamma$. But since he does not know how trader i assigns prior probability to the elements of Ω, trader j could assign some positive probability in his second-order belief distribution ρ_j^2 to the possible priors (.3, .2, .1, .4); (.2, .2, .2, .4). For both of these possible priors, trader j's posterior for E of 4/6 would indicate he received the signal $\Phi_j(\omega) = \beta\delta$.

Finally, the traders could draw the correct inference about the signals from erroneous assumptions about priors. For example, if trader *j* assigns positive probability to trader *i* using the prior (.1, .4, .3, .2) instead of trader *i*'s actual prior (.4, .1, .2, .3), trader *j* might still correctly infer that *i*'s posterior for *E* of 4/5 means trader *i* received the signal $\Phi_i(\omega) = \alpha\beta$.

In principle, it is possible to define *third-order beliefs*, which would be a probability distribution over second-order beliefs, and so on for an infinite regression. Third- and higher-order beliefs in finance theory date back to Keynes' classic beauty contest analogy to stock market investment:

> [P]rofessional investment may be likened to those newspaper competitions in which the competitors have to pick out the six prettiest faces from a hundred photographs, the prize being awarded to the competitor who choice most nearly corresponds to the average preferences of the competitors as a whole; so that each competitor has to pick, not those faces which he himself finds prettiest, but those which he thinks likeliest to catch the fancy of other competitors, all of whom are looking at the problem from the same point of view. It is not a case of choosing those which, to the best of one's judgment, are really the prettiest, nor even those which average opinion genuinely thinks the prettiest. We have reached the third degree where we devote our intelligences to anticipating what average opinion expects the average opinion to be. Keynes (1936), p.156.

Chapter 6 develops a Cartesian product space framework to represent higher-order beliefs more rigorously.

In the two-person example, with traders *i* and *j*, the second-order beliefs for trader *i* have been reduced from a probability distribution over the (*n*-1)-tuple $(\rho_i^1, \ldots, \rho_{i-1}^1, \rho_{i+1}^1, \ldots, \rho_n^1)$, to simply a probability distribution over ρ_j^1. Similarly, ρ_j^2 is now a probability distribution over ρ_i^1. By induction the third-order beliefs of trader *i*, ρ_i^3, distribute probability over the possible values of ρ_j^2.

Common knowledge is the opposite extreme of complete intrinsic uncertainty. For the mathematics of higher-order beliefs, common knowledge first-order beliefs imply mass points on the higher-order beliefs: all probability will be assigned to the known value of the first-order belief.

If trader i assigns probability to more than one probability distribution in his second-order belief for trader j, then he must not know the first-order probability distribution employed by trader j. Hence, traders i and j cannot 'know' they agree if their respective second-order beliefs for each other assign positive probability to more than one first-order belief. The following definitions apply to a two-person model with traders i and j, and $E \subset \Omega$.

Definition 3: j is said to *know* $\rho_i^1(E) = c$ if and only if $\rho_j^2(E) = c$.

Definition 4: i is said to *know j knows* $\rho_i^1(E) = c$ if and only if $\rho_i^3(E) = \rho_j^2(E) = \rho_i^1(E) = c$.

Definition 5: j is said to *know i knows j knows* $\rho_i^1(E) = c$ if and only if $\rho_j^4(E) = \rho_i^3(E) = \rho_j^2(E) = \rho_i^1(E) = c$.

Definition 6: The first-order posterior $\rho_i^1[E|\Phi_i(\omega)] = c$ is common knowledge between i and j at ω if and only if for any even integer K, and any odd integer L, $\rho_j^K[E|\Phi_i(\omega)] = \rho_i^L[E|\Phi_i(\omega)] = \rho_i^1[E|\Phi_i(\omega)] = c$.

Note that in Definition 6 the conditioning event $\Phi_i(\omega)$ is actually known only to trader i. The posterior for trader j conditioned on trader i's signal corresponds to the posterior j would assign to the event given what j believes i has been informed.

4.3 Illustration of Intrinsic Uncertainty with Homogeneous Beliefs

This section presents some additional numerical examples that point out the distinction between homogeneous beliefs, agreed common knowledge beliefs, and common knowledge (posterior) beliefs that are not equal.

Example 1: Homogeneous Beliefs, Homogeneous Posteriors

Suppose the numerical values of the common (homogeneous) prior for i and j is set equal among the four possible states of the world. Take $\Omega = \{\alpha,\beta,\gamma,\delta\}$, $\Phi_i = \{\alpha\beta,\ \gamma\delta\}$, $\Phi_j = \{\alpha\gamma,\ \beta\delta\}$, $E = \alpha\delta$, and $\omega = \alpha$. But now let both i and j assign equal prior probability of 1/4 to all four states. Then

$$\rho_i^1[E|\Phi_i(\omega)] \equiv \rho_i^1(\alpha\delta\,|\,\alpha\beta) = \frac{1/4}{1/2} = \frac{1}{2}, \text{ and } \rho_j^1(\alpha\delta\,|\,\alpha\gamma) = \frac{1}{2}\,.$$

The traders would have equal posteriors without any further revising, unlike the numerical example of Section 4.2 in which the posteriors remained unequal. Yet, even for this case, the traders cannot know whether their equal posteriors stem from having the same priors or having different priors and different information. The traders still face intrinsic uncertainty and agree upon the posterior probability by chance.

Example 2: Homogeneous Beliefs, Different Posteriors

Suppose i and j have the same prior belief for the state of the world in a model with only two possible states S_1 and S_2; the prior probability for S_1 is 1/2 and the prior for S_2 is 1/2. Let E represent the event that S_1 will appear in the next trial. Suppose that each person can observe one previous outcome, and that these trials came up S_1 for trader i and S_2 for trader j. If each trader's information consists solely of his endowed prior distribution and the outcome of his one observation, then the posteriors for E will be 2/3 for trader i and 1/3 for trader j.

If each one then informs the other of his posterior, what will they conclude about the previous outcomes? The common knowledge literature suggests that trader j would can immediately infer that i's observation came up S_1 and that i would infer j's trial came up S_2, so that both people would revise their posteriors to 1/2.

But, in the face of intrinsic uncertainty, how could trader i infer anything from trader j's posterior without knowing j's prior as well? Neither trader would know how many trials the other observed, let alone the outcome of these trials. Therefore, the 2/3 and 1/3 posteriors may remain divergent.[7]

Example 3: Same Prior, Different Posterior, Further Refinement

When the agents' posteriors are announced and common knowledge, then each agent has three pieces of information. He knows his own prior, his own private signal (in the form of a class of his partition), and he knows both his and the other trader's posterior is common knowledge. For many problems this amount of information may suffice to lead to posterior revision and equality, even when the priors are only the same but *not* common knowledge.

Consider $\Phi_i = \{1,2,3\}, \{4,5\}, \{6,7,8,9\}$; $\Phi_j = \{8,1,4\}, \{2,5,7,9\}, \{3,6\}$; $\omega = 6$; $\Phi_i(\omega) = \{6,7,8,9\}$; $\Phi_j(\omega) = \{3,6\}$; $E = (3,7)$; and both i and j assign equal (1/9) probability to the nine events in Ω.

Both trader i's and trader j's posterior for E, $\rho_i^1(E|6,7,8,9) = 1/4$ and $\rho_j^1(E|3,6) = 1/2$, are common knowledge. The traders' partitions are also common knowledge. Thus, when trader j calls out positive probability for the event (3,7) given his private signal, it becomes common knowledge that $\Phi_j(\omega) \neq \{8,1,4\}$ since $E \bigcap \{8,1,4\} = \phi$. Similarly, it becomes common knowledge that $\Phi_j(\omega) \neq \{4,5\}$.

Define the set $C = \{\omega': \rho_j^2[E|\Phi_i(\omega')] = 1/4\}$ and analogously define the set $D = \{\omega': \rho_i^2[E|\Phi_j(\omega')] = 1/2\}$. It follows that $\{8,1,4\} \not\subset D$ and $\{4,5\} \not\subset C$, so these states would be removed from consideration when the posteriors are common knowledge. From Definition 6, j knows i assigns zero probability to the set $\{4,5\}$ implies $\rho_j^2[4,5|\Phi_i(\omega)] = 0$, and the fact that i knows j knows i assigns zero posterior probability to $\{4,5\}$ means $\rho_i^3[4,5|\Phi_i(\omega)] = 0$, so that

$$\rho_j^K[4,5|\Phi_i(\omega)] = \rho_i^L[4,5|\Phi_i(\omega)] = 0,$$

where K is an even integer, and L is an odd integer.

Previously, with only their private signals, the set of states that were common knowledge between i and j at ω was given by $\{1,2,3,4,5,6,7,8,9\}$, which is the join of the classes of the two partitions $\Phi_i(\omega)$ and $\Phi_j(\omega)$ as defined in the Appendix. Now that the posteriors for E are common knowledge as well, the set of possible states that are common knowledge has been refined to $\{2,3,6,7,9\}$. Then i knows that the element '8' of his informed class $\{6,7,8,9\}$ is not possible. Trader

i thus revises his posterior to $\rho_i^1(E|6,7,9) = 1/3$.

At this stage, i's posterior remains at 1/3 conditioned on his original informed signal, the refinement of the state space, and a posterior for j of 1/2. The two have moved closer to consensus but have not reached equality. In some examples, the revision process may lead to consensus, but there is no guarantee.

To illustrate how the traders reach agreement in the present example, suppose the traders not only have the same priors but that these priors are common knowledge as well: the traders have agreed common knowledge prior beliefs.

If trader i's prior was common knowledge, then by Definition 6

$$\rho_j^K(\omega) = \rho_i^L(\omega) = \rho_i^1(\omega) \tag{4.1}$$

where K is any even integer and L is any odd integer, and condition (4.1) holds for all $\omega \in \Omega$. Similarly, if trader j's prior is common knowledge, then

$$\rho_i^K(\omega) = \rho_j^L(\omega) = \rho_j^1(\omega). \tag{4.2}$$

The traders have 'agreed' priors if their priors are equal:

$$\rho_j^1(\omega) = \rho_i^1(\omega), \tag{4.3}$$

again for all $\omega \in \Omega$. Combining equations (4.1), (4.2), and (4.3) means that every first- and higher-order belief of trader i equals every first- and higher-order belief of trader j for a particular event under consideration. The notation in the following definition applies to a two-person model.

Definition 7: i and j have *agreed common knowledge priors* (ACKP) when for any pair of natural numbers, N and M, and $\omega \in \Omega$,

$$\rho_j^N(\omega) = \rho_i^M(\omega). \tag{4.4}$$

Alternatively, using set theory concepts, i and j have ACKP if condition (4.3) is met and both $\rho_i^1(\omega)$ and $\rho_j^1(\omega)$ are $\Phi_i(\omega) \cap \Phi_j(\omega)$-measurable.

We will return to the σ-field measurability property in Chapter 6.

With ACKP in the preceding example, hearing the posterior

$\rho_i^1[(3,7)\,|\,\Phi_i(\omega)] = 1/4$ immediately informs trader j that i received the informed signal $\Phi_i(\omega) = \{6,7,8,9\}$. Similarly, i knows j received the signal $\{3,6\}$ when he hears the posterior $\rho_j^1[(3,7)\,|\,\Phi_j(\omega)] = 1/2$. Then each individual can determine that $\omega = 6$, in this particular example, by taking the intersection of $\{3,6\}$ and $\{6,7,8,9\}$. Thus, both traders i and j would then assign zero posterior probability to (3,7) conditioned on ACKP, their respective informed class of their partitions, common knowledge partitions, and the common knowledge posteriors.

4.4 The Consensus Propositions

Let J denote the join or 'finest common coarsening' of the partitions $\Phi_1, \Phi_2, \ldots \Phi_n$, and let $J(\omega)$ be that element of the join containing ω.

Definition 8: An *event E* is *common knowledge* at ω if $J(\omega) \subset E$. [8]

Note that Definition 8 applies only to events, not to beliefs.

The common knowledge literature's lattice partition framework requires additional constraints on the admissible set of elements for the join to develop the notion of common knowledge beliefs. Define $\Psi_i = \{\omega' \in \Omega\colon \rho_i^1[A\,|\,\Phi_i(\omega')] = c\}$, and let $J_{ij}(\omega)$ be the element of the join of Φ_i and Φ_j that contains ω. Geanakoplos and Polemarchakis (1982) have shown that a necessary condition for the posterior $\rho_i^1[A\,|\,\Phi_i(\omega)] = c$ to be common knowledge between i and j is that $J_{ij}(\omega) = A$.

To see the severity of this restrictive condition in a contingent claims economy, suppose the model contains six states of the world numbered 1 through 6. If $J_{ij}(\omega) = \{1,2,3,4,5,6\}$, and $\Phi_i = \{1,2\}, \{3\}, \{4,5,6\}$, then only a posterior such as $\rho_i^1[1,2,3,4,5,6\,|\,\Phi_i(\omega)] = 1$ can be common knowledge before the agents start calling out their beliefs back and forth. Surely contingent claims analysis requires a framework that can depict more than just the probability of the whole universe is 1.

In Section 4.2, when the true state of the world is ω, trader i is given the private signal $\Phi_i(\omega)$, and trader j is similarly informed the true state lies within the class $\Phi_j(\omega)$. It is then common knowledge between i and

j that the true state lies within $J_{ij}(\omega)$. When the agents receive further information about a posterior for some specific event E, they typically cannot refine the set $J_{ij}(\omega)$ unless they know the prior upon which the posterior is based. The following proposition states this fact more formally.

Proposition 1: Let $\omega, \omega' \in \Omega$, and let $c \in [0,1]$ and $d \in [0,1]$. Define the set $C = \{\omega': \omega \in J_{ij}(\omega) \text{ and } \rho_j^2[E|\Phi_i(\omega')] = c\}$, and similarly define the set $D = \{\omega': \omega' \in J_{ij}(\omega) \text{ and } \rho_i^2[E|\Phi_j(\omega')] = d\}$. Let the posteriors $\rho_i^1[E|\Phi_i(\omega)] = c$ and $\rho_j^1[E|\Phi_j(\omega)] = d$ be common knowledge between i and j at ω. Then $c \neq d$, if

$$\rho_i^2[E \cap D] / \rho_i^2[D] \neq \rho_j^2[E \cap C] / \rho_j^2[C].$$

Proof: See the Appendix.

Proposition 1 shows that even when (two) traders have common priors and their posteriors for an event E are common knowledge, as when they both call out their posteriors,[9] then their posteriors may remain unequal. Intrinsic uncertainty may lead to an equilibrium in which the traders disagree and have no basis for further iteration toward consensus.

In contrast, the common knowledge literature has reached precisely the opposite conclusion. The subtle distinction between 'common priors' and common knowledge priors has somehow been largely overlooked in finance theory and, ironically, confused in the literature on common knowledge. Aumann (1987, p.10) asserts that in all games of incomplete information, the priors are common knowledge. 'If it were not, then the description of ω would be incomplete; we would be able to split ω into several states, depending on the various possibilities for $\rho^1(\omega)$.' Thus Aumann's treatment expands the state space to include a description of investor beliefs as well as a state of nature. Aumann then seems to contradict himself on the same page when he asserts 'neither a partition nor a prior is an event.' Events are subsets of the state space.

Brandenberger and Dekel (1993) found a more reasonable way of treating common knowledge priors as attributes of a particular type of person. They suggest Aumann's expanded state space should be the product of the underlying states of nature times the possible type spaces of each individual. 'i is of a type that assigns probability 1 to j being of a type that assigns probability 1 to E, and so on.' (p.197) Yet they go on to interpret common knowledge of the information structure — including the prior and thus higher-order beliefs of other market participants — as imposing no 'loss of generality.' I cannot agree. Common knowledge prior beliefs is a highly restrictive assumption that was not intended and need not be imposed on many (game theoretic) models of differential information. Chapter 6 proves that a large class of arbitrage pricing models with incomplete information only requires the weaker common priors or homogeneous beliefs assumption. The long history of Arrow-Debreu contingent claims and securities models outlined in Chapter 2 contains common knowledge assumptions about future prices, but not necessarily about prior beliefs.

Aumann argues that if game players know the structure of a game, then priors are automatically common knowledge. As Proposition 1 shows, this argument is invalid. We can have meaningful discussions of games of incomplete information in which the priors of players are not common knowledge. The common knowledge literature's consensus results and no trading theorems depend critically and explicitly on a common knowledge priors assumption. This assumption should be stated up front and not relegated to some murky discussion of 'information structure,' on which reasonable people might disagree about what is and is not included.[10]

A related article by Shin (1993) formalizes the notion that to claim one knows something implies that person can justify the claim by showing a proof. Shin finds that a statement will be common knowledge at ω only if there exists an event proving that statement in the (join) of the partitions. It is difficult to conceive of such an event in the join of the partitions that could be used to prove a statement such as 'individual i's prior is ....' No such events are mentioned by Shin, although he does find some events related to common knowledge information partitions.

By imposing ACKP as an assumption, we arrive at the following corollary to Proposition 1.

Proposition 2: If i and j have ACKP, and their posteriors $\rho_i^1[E|\Phi_i(\omega)] = c$ and $\rho_j^1[E|\Phi_j(\omega)] = d$ are common knowledge between i and j at ω, then $c = d$.

Proof: See the Appendix.

Proposition 2 follows directly from Aumann (1976), but it settles a lingering question on the fundamental assumptions necessary to derive consensus. Following Aumann's original proposition, a series of no-trading theorems were proposed by Milgrom and Stokey (1982), Tirole (1982), and Geanakoplos and Polemarchakis (1982). These papers allege that with *common priors*, the mere willingness of others to trade should convince at least one trading partner that his own position must be disadvantageous.[11] Hence all the required trading partners would allegedly never agree to the trade. In general, the no trading results will only hold if the traders' priors are common knowledge.

4.5 Heterogeneous Common Knowledge Beliefs

Section 4.4 emphasized *agreed* common knowledge priors. Market participants could conceivably have unequal yet common knowledge priors. It could be common knowledge between i and j that $\rho_i^1(\omega) \neq \rho_j^1(\omega)$, for $\omega \in \Omega$. Differing common knowledge beliefs are a form of heterogeneous beliefs. Market traders with heterogeneous beliefs that are not common knowledge still face intrinsic uncertainty over the unknown beliefs of others.

It may be helpful to list possible individual belief assumptions in decreasing order of restrictiveness:

1. agreed common knowledge priors;
2. agreed priors ≡ common priors ≡ homogeneous priors ≡ homogeneous beliefs ≡ equal priors;
3. heterogeneous common knowledge priors; and
4. heterogeneous priors.

Does it make sense in financial markets to talk about beliefs that are common knowledge but heterogeneous, as in number 3 above? In the real world, two equally intelligent and knowledgeable mutual fund managers may have different and common knowledge beliefs about the market's future performance. Both mutual fund managers would seem to have access to similar financial reports, yet one may be bullish and one may be bearish on the market. When these conflicting prognoses for the market are publicly announced, their heterogeneous beliefs become common knowledge.

To maintain heterogeneous common knowledge beliefs in this pooling equilibrium, each mutual fund manager must consider himself either a better analyst or the recipient of better information than the party with whom he disagrees. Each must believe that in the final analysis he will be proven correct. This willingness to disagree openly also raises some interesting behavioral questions about aggressiveness and self-confidence (in one's own priors) that have not been addressed to date in the consensus literature.

4.6 Conclusions and Issues for Future Research

This chapter has focused on the standard 'homogeneous beliefs' assumption that permeates finance theory. Under this assumption, individuals typically do not know the beliefs of others in the market. Several numerical examples were developed that employ homogeneous beliefs but focus on how intrinsic uncertainty over priors can still arise: individuals can agree without knowing *a priori* they agree.

Intrinsic uncertainty has nothing to do with 'innate' differences in priors; it arises whether the priors are equal or unequal. Intrinsic uncertainty depends on how much each individual knows about the rest of the market.

This chapter has also presented two propositions. The first states if (any) two people have common priors and their posteriors (after receiving private information) for an event are common knowledge, then these posteriors may be unequal. The second proposition states that with agreed common knowledge priors (ACKP) and common knowledge posteriors, the posteriors must be equal.

Future research should explore some of the interesting behavioral issues raised in the analysis. First, we assumed that the individuals will honestly reveal their true posteriors. In financial markets, traders have every incentive to conceal their true beliefs until after they have traded. Furthermore, we assumed the individuals cooperate and actually want to reach consensus. If one person adamantly refuses to update his beliefs, e.g., because he feels he has superior information or simply because he is stubborn, then another person listening to him repeatedly call out the same posterior may draw incorrect inferences. Again, in financial markets, firms could obviously lose potential profits from sharing information with their competitors.

Not all theories require highly restrictive market belief assumptions. The common knowledge literature does for its key agreement results. However, Chapter 6 shows that a large class of arbitrage pricing models actually need only the weaker assumption of homogeneous beliefs. Therefore, the reader should exercise caution before replacing a homogeneous beliefs assumption with an ACKP assumption in his or her own models.

Appendix

This Appendix contains some illustrations of the lattice theory concepts used in the common knowledge literature, and proofs of Propositions 1 and 2.

Illustration of Meet and Join

The common knowledge literature uses relatively sophisticated notation and concepts from lattice theory. This section attempts to explain some of these concepts. Let J denote the join of the partitions Φ_1, Φ_2,, . . . Φ_n, where the *join of the partitions*, as distinguished from the *join of the elements* of a set, is defined in lattice theory as the 'finest common coarsening' of the partitions. Let $J(\omega)$ be that element of the join containing ω .

The basis for *meets* and *joins of partitions* in lattice theory becomes coarsenings and refinements of those partitions. Donnellan (1968), pp.18-19, provides the following illustration. If a set *(abcd)* is partitioned into P_1 = *(abc/d)* and P_2 = *(ab/cd)*, then the *meet of* P_1 and P_2, written $P_1 \wedge P_2$, is *(ab/c/d)*. The *meet of the partitions* is the coarsest common refinement of the partitions. The partition P_1 contains two *classes:* *(abc)* and *(d)*.

If P_3 = *(a/b/cd)* and P_4 = *(ab/c/d)*, then the *join of* P_3 *and* P_4, written $P_3 + P_4$ or $P_3 \vee P_4$, is *(ab/cd)*. The *join of the partitions* gives a coarsening of either partition. $P_3 + P_4$ is characterized as the most refined partition having the property that overlapping classes of P_3 and P_4 are wholly contained in just one of the classes: the finest common coarsening.[12]

Consider $\Phi_i = \{1\}, \{2,3\}, \{4,5\}, \{6\}$; $\Phi_j = \{1,2\}, \{3,4,5\}, \{6\}$; $\omega = 3$; $\Phi_i(\omega) = \{2,3\}$; and $\Phi_j(\omega) = \{3,4,5\}$. The following set of statements applies to knowledge about what state of the world can occur:

i knows {2,3};
j knows {3,4,5};
i knows *j* knows either {1,2} or {3,4,5}, but not both;
j knows *i* knows either {2,3} or {4,5}, but not both;
i knows *j* knows *i* knows {1} or {2,3} or {4,5}, but only one of them; and

j knows i knows j knows $\{1,2\}$ or $\{3,4,5\}$, but not both.

By the third-order beliefs, we have reached a consensus over the range of possible states. When the true state $\omega = 3$, each agent is informed the true state lies in that class of his partition that contains 3: $\{2,3\}$ for agent i and $\{3,4,5\}$ for agent j. Agent i does not know whether the true state is 2 or 3. If the true state is 2, then i knows j would have been informed with the class $\{1,2\}$. If the true state is 3, then i knows j would have been informed with the class $\{3,4,5\}$. Therefore, as his second-order belief, $\rho_i^2(\omega \mid \{2,3\})$, agent i knows j was informed either $\{1,2\}$ or $\{3,4,5\}$. A similar logic applies to agent j's second-order belief.

At the third-order, if j was in fact informed $\{1,2\}$, then i could reason that j would know i was informed either $\{1\}$ if $\omega = 1$, and $\{2,3\}$ if $\omega = 2$. Remember, neither agent knows with certainty the exact value of ω. If j was in fact informed $\{3,4,5\}$, then i could reason that j would know i was informed either $\{2,3\}$ or $\{4,5\}$. Thus agent i's third-order belief, $\rho_i^3(\omega \mid \{2,3\})$, comprises $\{1\}$, $\{2,3\}$, or $\{4,5\}$.

In assessing the higher-order beliefs of each agent, we first look to each agent's informed signal. The second-order beliefs depict those classes of the other agent's partition that share any element in common with the original agent's informed signal. Once we have the second-order beliefs, we again iterate to find the range for the third-order beliefs. This time we look for classes with any overlapping elements in the (expanded) second-order belief range. Fourth-order beliefs would be defined over classes with overlapping elements of the third-order beliefs, and so on.

At the third-order stage, we have defined a common range of $\{1,2,3,4,5\}$ for both agents i and j. It turns out that all higher-order beliefs will use this same range as well; this range must then be common knowledge by defintion. This process of looking for classes with elements that overlap with some range of interest is merely the lattice theory concept of coarsening. The fincst common coarsening, or the *join*, of $\Phi_i(\omega)$ and $\Phi_j(\omega)$ is $\{1,2,3,4,5\}$ in this example: it is common knowledge between i and j that the true state of the world is in the set $\{1,2,3,4,5\}$. Due to the way the partitions isolated the element $\{6\}$, the coarsening will not include it. Thus it is also common knowledge between i and j that the true state will not be '6.'

Proof of Proposition 1

Since $\rho_i^1[E|\Phi_i(\omega)] = c$ is common knowledge between agents i and j at ω, then in general

$$c = \rho_i^1[E|\Phi_i(\omega)] = \rho_j^K[E|\Phi_i(\omega)] \qquad \textbf{(A4)}$$

where K is an even integer, and in particular

$$c = \rho_i^1[E|\Phi_i(\omega)] = \rho_j^2[E|\Phi_i(\omega)]. \qquad \textbf{(A5)}$$

By definition, $C = \{\omega': \omega' \in J_{ij}(\omega)$ and $\rho_j^2[E|\Phi_i(\omega')] = c\}$ and $D = \{\omega' : \omega' \in J_{ij}(\omega)$ and $\rho_i^2[E|\Phi_j(\omega')] = d\}$. Let $C = \bigcup_y \Phi_i(\omega)^y$. Since the classes $\Phi_i(\omega)^y$ are disjoint and $\rho_i^2[E|\Phi_j(\omega)] = c$ throughout C, then

$$\begin{aligned} c &= \rho_j^2\left[E|\Phi_i(\omega)^y\right] \\ &= \rho_j^2\left[E \bigcap \Phi_i(\omega)^y\right] / \rho_j^2\left[\Phi_i(\omega)^y\right] \\ &= \rho_j^2[E \cap C] / \rho_j^2[C] \end{aligned} \qquad \textbf{(A6)}$$

Similarly, it follows that $\rho_i^2[E \cap D] / \rho_i^2[D] = d$. Therefore $c \neq d$, if

$$\rho_i^2[E \cap D] / \rho_i^2[D] \neq \rho_j^2[E \cap C] / \rho_j^2[C]$$

and $c = d$ if

$$\rho_i^2[E \cap D] / \rho_i^2[D] = \rho_j^2[E \cap C] / \rho_j^2[C].$$

Proof of Proposition 2

By statement in the proposition, the two traders i and j have ACKP and their posteriors $\rho_i^1[E|\Phi_i(\omega)] = c$ and $\rho_j^1[E|\Phi_j(\omega)] = d$ are common knowledge at ω. It follows that $\rho_i^2[E|\Phi_j(\omega)] = d$ and $\rho_j^2[E|\Phi_i(\omega)] = c$, and indeed $\rho_i^K[E|\Phi_j(\omega)] = d$ and $\rho_j^K[E|\Phi_i(\omega)] = c$, for any integer K. Define the set $C = \{\omega' : \omega' \in J_{ij}(\omega),\ \rho_i^1[E|\Phi_i(\omega)] = c\}$. By the *agreed* part of the ACKP assumption, $\rho_i^1[E|\Phi_i(\omega)] = c$. The partitions for i and j are common knowledge, so that j knows the elements of the set C. Agent j knows what elements are contained in each of i's partitions; consequently, j knows which of i's partitions are contained in C since they must also satisfy the condition $\rho_j^1[E|\Phi_i(\omega)] = c$. Similarly, define the set $D = \{\omega' : \omega' \in J_{ij}(\omega),\ \rho_j^1[E|\Phi_j(\omega)] = d\}$, and both i and j will know all the elements of the set D (by the ACKP assumption). The elements of C and D must be in $J_{ij}(\omega)$, since the posteriors are common knowledge *at* ω by assumption and it is common knowledge between i and j that the true event lies within $J_{ij}(\omega)$.

Write $C = \bigcup_y \Phi_i(\Omega)^y$. Since the partitions $\Phi_i(\omega)^y$ are disjoint and $\rho_i^1[E|\Phi_i(\omega)] = c$ throughout C, then $c = \rho_i^1[E|C]$. Similarly, throughout D, $\rho_j^1[E|\Phi_j(\omega)] = d$, so that $d = \rho_j^1[E|D]$. The intersection of C and D is nonempty, since it must include ω. Since $\{C \cap D\} \subset C$ and $\{C \cap D\} \subset D$, then

$$c = \rho_i^1[E|C \cap D], \tag{A7}$$

and

$$d = \rho_j^1[E|C \cap D]. \tag{A8}$$

The right-hand sides of (A7) and (A8) are equal from the 'agreed' part of the ACKP assumption. This result establishes Proposition 2.

Notes

1. This chapter expands an article that originally appeared in the *Journal of Financial Research*, Vol. XII, No. 4 (Winter 1989), pp. 269-283. The permission of the *Journal of Financial Research* to reprint in this volume is gratefully acknowledged. Jack Hirshleifer provided me with the quotation by Patmore.

2. Aumann (1987), Tirole (1982), Milgrom and Stokey (1982), Geanakoplos and Polemarchakis (1982), and Sebenius and Geanakoplos (1983) use the terms 'common priors' and 'common knowledge priors' interchangeably. These same works go to great lengths, by contrast, to point out the distinction between common posteriors and common knowledge posteriors.

3. Common priors are used synonymously with 'homogeneous priors' or 'homogeneous beliefs' in finance theory and in this chapter.

4. The consensus not to 'agree to disagree' requires underlying behavioral assumptions that market participants honestly reveal their posterior beliefs and do not stubbornly refuse to update their probability beliefs.

5. When Ω is finite, the σ-field $\mathscr{F}$ is taken to be the power set 2^{Ω}.

6. No homeomorphism exists between the first-order, second-order, or any higher-order beliefs of an individual. Theoretically, each higher-order belief can be defined as a separate random variable on a separate probability space.

7. Even if each knew the number of trials the other one observed, their posteriors still might diverge, since each person would be uncertain about the other's prior before witnessing any trials.

8. Based on Aumann (1976), with the 'join' corrected for 'meet.'

9. DeGroot (1974) described a revision process where agents, with different information about the unknown value of some parameter θ, call out their probability beliefs back and forth and then successively update the measures based on the posteriors they hear. As shown in Proposition 1, this consensus result typically only

holds for the limiting case where the agents' priors are equal and common knowledge.

10. Reny (1993) has found another limitation on assuming the information structure is common knowledge: two-person games with complete information where the fact that the players maximize expected utilty cannot be common knowledge.

11. Other theorists have noted the confusion in the common knowledge literature:

    (The) conclusion, that this process leads inevitably to agreed beliefs and thus to non-trading is a special result with very little robustness. For one thing, and Tirole (1982) concedes this, it fails if the traders' *priors* differ. And indeed, for the validity of the non-trading theorem something even stronger than agreed priors is needed: the parties' priors must not only be agreed but must be 'common knowledge' in the sense of Aumann (1976) - i.e., each must know the other shares his beliefs, must know that the other knows he knows, etc. This point is due to Guth (1984, published 1989), who has also analyzed the implications for speculation theory of shared priors that are *not* common knowledge....Even the classic statement by Aumann (1976) appears defective on this score. Aumann emphasizes that the *posteriors* must be common knowledge; he requires only that the agents have the same priors. But the information-transmission process he describes will work only if the parties have common knowledge about their shared *priors* as well. Hirshleifer (1984, published 1989), p.295, and Note 5.

    In fact, the common knowledge literature's 'no trading theorem' essentially attempts to restate necessary conditions for Akerlof's (1970) no trading of 'lemons' theorem.

12. The reader should take caution that the common knowledge literature has used the term 'meet' to stand for the finest common coarsening. For clarification see Donnellan (1968), Birkhoff (1961), or Szasz (1963).

References

Akerlof, George, (1970), ''The Market for 'Lemons': Qualitative Uncertainty and the Market Mechanism,'' *Quarterly Journal of Economics*, Vol. 84, pp. 488-500.

Aumann, Robert J., (1976), 'Agreeing to Disagree,' *Annals of Statistics*, Vol. 4, pp. 1236-1239.

(1987), 'Correlated Equilibrium as an Expression of Bayesian Rationality,' *Econometrica*, Vol. 55, pp. 1-18.

Birkhoff, Garret, (1961), *Lattice Theory*, American Mathematics Society, New York.

Brandenberger, Adam, and Eddie Dekel, (1993), 'Hierarchies of Beliefs and Common Knowledge,' *Journal of Economic Theory*, Vol. 59, pp. 189-198.

Brieman, L., (1968), *Probability Theory*, Addison-Wesley, Reading, Massachusetts.

DeGroot, Morris H., (1974), 'Reaching a Consensus,' *Journal of the American Statistical Association*, Vol. 60, pp. 118-121.

Donnellan, Thomas, (1968), *Lattice Theory*, Pergamon Press, London.

Geanakoplos, John D., and Heraklis M. Polemarchakis, (1982), 'We Can't Disagree Forever,' *Journal of Economic Theory*, Vol. 28, pp. 192-200.

Guth, Michael A. S., (1984, published 1989), 'Intrinsic Uncertainty and Common-Knowledge Priors in Financial Economics,' *Journal of Financial Research*, Vol. 12, No. 4, pp. 269-283.

Hirshleifer, Jack, (1984, published 1989), 'Two Models of Speculation and Information,' in J. Hirshleifer, *Time, Uncertainty, and Information*, Basil Blackwell, Inc., New York.

Keynes, John Maynard, (1936), *The General Theory of Employment, Interest, and Money*, McGraw-Hill, New York.

Mertens, J. F., and S. Zamir, (1985), 'Formulation of the Bayesian Analysis for Games with Incomplete Information,' *International Journal of Game Theory*, Vol. 14, pp. 1-29.

Milgrom, Paul, and Nancy Stokey, (1982), 'Information, Trade, and Common Knowledge,' *Journal of Economic Theory*, Vol. 26, pp. 17-27.

Reny, Philip J., (1993), 'Common Belief and the Theory of Games with Perfect Information,' *Journal of Economic Theory*, Vol. 59, pp. 257-274.

Sebenius, James K., and John Geanakoplos, (1983), 'Don't Bet On It: Contingent Agreements with Asymmetric Information,' *Journal of the American Statistical Association*, Vol. 78, pp. 424-426.

Shin, Hyun Song, (1993), 'Logical Structure of Common Knowledge,' *Journal of Economic Theory*, Vol. 60, pp. 1-13.

Szasz, Gabor, (1963), *Introduction to Lattice Theory*, Academic Press, New York.

Tirole, Jean, (1982), 'On the Possibility of Speculation Under Rational Expectations,' *Econometrica*, Vol. 50, pp. 1163-1181.

Comment

Although useful in developing many of the valuable insights into features of market equilibrium, the stylized fiction of 'homogeneous beliefs' has already fallen by the wayside on many important empirical and theoretical fronts. It has been superseded by variations of 'information asymmetry,' as first applied theoretically to problems of agency and incentive contracting, but more recently to empirical issues related to understanding volatility in financial markets.

In regard to volatility, the issue is the manner and extent of information arrival, where information arrival may include information-revealing market transactions which may either increase or reduce the heterogeneity of beliefs between 'players' in financial markets (see references). Indeed, in a semi-strong form efficient market, information asymmetry (heterogeneity of beliefs) is necessary for profitable (and market informing) private trades. As the degree of information asymmetry increases (decreases), the potential for informative private trades increases (decreases).

The emphasis of recent finance theory and empirics is on the *process* of moving toward an equilibrium, as opposed to describing conditions of equilibrium (though the latter are of interest in a limiting case sense). What is of interest in the current work is its implications for the role of common knowledge beliefs in that process; specifically, whether the process involves evolution of beliefs toward common knowledge. (It most surely does not begin with common knowledge beliefs.) The value of this effort lies in its potential to yield insights into the underlying process of updating of beliefs, and reveal conditions under which posteriors 'converge' to common knowledge.

Ronald E. Shrieves
Department of Finance
University of Tennessee, Knoxville

References

Damodaran, A., (1985), 'Economic Events, Information Structure, and the Return Generating Process,' *Journal of Financial and Quantitative Analysis*, Vol. 20, pp. 423-434.

Ederington, L. H., and J. H. Lee, (1993), 'How Market Process Information: News Releases and Volatility,' *Journal of Finance*, Vol. 48, pp. 1161-1191.

French, K. R., and R. Roll, (1986), 'Stock Return Variances: The Arrival of Information and the Reaction of Traders,' *Journal of Financial Economics*, Vol. 17, pp. 5-26.

Grossman, S. J., and J. E. Stiglitz, (1976), 'Information and Competitive Price Systems,' *American Economic Review*, Vol. 66:2, pp. 246-253.

Grossman, S. J., and J. E. Stiglitz, (1980), 'The Impossibility of Informationally Efficient Markets,' *American Economic Review*, Vol. 70, pp. 393-408.

Roll, R., (1988), 'R^2,' *Journal of Finance*, Vol. 43, pp. 541-566.

Ross, S. A., (1989), 'Information and Volatility: The No-Arbitrage Martingale Approach to Timing and Resolution Irrelevancy,' *Journal of Finance*, Vol. 44, pp. 1-18.

5 Homogeneous beliefs and speculation in asset pricing paradigms

> [A] major problem of finance theory is an overreliance on the assumption of common beliefs. I have a suspicion, (and it is *only* a suspicion), that this assumption is behind the failure of theory to explain much of the observed empirical behavior in markets. It is difficult, however, to figure out how to proceed in relaxing this assumption.
>
> Richard Roll, 1988

5.1. Introduction[1]

Most asset pricing theories assume investors hold common or homogeneous beliefs. These assumptions permit theorists to aggregate individual valuation formulas into a market-level expression. Recently, common knowledge belief assumptions have begun replacing the older homogeneous beliefs assumptions. If beliefs are common knowledge, then everyone knows everyone knows .... everyone's beliefs. Without common knowledge assumptions, investors in these models face intrinsic uncertainty over which firms the rest of the market regarded as undervalued or overvalued. Investors might also face uncertainty over how the market's beliefs will change with the arrival of new information. This uncertainty can affect future prices; consequently, it figures in any capital gains (loss) estimate.

Stock prices largely reflect real earnings for the past year coupled with expected earnings for the out year or two. Investor beliefs partially determine forecasts for future earnings and play an even larger role in the equilibrium price-to-earnings ratio for each firm's stock. This chapter examines whether Modigliani-Miller (MM) arbitrage, the Capital Asset Pricing Model (CAPM), and Ross's Arbitrage Pricing Theory (APT) need to employ common knowledge investor belief assumptions.

Although we could apply these concepts to any asset valuation theory, this chapter emphasizes the celebrated Modigliani-Miller (1958) paradigm. The MM arbitrage strategy has a common thread to most of the other asset pricing theories. The paradigm's thirty year anniversary in 1988 spawned several MM theory retrospectives, which surprisingly omitted any discussion of embedded common knowledge assumptions in the model.

Concerning the informational structure of the paradigm, Miller (1988) writes 'one of the key assumptions of both the leverage and dividend models (was) that all capital market participants, inside managers and outside investors alike, have the same information about the firm's cash flows.' Once this assumption is relaxed, it is well known that the MM results do not hold under asymmetric information. An extensive literature deals with this issue dating back to Ross (1977a) and Leland and Pyle (1977),[2] who showed how managers with inside information might have incentives to 'signal' the market about the firm's future earnings through either the firm's debt-equity ratio or dividend policy. In general, this literature focuses on the related topic of managerial incentives but does *not* explore the theoretical underpinnings of the MM propositions.

Recent developments on common knowledge raise questions about the robustness of the MM results as the model is currently formulated. How are the MM results affected if investors agree (on the cash flows of a firm) without knowing they agree?[3] Would some investors want to speculate that the market diverges from their own beliefs? Stiglitz (1969, 1974) has argued that the MM paradigm remains valid even if heterogeneous beliefs are admitted into the model. However, his two-period (1969) model was inadequate to consider the problems posed by speculation, where traders plan to buy and resell knowing information will arrive before the state of the world is revealed. His multiperiod (1974) model conveniently assumes that all the well-known aggregation problems with diverse individual beliefs have somehow sorted themselves out, and the economy starts in a market-clearing equilibrium.

Our analysis can be distinguished from the older, pre-common knowledge era literature on asymmetric information. The older literature examined the impact of *heterogeneous* beliefs based on insider information, with managers or existing shareholders better informed than the rest of the market. This chapter focuses on an MM world in which everyone is equally well informed. Investors in our formulation will not know if their beliefs are homogeneous or heterogeneous.

In studying the role of common knowledge in the MM paradigm, one finds a gap even in modern restatements of debt-equity irrelevancy.

Modern restatements are based on *income* arbitrage: people switching from one asset to another to achieve a greater cash flow from earnings. In fact, they can also receive cash flows from capital gains. For example, speculation and capital gains considerations do not enter into the following analysis.

> The values of debt and equity, in turn, are based on the cash flows that are expected to go to each. Since the cash flow of the firm must go either to debt or to equity and since linearity assures us that the sum of their values is the value of the sum of their cash flows, it follows that the total value of the firm depends simply on the total cash flow to the firm, regardless of the debt-equity mix chosen by that firm. Ross (1988), p.128.

Intelligent investors know the market values of firms depend on more than just accounting identities; market values depend on (changing) beliefs about the future. We will assess the impact these speculative considerations have on MM-style arbitrage, the CAPM, and the APT.

The CAPM is an equilibrium model, whereas the MM paradigm and the APT are arbitrage models.[4] The absence of arbitrage opportunities permits market clearing in the latter two models. The reader may be surprised to learn that we find the MM paradigm does not require investor beliefs to be common knowledge. The CAPM implicitly makes beliefs common knowledge by endowing investors with perfect foresight about asset returns. The APT needs common knowledge belief assumptions for its validity. Thus the need for common knowledge belief assumptions depends on features of individual models, not on the equilibrium solution concept.

Section 5.2 discusses MM's attempts to deal with intrinsic uncertainty and explains how it might lead to speculative investments in the opposite direction of *income* arbitrage. Section 5.3 illustrates the logical intuition in the original MM framework. Section 5.4 presents a numerical example again based on the MM paradigm. The necessity for common knowledge belief assumptions is examined for the Capital Asset Pricing Model in Section 5.5 and for Ross's Arbitrage Pricing Theory in Section 5.6. Section 5.5 derives the CAPM from basic constructs; most finance textbooks merely state the CAPM without deriving it. Section 5.7 examines whether the MM and APT pardigms can incorporate heterogeneous beliefs, as some have suggested, and remain valid. Section 5.8 presents our conclusions and some observations about real world arbitrage.

5.2. MM's Missing Assumption and Speculative Investment

MM-style arbitrage opportunities imply that when securities are either undervalued or overvalued, an investor should be able to buy and sell stocks and bonds in such a way that he increases the income he would have received from his original portfolio position. In focusing on income, MM neglected the capital gains motive.

MM sensed their original proof of the debt-equity propositions left open the possibility for price speculation. Although some investor personally regards a firm as overvalued, he may fear the rest of the market views that same firm as fair valued or even undervalued. That concern led MM to include a missing 'imputed rationality' assumption in their subsequent (1961) dividend paper:

> [W]e shall say that an individual trader 'imputes rationality' to the market or satisfies the postulate of 'imputed rationality' if, in forming expectations, he assumes that every other trader in the market is (a) rational in the previous sense of preferring more wealth to less regardless of the form an increment in wealth may take, and (b) imputes rationality to all other traders... Our postulate thus rules out, among other things, the possibility of speculative 'bubbles'... MM (1961).

By imputed rationality, MM sought to eliminate self-fulfilling equilibria, in which investors take dividends into account simply because they believe others will do so. MM obviously intended that subsequent formulations of the capital structure paradigm assume imputed rationality as well. Since prices are determined endogenously in capital markets, the beliefs of market participants will materially affect each person's own opportunity set, whether these beliefs hold that debt-equity ratios, dividends, or sunspots are relevant to firm valuations.

This missing assumption appears to have been noted by only one previous paper in the vast MM literature:

> MM clearly read much more into this assumption than a statement of the assumption seems to warrant....Thus by 'rationality' MM apparently mean than an individual ignores capital gains aspects of security purchases - but this is never stated explicitly....And what this amounts to is an assumption that individuals behave in the market on the basis of earnings expectations (income prospects) and not on the basis of wealth considerations based on prospective future values of shares or bonds....[W]hen an obviously important

> (and perhaps dominant) feature or aspect of behavior is assumed away, or must be assumed away, to prove a proposition, there is a presumption of problems for the proposition itself. We might also note that MM agree their use of the term 'rational' to refer to behavior based solely on the earnings prospects is much more debatable than, say, the use of the term 'rational' to refer to consistent behavior by consumers in (economic theory). Burness, Cummings, and Quirk (1980), pp.40-42.

Stiglitz (1974) previously spoke about problems with self-fulfilling equilibria when he concluded 'if individuals believe that financial policy affects firm valuation, then it will.' Without using the term 'common knowledge,' Stiglitz nevertheless implied that a common knowledge beliefs assumption was required to prevent 'expectations of real returns dependent on firm financial policy.' An interested reader would be left confused as to whether Stiglitz was assuming the very object of his proof: debt-equity ratios are irrelevant.

But in the final analysis, after more than two dozen separate proofs in alternative variants of the original MM model, the MM literature concluded that investor beliefs must be homogeneous (as to firm earnings and therefore risk classes) and common knowledge. Otherwise, the MM propositions were susceptible to disproofs of the kind outlined below:

> Stiglitz (1974) seems to argue that only if investors think that financial policy will affect the 'real' returns -- presumably earnings and/or dividends of a firm -- will this be a factor in determining market value. But of course all that is required for financial policy to affect market value is the belief on the part of any investors that *other* investors value firms in part on the basis of the debt-equity ratio of the firm, regardless of whether the financial policy has any effect at all on earnings and/or dividends....Stiglitz is underestimating the importance of the problems posed by speculative considerations so far as the MM proposition is concerned. We are in what might be called an *emperor's clothes* situation; the MM proposition is correct only so long as all investors believe it is correct, and once any non-infinitesimal group of investors believes it is wrong, it is wrong. In order to clear the air, and settle the matter once and for all, we would like to announce that we do not believe the MM proposition is correct. Since we have modest (but non-infinitesimal) investments in the market, we have now disproved the theorem. We would be interested in alternative proofs that bypass

the problems posed by our approach. Burness, Cummings, and Quirk (1980), pp. 63-65.

We agree with the reasoning of Burness, Cummings, and Quirk, but not their conclusion.[5] The above quotation correctly points out that in a multiperiod economy the absence of common knowledge can lead investors to speculate in a manner differing from the arbitrage predicted by the MM literature.[6] However, even if some non-infinitesimal group believes debt-equity ratios matter, the MM strategy continues to lock in a sure-profit, provided the investor can hold his position long enough for earnings to be reported. This group's actions in no way eliminate the arbitrage opportunities available in the market. Thus, markets would not clear. Fluctuations in security prices during the intermediate periods - before earnings are realized - represent an opportunity cost, not a real loss.[7]

5.3. Capital Gains in the Original MM Model

Ross (1989) describes how more modern developments in arbitrage pricing have improved the original MM formulation of their paradigm. However, the original MM formulation is easier to understand than much of the modern theory.[8] This section the capital gains motive in the original MM framework. Let X_{is} denote the earnings of firm *i* in state of the world *s*, e_i the price of firm *i*'s shares, and S_i the total number of shares. Suppose firm *1* and firm *2* belong to the same risk class: $X_{1s} = c\, X_{2s}$, across every state *s*. For simplicity, set the constant $c = 1$, so that

$$X_{1s} = X_{2s} \equiv X_s. \tag{5.1}$$

Let the first firm be capitalized with only equity so that its market value $V_1 = E_1 = e_1\, S_1$, while the second firm has both debt and equity so that its market value $V_2 = e_2\, S_2 + B_2$. Suppose $V_1 < V_2$. MM showed that owners of firm *2* shares could sell off their holdings, purchase shares in firm *1*, and achieve higher cash flows for the same dollar investment.

To see this, let some investor hold $\alpha\%$ of firm *2*'s outstanding stock. Then the income, Y_{2s}, the investor receives from his firm *2* shares in state of the world *s* is

$$Y_{2s} = \alpha\, (X_{2s} - r_2\, B_2)$$

$$= \alpha\,(X_s - r_2\,B_2), \qquad \textbf{(5.2)}$$

where r_2 is the market rate of return firm *2* must pay on its bonds. Suppose the investor sells his shares in firm *2* and borrows $\alpha\,B_2$ dollars using these combined proceeds to invest in firm *1* shares. Let β denote the percentage of firm *1* shares he purchases. Thus

$$\beta\,E_1 = \alpha\,(e_2\,S_2 + B_2) = \alpha\,V_2.$$

The income he receives from holding these shares in firm *1* and paying interest on his borrowed funds, again noting that $X_{1s} \equiv X_s$, is

$$\begin{aligned} Y_{1s} &= \beta\,X_s - \alpha\,r_2\,B_2 \\ &= (\alpha\,V_2/E_1)\,X_s - \alpha\,r_2\,B_2 \\ &= \alpha\,[(V_2/V_1)\,X_s - r_2\,B_2] \qquad \textbf{(5.3)} \end{aligned}$$

Since $V_2 > V_1$ by hypothesis, then from comparing (5.2) and (5.3), $Y_{1s} > Y_{2s}$ for every state of the world *s*. Thus all investors find it profitable, whatever their preferences toward risk, to sell their 'overvalued' shares in firm *2* and acquire shares in the 'undervalued' firm *1*. So far so good from an *income* perspective.

A few comments are in order on the nature of the MM riskless profit. First, as already mentioned, it assumes the investor will not have to liquidate his holdings before realizing the earnings X_s in some future period *s*. Second, equation (5.3) contains the term r_2, which implies the 'homemade leverage' idea that individuals can borrow at the same rate as firms. For the arbitrage trading group of a commercial or investment bank, this assumption is trivial. For individual investors in the real world, this assumption generally will not hold.

But what happens if the investor wants to continue holding the overvalued firm *2* shares, or even buy additional firm *2* shares, because he believes he can realize an intermediate capital gain before the state is revealed in some future period. Let $E_T(V_i)$ denote the individual's conditional expectation for the market value of firm *i* in period *T* given the value of V_i in period *1*. If the same investor believes

$$\alpha\,[E_T(V_2) - V_2] - \beta\,[E_T(V_1) - V_1] > Y_{1s} - Y_{2s} \qquad \textbf{(5.4)}$$

then he may hold the overvalued shares with the speculative intent of realizing an intermediate capital gain. This combined treatment of capital gains and wealth apart from income is largely missing in both the MM literature and the arbitrage pricing literature to date.

A few comments are also necessary about condition (5.4). The expectation operator in (5.4) would typically be conditioned on the individual's information set. However, to assure that everyone has access to the same information, we have restricted the information set to the publicly known market values in period *1*. Even with the inequality expressed in (5.4), the fact remains that $Y_{1s} > Y_{2s}$, and others in the market will want to exploit this arbitrage condition. Therefore, expression (5.4) suggests why someone may seek intermediate capital gains, but it fails to eliminate the arbitrage opportunities, a condition necessary for market clearing in the MM world.

5.4. A Numerical Example

This numerical example will first derive conditions under which an investor may want to continue holding 'overvalued' shares in a firm. Second, we will show that under these conditions, an arbitrage opportunity exists - even if the investor still wants to hold the overvalued shares. Consider two firms, Firm *A* and Firm *B*, with identical earnings per share of either 1, 2, 3, 4, or 5 and a sequence of events as follows. Initially traders have a prior round equilibrium based solely on their prior beliefs for earnings. Then after markets have cleared, Firm A changes its debt-equity ratio. The markets reopen and trading resumes. After markets have again closed, Firm B will announce a change in its debt-equity ratio. Trading resumes followed by information on the actual earnings of the two firms.

Just as in the original MM model, let all market participants have access to the same information and share 'homogeneous beliefs' in the form of a common prior over the five possible states for earnings/share.[9] Define this common prior as Pr(1) = 0.6, Pr(2) = 0.1, Pr(3) = 0.2, Pr(4) = 0, and Pr(5) = 0.1, where Pr(*s*) denotes the common probability assigned to earnings/share *s*.

With the prior belief distribution (.6, .1, .2, 0, .1), the market fundamental[10] of this firm's equity is 6 in period 0. To simplify the calculations, suppose both firms' shares trade at a price/earnings ratio of 10. Thus in the prior trading round, both Firm *A* and *B* shares clear the market at a price of \$19. Next suppose Firm *A* changes its debt-equity ratio, and this change is publicly announced (so everyone has access to the same information). Suppose some non-infinitesimal group decides that debt-equity ratios matter to them, and they are willing to sell Firm *A* shares now for \$17/share. The rest of the market would willingly purchase from the group at that price, i.e., the group could easily find one or more trading partners. Therefore, this group may sell their block of shares in Firm *A* at \$17/share. The price of Firm *B* shares continues to rest at \$19/share.

For the rest of the market Firm *A* shares now look undervalued relative to Firm *B* shares, and the MM arbitrage strategy suggests selling off Firm *B* shares and borrowing to buy Firm *A* shares until the two shares are again selling for the same price. Any price discrepancy between these two firm's share prices is an arbitrage opportunity. MM define their equilibrium as the absence of arbitrage for *any* investor. This arbitrage exists by virtue of the firms having the same earnings across possible states of the world; the lack of common knowledge about investor prior beliefs in no way limits the arbitrage. Thus, while some block of shares may trade at \$17/share, this price cannot remain the market clearing price in this period. Firm *A* shares will most likely be bid up again to \$19/share.

If we pursue the numerical example further, we may illuminate some features of condition (5.4). We see from the prior distribution (.6, .1, .2, 0, .1) that investors assign the most probability to earnings/share equal to 1. However, suppose some individual believes that other people believe the earnings/share will most likely turn out to be 3. In that case, both Firm *A* and Firm *B* shares will eventually sell for \$30/share. Applying these numbers to condition (5.4), and noting the \$2 price discrepancy, would yield

$$\alpha\,[30-17] - \beta[30-19] > 2. \tag{5.5}$$

For condition (5.5) to be met, α would have to be much greater than β: Firm *A* must have many fewer shares outstanding than Firm *B*. Even then the condition does not guarantee any individual will actually speculate on capital gains. Finally, if both Firms *A* and *B* did not trade at \$30/share when they both report earnings of \$3/share, then they would not belong to the same risk class (assuming $c = 1$ in equation (5.1)). Thus another of the MM assumptions would have been violated.

5.5. The Capital Asset Pricing Model

Like the MM paradigm, common knowledge prior beliefs are *not* required for the standard formulation of the Capital Asset Pricing Model (CAPM). The CAPM, developed by Sharpe (1964), Mossin (1966), Lintner (1969), and others, equates market demand (given expected returns) with the supply of assets to solve for equilibrium prices. In practice, finance professionals have frequently taken prices in real financial markets as given and then used the β of the CAPM to compute the return expected on individual assets (compared to the overall market's return).

The empirical assignment of CAPM betas to firms has proven useful for guiding investment choices and evaluating the performance of firms. In other respects, the CAPM theory had widely disconfirmed implications, e.g., that everyone should hold exactly the same proportionate mix of stocks in the risky portion of his portfolio. Other implications of the CAPM, such as quadratic utility functions so that individuals are guided soley by the mean and variance of an asset's return or independent and normally distributed asset returns, have also been disproved.

This section explains why investors in the CAPM paradigm do not face intrinsic uncertainty. The CAPM assumes investor beliefs are homogeneous but not common knowledge. Significantly, our finding thus negates the claim that theorists needed or meant to 'common knowledge beliefs' for 'homogeneous beliefs' all along.

The 'homogeneous beliefs' assumption has crucially simplified mean-variance asset pricing theory and related empirical works. By homogeneous beliefs financial theorists assume

> every investor attaches the same values for the mean m_x and standard deviation s_x for the distribution of returns of every security and for the correlations r_{xy} among the returns. It follows from this that the opportunity sets of all individuals have the same proportionate shape, differing from one another by only the scale factor of individual endowed capital K_0. (Hirshleifer (1970), p.289)

Although Sharpe (1964) acknowledged the homogeneous beliefs assumption was 'highly restrictive and undoubtedly unrealistic,' he nevertheless defended its use. 'Since these assumptions imply equilibrium conditions which form a major part of classical financial doctrine, it is far from clear that this formulation should be rejected - especially in view of the dearth of alternative models leading to similar results.' (Sharpe (1964), p.434)

The two-period CAPM assumes investors know the return on assets, and this return includes both dividends and capital gains potential. Now purchases and sales of assets by other investors clearly affect everyone's opportunity set. Therefore, implicitly, investors in the CAPM must know the purchasing behavior of the rest of the market. Otherwise, they could not calculate with certainty any asset's expected capital gains (losses). Common knowledge beliefs assumptions would eliminate speculative changes in market prices due to changing beliefs. The two-period CAPM has substituted perfect knowledge (and indeed common knowledge) about capital gains in place of an agreed common knowledge beliefs assumption over the possible states of the world. Actually, the two assumptions are logically equivalent.

The multiperiod CAPM, derived by Merton (1973) and extended by Breeden (1979), assumes price trajectories into the future are known. It can be shown that intermediate period prices are common knowledge in period 0 only when individuals have agreed common knowledge priors (ACKP) about the state space. Without ACKP individuals might not reach consensus agreement about what future prices will prevail. In contrast, the two-period CAPM eliminates intrinsic uncertainty by assuming individuals know the correct capital gains value of assets.

In his classic beauty contest analogy, Kenyes (1936) reveals why estimates about other investors beliefs are crucial to stock market speculation. Since stock market investors realize other investors revise their portfolios according to changes or perceived changes in market expectations, investors need to choose stocks which they think average opinion thinks average opinion thinks will perform well. This thought process is known as 'metathinking.' In general, investors second and third-order beliefs could differ, and consequently one would expect investors to hold differing quantities of a given asset depending on which higher-order beliefs guide their portfolio revision.

Both the two-period and multiperiod CAPM cleverly avoid financial metathinking behavior by simply assuming investors know the assets' returns with certainty. Once they know these returns, which may depend on higher-order beliefs or a lack thereof, they have all the information they need to minimize the variance of their portfolios for a given expected return.

Chapter 4 showed that when investors agree without knowing they agree, intrinsic uncertainty is still present. If CAPM investors agreed on assets' returns without knowing they agree, one might expect speculative trades to arise in the CAPM as well. Keynes would argue that stock market investors cannot know assets' returns unless they know the higher-order beliefs of other market traders. The CAPM simply assumes that do know the returns. Let us turn now to a derivation of the CAPM and see where investor belief assumptions enter the model.

The standard CAPM equation derives from the minimization problem,

$$\underset{X_{ik}}{MIN} \sum_i \sum_j X_{ik} X_{jk} \, COV(\tilde{R}_i, \tilde{R}_j) + \lambda_k \left[\sum_i X_{ik} E(\tilde{R}_i) + (1 - \sum_i X_{ik}) R_f - E(\tilde{R}_p) \right]. \tag{5.6}$$

where X_{ik} represents the proportion of individual k's portfolio held in asset i; $\tilde{R}_i$ and $\tilde{R}_j$ are the returns on assets i and j, respectively, where the return denotes the summed capital gain, dividends, and interest payments divided by the asset's price when the period commenced; λ_k is the Lagrange multiplier associated with individual k's wealth, R_f is the riskless rate of interest, and $E(\tilde{R}_p)$ is a constant denoting individual k's expected return on his portfolio.

The first-order interior condition stated for individual k is

$$\sum_j X_{jk} \, COV(\tilde{R}_i, \tilde{R}_j) + \lambda_k [E(\tilde{R}_i) - R_f] = 0. \tag{5.7}$$

Let W_k denote the fraction of total market wealth individual k holds. Then

$$\sum_j \sum_k W_k \, X_{jk} \equiv \sum_j X_{jm}, \tag{5.8}$$

and

$$\sum_j X_{jm} \tilde{R}_j \equiv \tilde{R}_m, \tag{5.9}$$

where X_{jm} denotes asset j's fraction in the total market portfolio, and R_m is the market's return on all assets taken together. Multiplying each term in (5.7) by W_k, summing over k, and substituting (5.8) into the first term after switching the order of summation yields

$$\sum_j X_{jm} \, COV(\tilde{R}_i, \tilde{R}_j) + \sum_k W_k \, \lambda_k \, [E(\tilde{R}_i) - R_f] = 0. \tag{5.10}$$

Next, we substitute (5.9) into (5.10) and let the variable Z denote $\sum_k W_k \lambda_k$. Then the first-order condition becomes

$$COV(\tilde{R}_i,\tilde{R}_m) + Z\,[E(\tilde{R}_i - R_f)] = 0. \qquad \textbf{(5.11)}$$

Let $\tilde{R}_i = \tilde{R}_m$ and observe that (5.11) is now

$$VAR(\tilde{R}_m) + Z\,[E(\tilde{R}_m - R_f)] = 0, \qquad \textbf{(5.12)}$$

and solving for Z yields

$$Z = -\,VAR(\tilde{R}_m)\,/\,[E(\tilde{R}_m) - R_f]. \qquad \textbf{(5.13)}$$

Again substituting this value of Z into (5.11) yields the familiar CAPM equation:

$$E(\tilde{R}_i) - R_f = \frac{COV(\tilde{R}_i,\tilde{R}_m)}{VAR(\tilde{R}_m)}\,[E(\tilde{R}_m - R_f)], \qquad \textbf{(5.14)}$$

$$= \beta_i\,[E(\tilde{R}_m - R_f)]. \qquad \textbf{(5.15)}$$

This result only requires investors to use, e.g., the same estimate for asset i's return, $\tilde{R}_i$. In equilibrium, when all agents revise their portfolios according to their beliefs about the returns, they will have mean-variance efficient holdings.

The expected value operator in equation (5.6) would likely be conditioned on each individual's information set. However, since the CAPM assumes investors know the returns, these expected (future) values are known constants, rather than some expected value over a genuine probability distribution. Again, the CAPM effectively eliminates any source for speculating over the beliefs of others.

5.6. Arbitrage Pricing Theory

The Arbitrage Pricing Theory (APT), introduced by Ross (1976) and (1977b), has now received considerable attention as an alternative to the CAPM. Like the MM model, the APT assumes investors have common prior beliefs. However, unlike the MM paradigm, the APT actually needs the more restrictive agreed common knowledge priors (ACKP) assumption for its validity.

The APT in its present form yields nonunique solutions to the market pricing model. Without common knowledge assumptions, the APT yields individual asset pricing equations that cannot guarantee that the rest of the market uses the same or even similar pricing relationships.

The logic behind the APT might be expressed as follows. The returns on a subset of assets in the market are governed by an M-factor model. Unfortunately, neither the list of factors, nor the specification, nor the subset of assets are ever definitively identified in the APT literature. This lack of a logical structure has led to numerous empirical problems, but we will focus here on the theoretical model.

The APT assumes investors have 'homogeneous' beliefs about the factor model generating asset returns. As Roll and Ross (1980) have suggested, '[t]he key point in aggregation is to make strong enough assumptions on the homogeneity of individual anticipations to produce a testable theory. To do so with the APT we need to assume that individuals agree on both the factor coefficients, β_{ik}, and the expected returns, $E(R_i)$.' Ross (1976) at page 356 indicated that the topic of investor belief assumptions is 'one of the most difficult and important areas for future research.' Ross concluded that relaxing the homogeneous expectations assumption would require study of disequilibrium dynamics and movement from *ex ante* expectations to *ex post* observations.

Since its introduction in 1976, the APT has been refined and extended by Huberman (1982), Chamberlain and Rothschild (1983), and Ingersoll (1984), among others.[11] Subsequently, Dybvig (1983) and Grinblatt and Titman (1983) independently derived upper bounds on the deviations from APT-predicted prices.

All of these papers begin with the same underlying assumption that asset returns are generated by a factor model.[12] Consider a market with Z risky assets and a riskless asset with return R_f. There exists a subset of the assets numbered 1 through T whose returns are governed by the factor model

$$R_j = E(R_j|\Phi) + \beta_{j1} F_1 + \cdots + \beta_{jM} F_M + \epsilon_j , \qquad (5.16)$$

where R_j = the return of asset j; Φ = the information set, upon which the expected value is conditioned; β_{jk} = sensitivity of asset j's return to movements in factor k; ϵ_j = mean zero idiosyncratic risk component of the jth asset, j = 1, ..., T. Assume that the error terms, ϵ_j, are independent of the factors, the returns, and of each other. Therefore, $cov(\epsilon_i,\epsilon_j) = 0$ for all $i \neq j$. Further assume that $T > M$, in order to ensure that the system of equations is determined.

Our model depicts the standard form of the APT with the addition of the information set Φ.[13] The theoretical intuition behind the APT is that for some subset of the assets under consideration, the returns will be a linear function of the factors in equation (5.16). In practice, these factors are 'grand aggregates' such as the employment level or the interest rate. Conversely stated, the APT implies that for a large enough subset of assets, the only possible common determinants of their returns could be the various grand aggregates, although empirical studies reveal little agreement on what these factors should be.

Each individual formulates his own measure of the market's expected return from assets. Under the homogeneous beliefs assumption investors in the APT, investors might agree on the returns and the *M*-factor model without knowing they agree. The intrinsic uncertainty in the APT can lead investors to question what factors, functional relationship, or information the rest of the market employs in deciding market values for assets.

An investor in the APT knows what factors and relationships he personally believes will affect asset returns, but he faces risk over the factors and relationships others feel are important. Consider now the following three factor equations. All three are possible candidates for the unknown factor model employed by the market, and all three are perfectly consistent with the existing assumptions of the APT.

First, we have

$$R_j = E(R_j|\Phi) + \beta_{j1}F_1 + \cdots + \beta_{jM-K}F_{M-K} + \epsilon_j , \qquad \textbf{(5.17)}$$

where the number of factors *M-K* is less than the *M* factors in (5.16). Second,

$$R_j = E(R_j|\Phi) + \gamma_{j1}F_1 + \cdots + \gamma_{jM}F_M + \epsilon_j , \qquad \textbf{(5.18)}$$

where $\gamma_{jk} \neq \beta_{jk}$, and third

$$R_j = E(R_j|\Psi) + \beta_{j1}F_1 + \cdots + \beta_{jM}F_M + \epsilon_j . \qquad \textbf{(5.19)}$$

The intrinsic uncertainty present in the original formulation of the APT would not allow any investor to exclude the possibility that other investors in the market employ any or all of these three factor models.

The first example (5.17) altered the number of factors believed to determine asset returns. Shanken (1982) has pointed out that financial economists have yet to determine empirically the precise number of factors in the APT. The statistical data on asset returns often reveal the great majority of variance to be explained by a single factor, and that the other factors though containing significant coefficients nevertheless account for a negligible amount of the variance.[14] If both the APT and the CAPM explain the variance in asset returns with primarily one factor, then these empirical observations raise questions about the utility of switching from the CAPM to the APT.

The specification problems encountered in trying to test the APT support the notion that the APT is not common knowledge, even among financial econometricians or arbitrage pricing specialists. The econometricians may have homogeneous beliefs; they may agree that an M-factor linear model governs asset returns. Yet uncertainty over what variables and factors the rest of the market might regard as relevant has led each of them to test for the significance of factors presumably not contained in their original M-factor model. The uncertainty over relevant factors faced by empirical researchers mirrors the uncertainty faced by investors in the APT model even under the homogeneous beliefs assumption.[15]

The second example (5.18) has replaced the factor coefficients, because although investors may objectively agree on the values of these coefficients, they do not know the values other investors assign to these coefficients. Again the empirical literature has arrived at no consensus on the factor coefficients. This lack of empirical agreement might well be explained by theoretical intrinsic uncertainty that investors do not know, and know everyone else knows, what the true coefficients are in the market model.

Finally, the third factor model (5.19) illustrates this same point for the expected returns. When $\mathbf{\Psi} \subset \mathbf{\Phi}$ in the third model, an investor believes he is better informed than at least some subset of the market; conversely, if $\mathbf{\Phi} \subset \mathbf{\Psi}$, an investor feels the market has additional information upon which to condition their expectation for the asset's return.

This section has been based on work published by Guth and Philippatos (1987). The latter work contains propositions that state (1) the sum of squared deviations from (5.16) is not bounded above as the number of assets increases; (2) the APT has multiple equilibria consistent with the homogeneous beliefs assumption; and (3) that imposing ACKP will yield a unique expression for the APT.

Finally, we conclude the section by noting that the standard APT return expression is a linear equation, and the APT cannot account for nonlinear relationships through interpreting the factors in the APT as nonlinear functions of real variables. Without common knowledge assumptions, any individual could personally believe these factors affect returns in a linear form but feel the rest of the market employs a nonlinear relationship.[16]

5.7. Heterogeneous Beliefs in the MM and APT Paradigms

Stiglitz (1969, 1974) and Stambaugh (1983) maintained that the MM and APT models, respectively, are valid even if investors have heterogeneous beliefs. We will consider their arguments sequentially.

In claiming to have generalized the original MM framework to include heterogeneous beliefs, Stiglitz asserts

> No assumption about the source of uncertainty is required. In particular, the distinction between technological uncertainty and price uncertainty...is of no consequence here. ...The argument of the proof does not require that individuals have the same expectations. The only agreement in expectations that is required is that the firm will not go bankrupt in any state of nature. Stiglitz (1974), p.861, 861n.

Stiglitz's claim that price uncertainty has no more consequence than technological uncertainty sounds suspicious. He seems to have overlooked speculative investments based on the unknown beliefs of others. But Stiglitz (1988) subsequently qualified his own remarks.

> It is often the unstated rather than the stated assumptions of a model which are critical, and so it is in the case of the MM theorems. A critical unstated assumption is that all market participants have full and equal information concerning the returns to the firm. However, the existence of asymmetric information gives rise to two problems: current owners may wish to convince potential borrowers that the firm is worth more; and managers can take actions which affect the returns to those who provide capital. Stiglitz (1988) pp. 123-124.[17]

Given the caveats that investors (1) assign zero probability to any firm going bankrupt and (2) have full and equal information concerning the returns to the firm, we will impose heterogeneous beliefs on Stiglitz's model and see whether the MM irrelevancy theorems still hold. Table 5.1 defines a subset of the variables used by Stiglitz.

Table 5.1. List of Relevant Variables in Stiglitz's (1974) Model

Symbol	Definition
$P^j(\theta(t))$	the probability investor j assigns to state $\theta(t)$.
$X_i(\theta(t))$	the profits to firm i at time t in state of the world $\theta(t)$.
$p(t,\tau)$	the price at time t in state $\theta(t)$ of a bond which promises to pay 1 dollar at time τ.
$B_i(t,\tau)$	the number of bonds for firm i outstanding at the end of period t with maturity at time τ.
$B^j(t,\tau)$	the jth individual's ownership of bonds maturing at time τ.
$E_i(t)$	the value of the shares outstanding in the ith firm at the end of period t.
$\alpha_i^j(t)$	$= E_i^j(t)/E_i(t)$, is the fraction of the ith firm held by the jth individual at the end of period t.

Two market clearing conditions characterize an equilibrium. The first states that ownership of shares in the ith firm equals the value of its equity:

$$\sum_j E_i^j(t) = \sum_j \alpha_i^j(t)\ E_i(t) = E_i(t) \qquad \forall\ t,\tau \qquad \textbf{(5.20)}$$

The second equates demand and supply of bonds at each maturity, τ:

$$\sum_i B_i(t,\tau) = \sum_j B^j(t,\tau) \qquad \forall\ t,\tau \qquad \textbf{(5.21)}$$

Note that condition (5.20) is equivalent to $\sum_j \alpha_i^j(t) = 1 \quad \forall\ t,i.$

Stiglitz's main theorem then states if (1) no firm goes bankrupt in any state of nature,[18] (2) the economy contains a liquid market for perfectly safe bonds of all maturities, (3) all firms have chosen their financing policy, (4) given a set of feasible consumption paths, every consumer always selects the same consumption path, and (5) the market is in a general equilibrium with all markets clearing; then there exists another general equilibrium in which any firm or group of firms has changed its financial policy, but in which the value of the firms and the price of all bonds of all maturities are unchanged. Individuals have adjusted their portfolios as follows:

$$\Delta B^j(t,\tau) = \sum_i \alpha_i^j(t) \Delta B_i(t,\tau) \qquad \forall\, t,\ \tau,\ j \tag{5.22}$$

i.e, each investor alters his holdings of bonds by exactly his stockholder's share of the change in debt of each maturity of all firms, and

$$\Delta \alpha_i^j(t) = 0 \qquad \forall\, i,\ j,\ t \tag{5.23}$$

or equivalently, each investor changes his equity holdings in proportion to the firm's change in total equity capital. Let us consider the two most natural forms of heterogeneous beliefs.

Case 1. For two or more representative individuals i and j, $P^i(\theta(t)) \neq P^j(\theta(t))$. The two individuals would therefore also disagree on the expected profits to each firm, since these profits are state-contingent. However, the individuals then disagree as to the returns to firms. Clearly, Stiglitz's model cannot handle the problems created by this situation, for it implies that the two individuals disagree on the fair price for virtually all, if not all, of the firms in the economy. If these two individuals represent the beliefs of sizable fractions of the population, then markets will never clear.

Alternatively, we could say the disagreement over profits to firms across states of the world violates Stiglitz's (1988) assumption of 'full and equal access to information on firm earnings.' Under this interpretation, Stiglitz's model again fails to accommodate the heterogeneous beliefs $P^i(\theta(t)) \neq P^j(\theta(t))$ by construction, rather than by implication.

Case 2. Assume the two individuals i and j agree on the probability distribution over states of the world so that $P^i(\theta(t)) = P^j(\theta(t))$ for all $\theta(t)$. However, i and j have different priors as to the profits of every firm n for each state of world: $\mathscr{E}^i[X_n(\theta(t))] \neq \mathscr{E}^j[X_n(\theta(t)]$ $\forall\, n$, where

$\mathscr{E}$ represents the expectation operator for each individual. Normally the expected value of a variable would be conditioned on each individual's information set. However, to adhere rigidly to Stiglitz's 'full and equal access' requirement, we will assume no one has received any information about earnings. The individuals are merely endowed with heterogeneous priors as to how profits are distributed across states of the world. Markets will never clear in this economy, because the individuals cannot agree on fair prices for stocks. One or more of the individuals will find mispriced stocks and want to buy more claims to those stocks than are available to the market; others may want to sell or supply more shares at that price than are available. Thus condition (5.20) will not be met.

In the Stiglitz (1974) multiperiod MM model, if investors maintain heterogeneous beliefs about the probability distribution over states of the world $[P^i(\theta(t)) \neq P^j(\theta(t))]$ or the distribution of profits to firms across states of the world $\{\mathscr{E}^i[X_n(\theta(t))] \neq \mathscr{E}^j[X_n(\theta(t)] \quad \forall\ n\}$, then markets will never clear. Thus Stiglitz's restated irrelevancy theorem has no consequence even for his own economy.

Stiglitz also abandoned the MM 'risk class' concept in favor of assumptions that consumers always select the same consumption path and expectations independent of financial policy. Stiglitz requires these two assumptions to motivate investors to undo the leverage or other financial policy change adopted by firms. By assuming that individuals believe financial policies have no effect on firm valuation, Stiglitz practically assumes the very object of his proof.

In contrast, we avoided this unwonted assumption by using the risk class concept. Section 5.3 shows the MM arbitrage locks in a sure profit even if some 'noninfinitesimal group,' or the rest of the market for that matter, believes financial policies matter. Without the risk class concept, Stiglitz is left with a theorem and a framework that applies only if the economy somehow, magically, reaches equilibrium. Homogeneous beliefs about each firm's earnings across states of the world clearly define arbitrage opportunities. Without homogeneous beliefs, individual investors could see arbitrage opportunities directly in conflict with one another.

Turning now to the APT, Stambaugh (1983) has argued that the APT applies even when investors have heterogeneous beliefs. The preceeding arguments concerning heterogeneous beliefs in Stiglitz's reformulation of the MM paradigm apply to Stambaugh's work as well. In particular, if two or more people disagree over the number of factors, or the returns to firms, or other specifications in the APT, somone may see arbitrage opportunities in prevailing market prices. In that case, markets will not clear.

Using a particular factor model (5.16), an individual may decide a given stock is overvalued. Another individual decides the same stock is undervalued using a different factor model (5.17). At any given price, one or both of the individuals will continue to show positive or negative excess demand.

How do we determine who is correct? Eventually when the state of the world is revealed and actual earnings become common knowledge, we will know which one correctly valued the firm. Perhaps neither did. After earnings are announced and their effect on the firm's stock price is revealed, the two would no longer have heterogeneous beliefs over that firm's earnings. They may continue to employ different factor models and continue to disagree on future earnings.

Since earnings and the state of nature could prove either of these individuals are correct, each faces some risk - whether he chooses to recognize it - that his own valuation may be wrong. In the APT with heterogeneous beliefs, everyone can personally believe he sees a riskless arbitrage opportunity, when in reality his investment amounts to risky speculation. Only an individual who assigns zero probability to his *M*-factor model being incorrect would be willing to serve as a price dictator and force prices to match his own valuation model.

In game theory terminology, the heterogeneous belief investors can each act as Stackelberg leaders. Without other parties agreeing that their own factor models are inferior and serving as followers, the disparate investors would continually bid against each other. Prices would continually move up and down with the bids and counter-bids. The resulting disequilibrium dynamics is known as Stackelberg warfare.

5.8. Conclusions and Issues for Future Research

This chapter has examined three asset pricing paradigms and found that common knowledge beliefs are not required for the MM model, implicitly assumed in the CAPM, and definitely required for the validity of the APT. The MM world depicts a stylized view of financial markets with certain simplifying assumptions, for example, no bankruptcy, firm risk classes, and personal borrowing at the same rate as corporate borrowing. In an effort to eliminate intrinsic uncertainty from their model, MM inserted an additional 'imputed rationality' assumption. As indicated in Section 5.2, the only previous paper to take notice of this missing assumption concluded that the MM results were invalid (unless investors had agreed common knowledge beliefs). We can relax the 'imputed rationality' assumption, which is tantamount to assuming investor beliefs are not only homogeneous but common knowledge, and the key results of the MM model are left intact. With this analysis, financial economics appears to have taken a step towards relaxing the restrictions on investor beliefs that has plagued the development of most asset pricing theories.

The absence of common knowledge creates an asymmetric information environment, but the MM arbitrage still holds under this particular dimension of uncertainty. Any individual can exploit cash flow arbitrage given sufficient resources and a suitably long investment horizon. Even if some 'non-infinitesimal' segment of the market believes debt-equity ratios matter, the MM strategy continues to lock-in a sure profit. This market segment can be used as a money pump by the rest of the market.

The CAPM assumes investors *know* the future returns on assets. This assumption effectively eliminates capital gains uncertainty and the source of speculation over the unknown beliefs of others. This strong assumption implies that investor beliefs are common knowledge. The APT employs homogeneous belief assumptions in an attempt to aggregate individual factor models into a market expression. However, this attempt falls short due to intrinsic uncertainty inherent in the APT.

Since the APT uses MM-style arbitrage, why would investor beliefs have to be common knowledge in the APT but not in the MM world itself? The answer may emerge from the response in Endnote 5 to the disproof the capital structure irrelevancy proposition. MM arbitrage focuses on identical cash flow streams; the APT emphasizes a murky *M*-factor model. Thus the objects of uncertainty are diverse. It would be like trying to compare the volume of ketchup in two bottles (an objective, measurable fact) with the ingredients that make ketchup taste good (an inherently subjective concept). Not all arbitrage theories are created equal, even though they employ some variant of MM arbitrage.

In contrast to Stiglitz (1988), we find that the 'risk class' concept is important for MM-style arbitrage, even in Stiglitz's general equilibrium framework. Without risk classes and homogeneous beliefs, we have no mechanism to eliminate arbitrage opportunities and clear markets. Without market clearing the applicability of Stiglitz's theorem, on moving from one general equilibrium to another, vanishes. By reinserting the risk class concept in Sections 5.3 and 5.4, we do not need to restrict individuals to adopt the same consumption path in every equilibrium or to form expectations independent of financial policy.

Assuming investors have 'full and equal access to information on earnings' effectively eradicates, by construction or by implication, the two most natural forms of heterogeneous beliefs: differing probabilities for states of the world or differing earnings expectations for a firm in a given state of the world. Thus, while not stated in his theorem, Stiglitz effectively assumes homogeneous investor beliefs like the original MM paradigm.

At least one issue remains unresolved. If an individual sees an arbitrage opportunity in either the MM or APT and executes the income arbitrage, what impact does he have on market prices? Under competitive assumptions, individuals take prices as given and have negligible impact on market prices. However, various arbitrage pricing models employ the 'price dictator' concept, in which any individual can sell an infinite quantity of some asset, if needed, to force the asset's price to adjust and thereby eliminate the arbitrage profit. If we assume no firm goes bankrupt, should we assume no individual can go bankrupt as well? If so, then an individual could borrow or sell infinite quantities of assets.

Intrinsic uncertainty is not merely a technical point but actually an important feature of real world financial markets. It is all too easy to fall into the trap of labeling certain assets as 'undervalued' or 'overvalued' or even 'a free lunch,' without appreciating the underlying risks involved. As a case in point, Japanese warrants in 1994 appear to be undervalued. They are undervalued in comparison to German warrants. They are undervalued in comparison to shorter term Japanese call options, and they are undervalued in comparison to their historical implied volatilities.

Nevertheless, only a foolhardy person would rush to buy 'undervalued' Japanese warrants based on these facts. The reasons were outlined in Sections 5.2 and 5.3. The market contains intrinsic uncertainty, which forces every rational investor to consider the resell potential of his assets based on changes in future market valuations. The Japanese warrant market could remain in a long-run 'undervalued' slump for years. Any financial institution that tries to execute income arbitrage could have its resources tied up with no return or worse, while it waited for earnings of underlying stocks to grow. To profit from Japanese warrant trading, arbitrageurs must accurately forecast not only the earnings of the underlying firms, but when these increases in earnings will be reflected in the long-term warrant prices.

There exists no perfect MM-style arbitrage with Japanese warrants. For example, German warrants are correlated to Japanese warrants, but anyone using German warrants as a hedge is exposed to risk that this correlation will change over time. Arbitrage desks of investment banks are in the business of managing *risks*, not simply pursuing 'free lunches.' The risks associated with the absence of common knowledge can be eliminated in the MM world; however, this perfect arbitrage strategy is rarely available in real financial markets. It is not surprising then that the capital gains motive affects asset prices, which are governed by market sentiment and other intrinsic factors aside from real earnings.

Having considered the need for common knowledge beliefs assumptions in three asset pricing paradigms, we might wonder how common knowledge assumptions affect the canonical arbitrage pricing model. The next chapter covers this topic. We prove a series of 'no price exists' propositions and relate the lack of common knowledge to the amount of information about higher-order beliefs revealed by prices. Chapter 3 emphasized that incomplete markets force everyone to speculate in the sense that optimal consumption bundles cannot be obtained from the available market instruments. Consequently, everyone plans to retrade. Chapter 6 shows that speculation based on uncertainty over other traders' (changing) beliefs will tend to be the norm rather than the exception.

Notes

1. I would like to thank Merton Miller, Ronald Shrieves, Robert Jarrow, and Jack Hirshleifer for helpful comments on earlier drafts. None of the above are responsible for any errors that remain.

2. See also Bhattacharya (1979), Myers and Majluf (1984), and Stiglitz (1988).

3. Indeed no mechanism in any of the major asset pricing theories transmits this information (about the beliefs of others) to individual investors.

4. Grinblatt and Titman (1983) and Stiglitz (1974) claim to have developed equilibrium formulations of the APT and MM paradigms, respectively. Their models still rely on arbitrage for price adjustments and the absence of arbitrage for market clearing.

5. The answer to the ''emperor's clothes disproof'' is as follows. If an 8 oz. bottle of ketchup sells for $1 and someone offers to buy 16 oz. of ketchup for $3, the market will supply the demander with as much ketchup at that price as he is willing to purchase. The fact that some 'non-infinitesimal' group steps forward to say the volume of ketchup (read earnings of a firm in a given risk class) in two 8 oz. bottles is not equivalent to the volume (read earnings of another firm in that same risk class) in a 16 oz bottle does not preclude the rest of the market from exploiting this arbitrage opportunity. In fairness, we should note that Burness, Cummings, and Quirk (1980) were aware of similar arguments and found them unpersuasive: 'in effect, this reduces things back to a two-period model, since market values in intervening periods (between now and doomsday) are irrelevant.' (p.62) Perhaps the matter will remain a philosophical disagreement.

6. An investor motivated by capital gains may buy into an 'overvalued' stock at present if he believes he can resell it at a profit. Alternatively, an investor may choose to sell 'undervalued' stock at present with the speculative intent of repurchasing the stock at an even lower price. From a wealth standpoint, this investment strategy is perfectly rational.

7. Durand (1989) has noted that pursuing speculative capital gains is more risky than collecting a known dividend. 'But with volatile stock prices, capital losses....are a real possibility. Dividends represent a bird in the hand; capital gains - representing only one bird in the bush if MM are to be taken literally - may never materialize.'

8. See, e.g., the vector analysis in DeMarzo (1988).

9. The numerical example also applies to the case of heterogeneous priors.

10. The market's collective judgement about the value of the firm measured as an expected value of future earnings.

11. However, these analyses were complex and their derivations of the APT formula lacked economic intuition, as articulated in the criticism by Shanken (1982).

12. Ross (1976) and Huberman (1982) went to some length to specify the necessary conditions that ensure arbitrage opportunities would apply to any asset deviating from the formula of the APT. These conditions include von Neumann-Morgenstern utility functions for investors, as well as assumptions on the factor and error distributions. Yet, as we show in this section, all these restrictive conditions failed to produce true arbitrage opportunities in the absence of common knowledge.

13. Note that we have assumed nothing about investor preferences of the objective function they seek to maximize.

14. Trzcinka (1987) has pointed out that the empirical tests of the APT often find seven or eight significant factors, but one factor predominantly accounts for the variance with the remaining portion split among the other factors tested.

    [I]t is clear from our analysis of the eigenvalues and our chi-squared tests that the question of how many factors (apply to the APT) is far from settled. Our partial and unsatisfying answer to this question is 'at least one.' In spite of this ambiguity, it is useful to know that the number probably is not zero. Trzcinka (1987), p.368.

In private correspondence, Richard Roll has disagreed with my characterization of the APT empirical literature as having found that one factor explains most of the return variance. That conclusion would be expected for empirical models of the return on a large diversified portfolio. However, for individual stocks, he has found that the first factor generally accounts for 20% of the total variance while the second and higher factors usually account for another 15 to 20 percent.

15. A similar problem crops up in trying to specify the factors relevant to an individual stock's return from a model applicable to a subset of stocks.

    [T]hese derivations of the APT have been relatively complex and lacking in economic intuition. Furthermore, the pricing equation obtained from them does not necessarily hold for any individual asset, even approximately. This has led some researchers to conclude that the empirical tests of Roll and Ross (1980), Chen ..., Oldfield and Rogalski..., and Brown and Weinstein... are not valid tests of theory....Our model suggests that the existing tests of the APT are appropriate in an economy with non-traded assets. Grinblatt and Titman (1983), pp.497, 505.

    Dhrymes, Friend, and Gultekin (1984) found that standard χ^2 tests of the APT require an increasing number of factors as more and more securities are analyzed. See also Roll and Ross's (1984) reply.

16. Chamberlain and Rothschild (1983) prove that a necessary and sufficient condition for returns to be generated by a K-factor *linear* model is that K eigenvalues of the covariance matrix of returns grow large as the number of securities increases.

17. Stiglitz's quotation reiterates what we stressed in Section 5.2: asymmetric information in the MM literature immediately translates into insider (manager or current shareholder) incentives. In fact, it applies to anyone who is concerned with wealth in addition to income.

18. Smith (1972) and Hellwig (1981) showed how the MM propositions could be extended in an economy that included possible firm

bankruptcy. We omitted a discussion of their models in this chapter, because it entails additional specifications for margin contracts.

References

Bhattacharya, Sudipto, (1979), ''Imperfect Information, Dividend Policy, and 'The Bird in the Hand' Fallacy,'' *Bell Journal of Economics*, Vol. 10:1, pp. 259-270.

Breeden, Douglas, (1979), 'An Intertemporal Asset Pricing Model with Stochastic Consumption and Investment Opportunities,' *Journal of Financial Economics*, Vol. 7, pp. 265-296.

Burness, Stuart, Ronald Cummings, and James Quirk, 'Speculative Behavior and the Operation of Competitive Markets Under Uncertainty: A Survey Article,' Staff Paper 80-11, Department of Economics, Montana State University, Bozeman, 1980.

Chamberlain, G., and Michael Rothschild, (1983), 'Arbitrage, Factor Structure, and Mean-Variance Analysis of Large Asset Markets,' *Econometrica*, Vol. 51, pp. 1281-1304.

DeMarzo, Peter M., (1988), 'An Extension of the Modigliani-Miller Theorem to Stochastic Economies with Incomplete Markets and Interdependent Securities,' *Journal of Economic Theory*, Vol. 45, pp. 353-369.

Dhrymes, P., I. Friend, and N. Gultekin, (1984), 'A Critical Examination of the Empirical Evidence on the Arbitrage Pricing Theory,' *Journal of Finance*, Vol. 39, pp. 323-347.

Durand, David, (1989), 'After Thoughts on a Controversy with Modigliani-Miller, Plus New Thoughts on Growth and the Cost of Capital,' *Financial Management*, Vol. 18:2, pp. 12-18.

Dybvig, Philip, (1983), ''An Explicit Bound on Individual Assets' Deviations from APT Pricing in a Finite Economy,' *Journal of Financial Economics*, Vol. 12, pp. 483-496.

Grinblatt, Mark, and Sheridan Titman, (1983), 'Factor Pricing in a Finite Economy,' *Journal of Financial Economics*, Vol. 12, pp. 497-507.

Guth, Michael A. S., and George C. Philippatos, (1987), 'A Reexamination of Arbitrage Pricing Theory (APT) under Common

Knowledge Beliefs,' *Rivista Internazionale di Scienze Economiche e Commerciali*, Vol. 36:8, pp. 729-746.

Hellwig, Martin F., (1981), 'Bankruptcy, Limited Liability, and the Modigliani-Miller Theorem,' *American Economic Review*, Vol. 71, pp. 155-170.

Hirshleifer, Jack, (1970), *Investment, Interest, and Capital*, (Englewood Cliffs, N.J.: Prentice-Hall, Inc.)

Huberman, Gur, (1982), 'A Simple Approach to Arbitrage Pricing Theory,' *Journal of Economic Theory*, Vol. 28, pp. 183-191.

Ingersoll, Jonathan E., (1984), 'Some Results in the Theory of Arbitrage Pricing,' *Journal of Finance*, Vol. 39, pp. 1021-1039.

Jarrow, Robert A., (1988), *Finance Theory*, Englewood Cliffs, N.J., Prentice-Hall, Inc.

Keynes, John Maynard, (1936), *The General Theory of Employment, Interest, and Money*, (New York: McGraw Hill).

Leland, H. E., and D. H. Pyle, (1977), 'Informational Asymmetries, Financial Structure, and Financial Intermediation,' *Journal of Finance*, Vol. 32, pp. 371-387.

Lintner, J., (1969), 'The Aggregation of Investors' Diverse Judgments and Preferences in Purely Competitive Security Markets,' *Journal of Financial and Quantitative Analysis*, Vol. 4, pp. 347-400.

Merton, Robert C., (1973), 'An Intertemporal Capital Asset Pricing Model,' *Econometrica*, Vol. 41:5, pp. 867-887.

Miller, Merton H., (1988), 'The Modigliani-Miller Propositions,' *Journal of Economic Perspectives*, Vol. 2, pp. 99-120.

Modigliani, Franco and Merton H. Miller, (1958), 'The Cost of Capital, Corporation Finance, and the Theory of Investment,' *American Economic Review*, Vol. 48, pp. 261-297.

Modigliani, Franco and Merton H. Miller, (1961), 'Dividend Policy, Growth and the Valuation of Shares,' *Journal of Business*, Vol. 34, pp. 411-433.

Mossin, Jan, (1966), 'Equilibrium in a Capital Asset Market,' *Econometrica*, Vol. 32, pp. 768-783.

Myers, S. C., and N. S. Majluf, (1984), 'Corporate Financing and Investment Decisions When Firms Have Information that Investors Do Not,' *Journal of Financial Economics*, Vol. 11, pp. 187-221.

Roll, Richard, and Stephen A. Ross, (1980), 'An Empirical Investigation of the Arbitrage Pricing Theory,' *Journal of Finance*, Vol. 35:5, pp. 1073-1103.

Roll, Richard, and Stephen A. Ross, (1984), 'A Critical Reexamination of the Empirical Evidence on the Arbitrage Pricing Theory: A Reply,' *Journal of Finance*, Vol. 39, pp. 347-350.

Ross, Stephen A., (1976), 'The Arbitrage Theory of Capital Asset Pricing,' *Journal of Economic Theory*, Vol. 13, pp. 341-360.

(1977a), 'The Determination of Financial Structure: The Incentive Signalling Approach,' *Bell Journal of Economics*, Vol. 8:1, pp. 23-40.

(1977b), 'Return, Risk, and Arbitrage,' in *Risk and Return in Finance*, edited by I. Friend and J. Bicksler, (Cambridge, MA: Ballinger).

(1988), 'Comment on the Modigliani-Miller Propositions,' *Journal of Economic Perspectives*, Vol. 2:4, pp. 127-133.

Shanken, Jay, (1982), 'The Arbitrage Pricing Theory: Is It Testable?,' *Journal of Finance*, Vol. 37, pp. 1129-1140.

Sharpe, William F., (1964), 'Capital Asset Prices: A Theory of Market Equilibrium under Conditions of Risk,' *Journal of Finance*, Vol. 19, pp. 425-442.

Smith, Vernon L., (1972), 'Default Risk, Scale, and the Homemade Leverage Theorem,' *American Economic Review*, Vol. 62, pp. 66-76.

Stambaugh, Robert, (1983), 'Arbitrage Pricing with Information,' *Journal of Financial Economics*, Vol. 12, pp. 357-369.

Stiglitz, Joseph E., (1969), 'A Reexamination of the Modigliani-Miller Theorem,' *American Economic Review*, Vol. 59, pp. 784-793.

(1974), 'On the Irrelevance of Corporate Financial Policy,' *American Economics Review*, Vol. 64, pp. 851-866.

(1988), 'Why Financial Structure Matters,' *Journal of Economic Perspectives*, Vol. 2, pp. 121-126.

Trzcinka, Charles, (1986), 'On the Number of Factors in the Arbitrage Pricing Model,' *Journal of Finance*, Vol. 46:2, pp. 347-368.

Comment

In reading through (an earlier draft of) the Chapter (5) you gave me, I was reminded of some discussions that Franco Modigliani and I had many years ago on a possible problem with our proof very similar in spirit to the one you point out. We did not use the term 'common knowledge,' of course; that term had not been invented yet. But we were very definitely aware of the problem. The missing assumption was noted and introduced not in the 1958 leverage paper, but in the 1961 dividend paper (see p. 427 and especially footnote 24). The treatment there is admittedly not very rigorous by present day standards. But at least we sensed an incompleteness that, somewhat to our surprise, no one seems to have followed up prior to your paper.

Merton H. Miller
Graduate School of Business
University of Chicago

6 Arbitrage pricing, common knowledge priors, and market completeness

6.1 Introduction[1]

Financial theorists' recent interest in common knowledge stems from the need to eliminate arbitrage opportunities in models of financial markets. Without implicit or explicit common knowledge assumptions, many so-called 'riskless arbitrage' trades in reality entail speculative exposure to risk from changing market beliefs and asset valuations.

Aumann (1976) introduced a mathematical definition of common knowledge using information partitions (σ-algebras) and coarsenings. Milgrom (1981) and Brandenberger and Dekel (1987) further developed the mathematical structure for representing common knowledge. The necessity of common priors has been studied for repeated communication by Geanakoplos and Polemarchakis (1982), Nielsen (1984), Aumann (1987), and more recently in imputed rationality to game players by Nau and McCardle (1990) and Nau (1992). This chapter examines the necessity for common knowledge priors in a contingent claims economy. The 'equilibrium' solution concept utilized in this chapter is the absence of arbitrage. This particular structure underpins much of contingent claims analysis, option pricing, and arbitrage pricing theory (see Babbs and Selby (1992) in this regard).

Our work also touches upon results found in Milgrom and Stokey (1982), Milgrom (1981), Tirole (1983) and Sebenius and Geanakoplos (1983). These papers relate common knowledge (of trader preferences and market structures) to no trading theorems in pure exchange economies with asymmetric information. Conversely, our paper investigates what the assumption of no trading of a particular type (arbitrage opportunities) implies about common knowledge (priors).

The no-trading proposition of Milgrom and Stokey (1982), Tirole (1983), and others asserts that if agents have common priors regarding the value of some assets, and receive private information about future values, then one agent's mere willingness to trade means no trading partner should complete the trade. The problem with this logic is that individuals with common priors have no way of knowing *a priori* that the rest of the market agrees with them. In fact, it would be just as reasonable for them to believe the rest of the market, or some fraction thereof, disagrees (at least in part) with their own priors. When priors are common but not common knowledge, the mere willingness to trade could indicate someone has (1) superior information or (2) apparently a different prior. No trader would be able to distinguish between these two cases *a priori*, and Chapter 4 demonstrated the formal proof of this lack of consensus.[2] Therefore, we draw an important distinction between priors being common (homogeneous) and common knowledge (leaving no uncertainty about how others hold their priors).

The condition for no arbitrage opportunities applied in this chapter leads to a series of no-price-exists results, which are analogous to the no-trading result of the common knowledge literature. For example, we show that when any trader knows with certainty that an asset poses limited liability, no positive price will exist for the asset.

Our work is also related to the more fundamental analysis of Nau and McCardle (1990). They formulate a new axiomatic foundation for rational behavior in a finite non-cooperative game, which takes as one of its basic axioms the absence of arbitrage. From this foundation, they deduce an equivalence theorem between 'correlated' equilibria (Aumann 1987) and strategies, which they call 'jointly coherent' (which require the absence of arbitrage). Further, they show that with an additional completeness hypothesis the identical common knowledge priors assumption is a consequence of their theory. Nau (1992) further explores the relaxation of this completeness assumption in a subsequent, related paper.

Our work uses similar concepts to Nau and McCardle, yet the focus differs significantly. Rather than exploring foundational issues, we take a state space, information partition (σ-algebra), and individual prior beliefs as given. From these, in a market context, we deduce what the absence of arbitrage (no trading) implies about the common knowledge of prior beliefs.

Our line of argument requires the construction of a universal beliefs space with consistent beliefs along the lines of Mertens and Zamir (1985) or Tan and Werlang (1988). In our construction, successively higher-order beliefs are independent of both lower order beliefs and the first-order beliefs over states of the world. Thus no individual is restricted into believing everyone else *must* assign the same probability as his own (subjective) priors. The construction uses well-known results from probability theory.

Consider a pure exchange economy where the universal beliefs space, its σ-algebra, individuals' information sets, and prices are all common knowledge, but where traders can have private information. We prove that the absence of arbitrage implies that prices partially reflect private information involving higher-order beliefs used in trading, and this partial information becomes common knowledge. (In another minor contribution, this chapter formulates a new and generalized definition of the no arbitrage condition when traders have private information.) Those events which traded securities can isolate as pure bets become common knowledge. Furthermore, the richer the set of traded securities, the more information about beliefs must be common knowledge. In the limiting case of complete markets (see Green and Jarrow (1987) for the relevant definition), common knowledge priors are a necessary condition of the analysis. Our definition of complete markets differs from the standard definition used in general equilibrium theory. Complete markets span not only the possible states of the world but also the possible distributions for higher-order beliefs over the states.

Market completeness plays a crucial role in the continuous time stochastic market models used to price contingent claims. These models require completeness in the strong sense used above and exclude speculation based on incomplete information about other traders' beliefs. Our analysis sheds considerable light on the restrictive nature (and perhaps inappropriateness) of this completeness assumption in many models in the options pricing literature.

The outline for the chapter is as follows. Section 6.2 provides the canonical arbitrage pricing model without imposing common knowledge priors. Section 6.3 generalizes the range of contingent claims to distinguish intrinsic uncertainty (a term coined in Guth 1989) from uncertainty over extrinsic events. Section 6.3 also constructs a hierarchy of higher-order beliefs into a universal beliefs space. Section 6.4 briefly applies the work in Section 6.2 and 6.3 to option pricing theory, and Section 6.5 concludes the chapter.

6.2. The Canonical Arbitrage Pricing Model

The canonical arbitrage pricing model extant consists of a single time period, starting at time 0 and ending at time 1. The state of the economy at time 1 is uncertain. The state space and possible events are represented by a measure space $(\Omega, \mathscr{F})$ with Ω an arbitrary set and $\mathscr{F}$

the associated σ-algebra.

There are a finite number of traders $\{1, 2, ..., I\}$, indexed by (a superscript) i, each with an information set F^i. The information set F^i is a σ-algebra contained in $\mathscr{F}$, the set of events. Let $\bigcap_i F^i$ denote the largest σ-algebra of sets containing the informed or true state across all the F^i. These information sets allow for infinite state spaces and, therefore, generalize the information partition concept applicable to finite state spaces used in the common knowledge literature. This added generality is needed to incorporate the universal beliefs space (an infinite set) as a possible set for Ω.

The fact that some set of events is known to individual i after he has received his private signal means that it is F^i-measurable. For that set to be common knowledge across all I individuals means that it must be $\bigcap_i F^i$-measurable.

The term 'common knowledge' can be used as a noun or an adjective. Thus, later when we speak of 'common knowledge price functionals', π, we mean the π are $\bigcap_i F^i$-measurable. Just as we use the expressions 'homogeneous beliefs' or 'common priors,' so can we use the term 'common knowledge beliefs' or 'common knowledge priors' to express the notion that each individual's prior is $\bigcap_i F^i$-measurable.

We assume that the state space Ω, the set of all possible events, $\mathscr{F}$, and the sets F^i for $i = 1, ..., I$ are common knowledge. Although the collection of sets F^i and $\mathscr{F}$ are common knowledge, those events (elements of these sets) containing the true state $\omega_0 \in \Omega$ are generally not common knowledge.

We say that individual i's information set, F^i, is common knowledge, when everyone knows everyone knows .... everyone else's information set. Mathematically, we could define a measure space for a random variable over possible values of the original information sets, F^i, for each individual. Each individual i would have another information set, say H^i, in this new measure space. We would then say an information set F^i is common knowledge when F^i is $\bigcap_i H^i$-measurable. Once it is recognized how to write mathematically that the information sets are common knowledge, we do not need to introduce the additional notation and carry it throughout the chapter. Alternatively, we could redefine our original event space to include not only states of the world but also a specification of each individual's information set.

Each trader is endowed with a probability measure p^i: $\mathcal{F} \rightarrow [0, 1]$ representing the trader's subjective prior beliefs. These probability measures p^i can differ across traders and need not be common knowledge. The necessity of this restriction, or the lack thereof, is the topic of this chapter.

In forming their time 0 trading decisions, individuals will condition on their information sets. To facilitate the analysis, we assume for all $i \in \{1, 2, ..., I\}$, $\omega \in \Omega$, and $A \in \mathcal{F}$, $p^i(A|F^i)(\omega)$ is a regular conditional probability of $\mathcal{F}$ given F^i, i.e., for fixed $\omega_0 \in \Omega$, $p^i(\cdot|F^i)(\omega_0)$ is a probability measure of $\mathcal{F}$, and for fixed $A \in \mathcal{F}$, $p^i(A|F^i)(\cdot)$ is F^i-measurable. We also assume p^i is posterior complete, i.e., F^i contains the $p^i(\cdot|F^i)(\omega)$ zero probability events for all $\omega \in \Omega$. Finally, we assume that p^i is proper (i.e., $p^i(A|F^i)(\omega) = 1_A(\omega)$ for every $A \in F^i$). These last two hypotheses ensure that our definition of common knowledge matches Aumann (1976) when beliefs are common knowledge (Brandenburger and Dekel 1987, Prop. 2.1).

In the economy, traders exchange financial securities entitling the owner to time 1 cash flows and the resale value of the paper claim (the capital gain). Let M represent a linear subspace of the $\mathcal{F}$-measurable functions mapping Ω into $\Re$. The linear subspace condition implies that if the assets m_1 and m_2 trade, then all portfolios with α shares of m_1 and β shares of m_2 trade as well (for all $\alpha, \beta \in \Re$). The set M must be common knowledge; otherwise, the traders do not know they are playing the same game. Consequently, the cash flows and prices that will prevail in each of the states are common knowledge.

The time zero value of the traded assets $m \in M$ are represented by a price functional π: $M \rightarrow \Re$, i.e., $\pi(m)$ denotes the time 0 price of asset $m \in M$. We require that the asset markets are frictionless in that π is linear, i.e., given $m_1, m_2 \in M$ and $\beta \in \Re$ then $\pi(m_1 + \beta m_2) = \pi(m_1) + \beta\pi(m_2)$. The price functional π is common knowledge.

For easy reference, we collect in a first assumption those quantities which are common knowledge.

Assumption 1: (Common Knowledge Parameters)

$(\Omega, \mathcal{F})$, $\{F^i: i = 1, ..., I\}$, M, and π are all common knowledge.

Let $\omega_0 \in \Omega$ represent the unknown, 'true' realization of the state space.

Define the sets $(M^+)^i(\omega_0) = \{ m \in M: p^i(m(\omega) \geq 0 \mid F^i)(\omega_0) = 1$ and $p^i(m(\omega) > 0 \mid F^i)(\omega_0) > 0\}$ and $(M^0)^i(\omega_0) = \{m \in M: p^i(m(\omega) = 0 \mid F^i)(\omega_0) = 1\}$. These sets represent special collections of traded assets, as seen by trader i. The first, $(M^+)^i(\omega_0)$, represents those traded assets which (under $\omega_0 \in \Omega$) the trader believes are nonzero and of limited liability since they always have non-negative payoffs at time 1. These assets will typically have zero payoffs for some states and positive payoffs in others. The set $(M^0)^i(\omega_0)$ represents those traded assets that trader i believes (under $\omega_0 \in \Omega$) have zero payoffs with probability one. The set $(M^0)^i(\omega_0)$ represents an equivalence class, under the ith investor's beliefs about assets with zero payoffs, i.e., it is the 'zero' element in the space of traded assets. Arbitrage opportunities are trader- and state-specific.

Definition (An Arbitrage Opportunity): $m \in M$ is called an *arbitrage opportunity for individual i under state* $\omega_0 \in \Omega$ if (1.a) $m \in (M^+)^i(\omega_0)$ and (1.b) $\pi(m) \leq 0$, or (2.a) $m \in (M^0)^i(\omega_0)$ and (2.b) $\pi(m) \neq 0$.

This definition of arbitrage is a straightforward extension to asymmetrically informed traders of that contained in the literature, see Jarrow (1987). An arbitrage opportunity is a traded asset which satisfies one of two conditions: either it is of limited liability with a non-positive price, or it is the 'zeroth' asset, but with a non-zero price. A well-functioning market (one that is in equilibrium) would not contain any of these opportunities, hence, we assume:

Assumption 2: (No Arbitrage Opportunities) Fix $\omega_0 \in \Omega$, (a) if $m \in \bigcup_i (M^+)^i(\omega_0)$ then $\pi(m) > 0$ and (b) if $m \in \bigcup_i (M^0)^i(\omega_0)$ then $\pi(m) = 0$.

This assumption implies that any individual, acting independently of the other traders, can force prices to be positive or zero, depending upon his beliefs. Any individual can act as a price dictator.

It is easy to show that if there exists an $m \in M$ such that $m \in \bigcap_i (M^+)^i(\omega_0)$, then Assumption 2(a) implies Assumption 2(b).[3] This condition is satisfied, for example, if a riskless asset trades ($1_\Omega \in M$ where $1_\Omega(\omega) = 1$ for all $\omega \in \Omega$).

Assumptions 1 and 2 impose these necessary conditions on common knowledge:

(*a*) if $m \in (M^+)^i(\omega_0)$ for some i, then
$-m \notin (M^+)^j(\omega_0)$ and $\in (M^0)^j(\omega_0)$ for all j.
(*b*) if $m \in (M^0)^i(\omega_0)$ for some i, then
$-m \notin (M^+)^j(\omega_0)$ and $\in (M^+)^j(\omega_0)$ for all j.

If some person believes with certainty an asset is of limited liability (condition *a*) or the 'zeroth' asset (condition *b*), then the absence of arbitrage implies that the other traders' beliefs must be minimally consistent. Indeed, if one trader believes with certainty an asset is of limited liability, then no one else can believe that shorting the asset is of limited liability or that it is a 'zero' cash flow security. Similarly, if one trader sees an asset as having 'zero' cash flows, then no one else can believe with certainty that it or its negative is of limited liability.

Consider the set of traded assets that everyone agrees has non-negative time 1 cash flows, i.e., $\bigcap_j \left[(M^+)^j(\omega_0) \cup (M^0)^j(\omega_0)\right]$. These assets, by Assumption 2, have non-negative prices. This set could be empty.

Define $\sigma(M)$ to be the smallest σ-algebra generated by all $m \in M$. These are the events in $\mathcal{F}$ relevant to asset payoffs. Next, define the set of events that generate potential arbitrage opportunities as D, where
$D \equiv \{ A \in \sigma(M): A = \{ \omega \in \Omega: m(\omega) > 0\}$ *for some* $m \in \bigcap_j [(M^+)^j(\omega_0) \cup (M^0)^j(\omega_0)] \}$. The set D could possibly contain only the empty set. If the I individuals trade, however, the set of traded assets D contains those assets that pay off \$1 in state A and 0 otherwise, denoted $1_A(\omega)$. These are analogous to 'Arrow-Debreu' securities.

Proposition 1 (Absolute Continuity of Beliefs): Given Assumptions 1 and 2 and $\omega_0 \in \Omega$, if $A \in D$, then $p^i(A|F^i)(\omega_0) = 0$ if and only if $p^j(A|F^j)(\omega_0) = 0$, $\forall j$.

Proof: If $D = \{\phi\}$ this is trivially true. If $D \neq \{\phi\}$, choose $A \in D$ such that $A = \{m > 0\}$ for some $m \in \bigcap_i [(M^+)^j(\omega_0) \cup (M^0)^i(\omega_0)]$. If $p^i(A|F^i)(\omega_0) = 0$ for some i, then $m \in (M^0)^i(\omega_0)$. By definition, $m \notin (M^+)^j(\omega_0)$ for any j. Hence, $m \in (M^0)^j(\omega_0)$ for all j, i.e., $p^j(A|F^j)(\omega_0) = 0$. QED.

Proposition 1 states that traders agree on zero probability events in the set of events D. This proposition generalizes a similar proposition contained in Jarrow (1987). Jarrow requires stronger assumptions on preferences and the market structure than that required in Proposition 1 above. As a special case of this proposition, if $D = \sigma(M)$, then traders agree on *all* the zero probability events relevant to asset payoffs. This is called a *complete* market (see Green and Jarrow 1987). Thus in complete markets, equivalent probability beliefs are a necessary and sufficient condition for the absence of arbitrage opportunities.

Our use of equivalent probability beliefs differs from the 'homogeneous or identical beliefs' assumption of mean-variance theory and the arbitrage pricing literature. Proposition 1 only implies that given an event $A \in D$, $p^i(A|F^i)(\omega_0) = 0$ if and only if $p^j(A|F^j)(\omega_0) = 0$ for all i, j. This assumption is also known as 'unconditional beliefs' in the literature. In contrast, homogeneous or identical beliefs are defined as $p^i(A) = p^j(A)$ for all i, j and $A \in \mathcal{F}$. With homogeneous beliefs, market traders objectively agree. However, the traders do not know they agree unless their beliefs are both equal *and common knowledge*.[4]

Proposition 2 (Common Knowledge Information Revealed by Prices): Given Assumptions 1 and 2 and $\omega_0 \in \Omega$, if $A \in D$ and $p^i(A|F^i)(\omega_0) = 0$ then A is common knowledge.

Proof: $p^i(A|F^i)(\omega_0) = 0$ implies $A \in F^i$. But, by Proposition 1, $A \in D$ and $p^i(A|F^i)(\omega_0) = 0$ implies $p^j(A|F^j)(\omega_0) = 0$ for all j. Hence, A is $\bigcap_j F^j$-measurable. QED.

Although the set of possible assets to trade, D, is common knowledge, individuals do not know *a priori* which contingent claims will actually be traded. This key proposition demonstrates that those events that can be bet upon (associated with traded assets) and that everyone agrees have non-negative cash flows ($A \in D$) become common knowledge through prices. The reason is that if someone assigns 0 probability to such an asset having positive cash flow, ($p^i(A|F^i)(\omega_0) = 0$ for some i), then this asset's price must be zero, or there is an arbitrage opportunity. But, the price being zero is common knowledge. If anyone else believes $p^j(A|F^j)(\omega_0) > 0$, then they would see an arbitrage opportunity, and these do not exist. Hence, as previously noted, everyone agrees that A can never occur, so A is common knowledge.

An important case of this proposition is for complete markets. In this case, $D = \sigma(M)$, since all 'Arrow-Debreu' securities trade ($1_A \in M$ for all $A \in \sigma(M)$). Here, all zero probability asset payoff relevant events will be common knowledge. This occurs, for example, in standard option pricing theory, see Section 6.4 below.

6.3 Extrinsic and Intrinsic Uncertainty

This section generalizes the canonical arbitrage pricing model to include uncertainty over investor beliefs in asset pricing. We call the initial state space governing the actual state of the world *extrinsic* uncertainty and the remaining part pertaining to the beliefs of other market traders *intrinsic* uncertainty. This distinction will clarify whether the absence of arbitrage opportunities requires common knowledge priors over extrinsic uncertainty.

Mertens and Zamir (1985) provide a formal model of Harsanyi's infinite hierarchies of beliefs by constructing a universal beliefs space generated by a compact state space Ω. They also examine consistency of a set of beliefs P over this universal beliefs space. The following development gives an alternative construction of such a universal beliefs space Ω and a consistent set of beliefs, P, for the case where Ω is a complete, separable, metric space. The results then follow from standard probability theory theorems (see Mertens and Zamir 1985, remark 2.18, p. 14). This construction, although not the analysis of this section, also resembles the work of Tan and Werlang (1988). Our higher-order beliefs are not artificially constrained to match first-order beliefs.

Let (Y_1, B_1) be a measurable space where Y_1 is a complete, separable, metric space (Parthasarathy 1967; p. 1) and B_1 is the Borel σ-algebra. The set Y_1 represents the *extrinsic* uncertainty in the economy. Extrinsic uncertainty is randomness due to exogenously-determined phenomena, independent of traders' beliefs, which has a real effect on earnings. Examples of extrinsic uncertainty are returns on firm investments, merger and acquisition policies, technological discoveries, etc. This definition is distinct from that of extrinsic uncertainty used by Cass and Shell (1983). 'Sunspot equilibria' can occur in our model through intrinsic uncertainty when traders believe others believe sunspots are relevant. This, however, is not the topic of the remaining analysis.

Each trader ($i = 1, 2, \ldots, I$) has a subjective probability measure P_1^i: $B_1 \rightarrow [0,1]$ defined over the extrinsic uncertainty. The traders may not know the other traders' probability beliefs; however, they know the population from which these beliefs are 'drawn.'

Let Y_2 be the space of all probability measures on (Y_1, B_1) endowed with the topology of weak convergence. Under this topology, Y_2 is a complete, separable, metric space (see Parthasarathy 1967; Theorem 6.2, page 43 and Theorem 6.5, page 46). Let B_2 be the Borel σ-algebra associated with Y_2. The I-cross product of Y_2 with itself $Y_2 \times Y_2 \times \ldots \times Y_2 = Y_2^I$ is the population from which the trader's beliefs $(p_1^1, p_1^2, \ldots, p_1^I)$ are 'drawn.'

Let $B_2 \times \ldots \times B_2 = B_2^I$ denote the product σ-algebra (see Parthasarathy 1967; Definition 1.2 and Theorem 1.10, p.6). Although each trader does not know the other traders' beliefs, he assigns a second probability measure $P_2^i: B_2^I \rightarrow [0,1]$ over the possibilities. This measure represents trader i's *second-order belief* over the first-order beliefs of the other traders (and for convenience himself as well).[3]

Continuing by induction for $n \geq 2$, let Y_n be the space of all probability measures on (Y_{n-1}^I, B_{n-1}^I) endowed with the topology of weak convergence. Again, this metric space is complete and separable. Let B_n be the Borel σ-algebra associated with Y_n. The I-cross product denotes the population of the traders' (n-1)-order beliefs. Define B_n^I as the I-cross product σ-algebra. The nth-order beliefs of trader i, $P_n^i: B_n^I \rightarrow [0,1]$, are defined over this set of events. Note that $P_n^i(Y_n^I) = 1$ since P_n^i is a probability measure and Y_n^I represents the entire population of the nth-order 'sample' points.

Traders thus experience uncertainty not only over the initial probability space Y_1, representing extrinsic uncertainty, but over $Y_2^I, Y_3^I, \ldots, Y_n^I$, as well. This latter uncertainty is over the beliefs (1st and higher-order) of other traders, and it is called *intrinsic* uncertainty. To capture this notion of an 'expanded' state space and to transform this model into the form of the canonical arbitrage pricing model, we construct the following space. This construction comes from Parthasarathy (1967;, pp. 135-139).

Fix a trader $i \in \{1, 2, \ldots, I\}$. Define $\bar{Y}_1 \equiv Y_1$, $\bar{B}_1 \equiv B_1$, and $\bar{P}_1^i \equiv P_1^i$. Next, define for $n \geq 2$, $\bar{Y}_n \equiv Y_1 \times Y_2^I \times \ldots \times Y_n^I = \bar{Y}_{n-1} \times Y_n^I$, $\bar{B}_n \equiv B_1 \times B_2^I \times \ldots \times B_n^I = \bar{B}_{n-1} \times B_n^I$, and $\bar{P}_n^i \equiv P_1^i \times P_2^i \times \ldots \times P_n^i = \bar{P}_{n-1}^i \times P_n^i$, where $\bar{P}_n^i$ is the n-fold cross product measure (see Breiman 1968; p. 399). By construction, since Y_n^I is a complete, separable, metric space for all $n \geq 1$, the set $\bar{Y}_n$ will be a complete, separable, metric space under the topology. Hence, $(\bar{Y}_n, \bar{B}_n)$ is a separable and standard Borel space for all $n \geq 1$.

Define γ_n: $\bar{Y}_{n+1} \to \bar{Y}_n$ as the projection map, i.e., $\gamma_n (y_1, y_2, \ldots, y_n, y_{n+1}) = (y_1, \ldots, y_n)$ where $y_1 \in Y_1$ and $y_j \in Y_j^I$ for $j \geq 2$. The expanded state space (Borel space) $(\Omega, \mathscr{F})$ is defined to be the inverse limit of the Borel spaces $(\bar{Y}_n, \bar{B}_n)$ for $n = 1, 2, 3, \ldots$. That is, $\Omega \equiv \{(\bar{y}_1, \bar{y}_2, \ldots)$: $\bar{y}_n \in \bar{Y}_n \; \forall \, n\}$, and $\mathscr{F}$ is the smallest σ-algebra of subsets of Ω such that $\tilde{\gamma}_n$: $\Omega \to \bar{Y}_n$ defined by $\tilde{\gamma}_n(\bar{y}_1, \bar{y}_2, \ldots) = \bar{y}_n$ is measurable for all n.

It is easy to see that the nth-order cross-product measure $\bar{P}_n^i$ satisfies $\bar{P}_n^i(A) = \bar{P}_{n+1}^i(\gamma_n^{-1}(A))$, $\forall \, A \in \bar{B}_n$, $\forall \, n$. Indeed,

$$\begin{aligned} \bar{P}_{n+1}^i(\gamma_n^{-1}(A)) &= \bar{P}_{n+1}^i(A \times Y_{n+1}^I) \\ &= \bar{P}_n^i \times P_{n+1}^i(A \times Y_{n+1}^I) \\ &= \bar{P}_n^i(A) P_{n+1}^i(Y_{n+1}^I) = \bar{P}_n^i(A). \end{aligned}$$

This consistency condition states that the modified probability beliefs at the nth step, $\bar{P}_n^i$, restrict the joint distribution of the beliefs at step $n+1$, $\bar{P}_{n+1}^i$. Hence, by Parthasarathy (1967; p. 139, Theorem 3.2), there exists a *unique* probability measure P^i defined on $(\Omega, \mathscr{F})$ such that $P^i(\tilde{\gamma}_n^{-1}(A)) = \bar{P}_n^i(A)$ for all $A \in \bar{B}_n$ and each $n = 1, 2, 3, \ldots$. This probability measure P^i, defined on the expanded Borel space $(\Omega, \mathscr{F})$, is the unique extension of the nth-order cross product measures $\bar{P}_n^i$ for all n. (This measure omits the subscript denoting the order of beliefs over extrinsic uncertainty.)

The σ-algebra $\mathscr{F}$ includes events with both intrinsic and extrinsic uncertainty. It is useful for the subsequent analysis to decompose $\mathscr{F}$ into those events which are either only extrinsic or intrinsic.

We claim that $\sigma\{\tilde{\gamma}_1^{-1}(A)$: $A \in B_1\}$, the smallest σ-algebra generated by the class of events $\{\tilde{\gamma}_1^{-1}(A): A \in B_1\}$, represents those events in $\mathcal{F}$ associated with *extrinsic* uncertainty alone. Indeed, by standard arguments, $\sigma\{\tilde{\gamma}_1^{-1}(A): A \in B_1\} = \tilde{\gamma}_1^{-1}(\sigma\{A: A \in B_1\}) = \tilde{\gamma}_1^{-1}(B_1)$. Recall that $\tilde{\gamma}_1$ is the projection of the universal beliefs space Ω into the extrinsic uncertainty space Y_1. Hence, the inverse mapping $\tilde{\gamma}_1^{-1}$ identifies all those events $A \in B_1$ with events in the corresponding universal beliefs space Ω. Since $\tilde{\gamma}_1$ is measurable, $\tilde{\gamma}_1^{-1}(B_1) \subset \mathcal{F}$. This proves the first claim. Denote $\xi \equiv \tilde{\gamma}_1^{-1}(B_1)$ for *extrinsic* events.

Secondly, we claim that $\sigma\{\tilde{\gamma}_n^{-1}(Y_1 \times A): A \in B_2^I \times B_3^I \times ... \times B_n^I \;\; \forall\, n \geq 2\}$ are those events in $\mathcal{F}$ associated only with intrinsic uncertainty. Indeed, $\sigma\{\tilde{\gamma}_n^{-1}(Y_1 \times A): A \in B_2^I \times ... \times B_n^I \;\forall\, n \geq 2\} = \sigma\{\tilde{\gamma}_n^{-1}(Y_1 \times B_2^I \times ... \times B_n^I) \;\forall\, n \geq 2\}$

$= \sigma\{\bigcup_{n=1}^{\infty} (Y_1 \times B_2^I \times ... \times B_n^I)\} \subset \mathcal{F}$ since each $\tilde{\gamma}_n$ is measurable. In this set of events, no information is revealed about extrinsic uncertainty since the events considered in the inverse mapping $\tilde{\gamma}_n^{-1}$ always take as given the first set Y_1. All that remains is information about higher beliefs. Define

$\Upsilon \equiv \sigma\{\bigcup_{n=1}^{\infty} \gamma_n^{-1}(Y_1 \times B_2^I \times ... \times B_n^I)\}$ for *intrinsic* events. It follows easily then that $\mathcal{F} = \sigma(\Upsilon \cup \xi)$.

Each trader $i = 1, 2, \ldots, I$ is endowed with an information set $F^i \subset \mathcal{F}$. To be consistent with the interpretation of the expanded state space, we add the following assumption.

Assumption 3: (Traders Know Their Own Beliefs)

$\{\omega \in \Omega: P_n^i \in A\} \in F^i \quad \forall\, A \in B_{n+1}^I,\; n \geq 1$, and $i = 1, \ldots, I$.

This assumption asserts that trader i has included in his information set all those events which contain his n^{th}-order beliefs (for all n). Finally, we assume that for each i, $P^i(A|F^i)(\omega)$ is a regular conditional probability measure, which is posterior complete and proper.

Thus, the probability space $(\Omega, \mathcal{F}, P^i)$ is a universal beliefs space in the sense of Mertens and Zamir (1985) which has consistent probability beliefs. To separate the influence of information about intrinsic uncertainty versus extrinsic uncertainty, we impose the following assumption.

Assumption 4: (Information Only Over Intrinsic Uncertainty)

For every trader i, ξ and F^i are independent σ-algebras with respect to P^i.

To understand Assumption 4 note that two σ-algebras are independent with respect to P^i if $P^i(A_1 \cap A_2) = P^i(A_1)P^i(A_2)$ for all $A_1 \in \xi$ and all $A_2 \in F^i$ (see Loeve 1977; p. 235). Hence, knowledge of the events in F^i provides no information about the extrinsic events in ξ. The individual could still receive a private signal about the extrinsic events ξ in this model, although it would be necessary to introduce new notation to distinguish this information set from F^i. In this section, we focus on information events about the other market participants. Assumption 4, therefore, indicates that F^i provides only information about intrinsic uncertainty Υ, i.e., higher-order beliefs.

We imposed Assumption 4 to highlight a fallacy in many 'private information' models, namely, that an individual's priors over other traders' higher-order beliefs depend on that individual's priors over the extrinsic events of the economy. Let's consider a simple two-state example of 'rain' or 'shine'. Just because one trader personally feels that 'shine' is three times more probable than 'rain,' he has no reason to assume everyone else shares his sunny disposition. This trader may have bad priors that need updating, or he may represent the market's view. Either case or any convex combination of the two is possible.

Assuming people agree with your own priors is no more rational/irrational than assuming they disagree with your priors. Assumption 4 allows traders the flexibility to formulate higher-order beliefs that may not correspond to their own priors over the extrinsic events. How do arbitrage opportunities relate to higher-order beliefs? The next proposition answers this question.

Proposition 3 (Common Knowledge Higher-Order Beliefs):

Given $A_1 \in B_1$, $A_2 \in B_2^I \times \ldots \times B_n^I$ for some $n \geq 2$. If $\tilde{\gamma}_n^{-1}$ $(Y_1 \, x \, A_2)$ is $\bigcap_i F^i$-measurable, then

$$P^i(\tilde{\gamma}_n^{-1}(A_1 \times A_2)\,|\,F^i)(\omega_0) = \begin{Bmatrix} P_1^i(A_1) \text{ if } \omega_0 \in \tilde{\gamma}_n^{-1}(Y_1 \times A_2) \\ 0 \quad \textit{otherwise} \end{Bmatrix}, \text{ a.e. } P^i.$$

Proof: First, $\tilde{\gamma}_n^{-1}(A_1 \times A_2) = \tilde{\gamma}_n^{-1}(A_1) \cap \tilde{\gamma}_n^{-1}(Y_1 \times A_2)$. Indeed, $\tilde{\gamma}_n^{-1}(A_1 \times A_2)$ $\tilde{\gamma}_n^{-1}(A_1 \times A_2) \subset \tilde{\gamma}_1^{-1}(A_1)$ and $\tilde{\gamma}_n^{-1}(A_1 \times A_2) \subset \tilde{\gamma}_n^{-1}(Y_1 \times A_2)$ are trivial. Conversely, if $\omega = (\bar{y}_1, \bar{y}_2, \ldots) \in \tilde{\gamma}_1^{-1}(A_1) \cap \tilde{\gamma}_1^{-1}(Y_1 \times A_2)$, then $\bar{y}_1 = y_1 \in A_1$ and $\bar{y}_n = (y_1, y_2, \ldots, y_n) \in Y_1 \times A_2$. Thus, $\bar{y}_n \in A_1 \times A_2$, i.e., $\omega \in \gamma_n^{-1}(A_1 \times A_2)$. Second, take $C \in F^i$, then

$$\int_C P_1^i(A_1)\, 1_{\{\tilde{\gamma}_n^{-1}(Y_1 \times A_2)\}}(\omega)\, dP^i(\omega) = P_1^i(A_1) P^i\left(\tilde{\gamma}_n^{-1}(Y_1 \times A_2) \cap C\right)$$

$$= \bar{P}_1^i(A_1) P^i\left(\tilde{\gamma}_n^{-1}(Y_1 \times A_2) \cap C\right)$$

$$= P^i\left(\tilde{\gamma}_1^{-1}(A_1)\right) P^i\left(\tilde{\gamma}_n^{-1}(Y_1 \times A_2) \cap C\right) \text{ by definition of } P^i(\cdot).$$

$$= P^i\left(\tilde{\gamma}_1^{-1}(A_1) \cap \tilde{\gamma}_n^{-1}(Y_1 \times A_2) \cap C\right) \text{ by Assumption 4.}$$

$$= P^i\left(\tilde{\gamma}_n^{-1}(A_1 \times A_2) \cap C\right) \text{ by the previous claim. QED.}$$

For clarity, let us write $\tilde{\gamma}_n^{-1}(Y_1 \times A_2)$ as '$Y_1 \times A_2$' and $\tilde{\gamma}_n^{-1}(A_1 \times A_2)$ as '$A_1 \times A_2$'. To understand the meaning of this proposition, consider the event '$A_1 \times A_2$'. It exhibits both extrinsic uncertainty $A_1 \in B_1$ and intrinsic uncertainty $A_2 \in B_2^I \times \ldots \times B_n^I$. Now we replace A_1 with Y_1, so that '$Y_1 \times A_2$' = 'A_2' reflects only the intrinsic uncertainty. If the event '$Y_1 \times A_2$' is common knowledge, then only uncertainty over the event 'A_1' remains. The proposition states that if 'A_2' is common knowledge then the individual assigns probability to the event '$A_1 \times A_2$' based on his *first-order probability* beliefs (over A_1) alone.

We say that *first-order beliefs* $\{P_1^i : i \in \{1, \ldots, I\}\}$ *are common knowledge* if each P_1^i is $\bigcap_i F^i$-measurable. A direct application of Proposition 3 yields the following corollary that only extrinsic uncertainty matters:[5]

Corollary 3.1: If first-order beliefs $\{P_1^i\}$ for all $i \in \{1, \ldots, I\}$ are common knowledge, then $\bar{P}_n^i$ is common knowledge for all i.

Corollary 3.1 indicates that if first-order beliefs are common knowledge, then all n-order beliefs can be shown to be common knowledge by induction. If first-order beliefs are common knowledge, then no intrinsic uncertainty remains over them. This certainty implies the second-order beliefs are fixed, known, and common knowledge, which in turn means third-order beliefs are fixed and common knowledge, etc.

When beliefs are homogeneous or identical, traders agree in the sense that their first-order beliefs happen to be equal. However, they need not know that everyone else knows that everyone knows ... they agree unless these beliefs are common knowledge. Corollary 3.1 also applies when traders' beliefs are *unequal and yet common knowledge*, as, for example, when the market knows that 2/3 of its members are bullish on future earnings and 1/3 of its members are bears.

Proposition 2 of Section 6.2 applied to the extrinsic/intrinsic state space gives the major result of this section.

Proposition 4 (Information About Prior Beliefs Revealed by Prices): Given $A_2 \in B_2^I \times ... \times B_n^I$ for some $n \geq 2$. If $\tilde{\gamma}_n^{-1}(Y_1 \times A_2) \in F^i$ for some i and $\tilde{\gamma}_n^{-1}(Y_1 \times A_2) \in D \equiv \{A \in \sigma(M): A = \{m>0\}$ for some $m \in \bigcap_j \left[(M^+)^j(\omega_0) \cup (M_0)^j(\omega_0)\right] \}$, then $\tilde{\gamma}_n^{-1}(Y_1 \times A_2)$ is common knowledge.

Proof: If $\tilde{\gamma}_n^{-1}(Y_1 \times A_2) \in F^i$ for some i, then

$$P^i\left(\tilde{\gamma}_n^{-1}(Y_1 \times A_2)|F^i\right)(\omega_0) = \left\{ \begin{array}{ll} 1 & \textit{if } \omega_0 \in \tilde{\gamma}_n^{-1}(Y_1 \times A_2) \\ 0 & \textit{otherwise} \end{array} \right\}.$$

By Proposition 2, $\tilde{\gamma}_n^{-1}(Y_1 \times A_2)$ is common knowledge. QED.

This proposition states that if individual i has private knowledge about higher-order beliefs that he can 'bet' upon with traded assets $\left(\tilde{\gamma}_n^{-1}(Y_1 \times A_2) \in D\right)$, then this information about higher-order beliefs is common knowledge.[7] The following two corollaries further illustrate this proposition's usefulness. If some individual i's priors can be 'bet' upon through traded assets, then these priors must be common knowledge.

Corollary 4.1: If $\{P_n^i \in A\} \in D$ for some $A \in B_{n+1}^I$ and some i, then

$\{P_n^i \in A\}$ is common knowledge.

Corollary 4.2: If $D = \sigma(M) = \mathscr{F}$, then first-order beliefs are common knowledge.

Proof: This corollary follows since if markets are complete, $\{P_n^i \in A\} \in D$ for all $A \in B_{n+1}^I$, all n, and all j. Hence, by Corollary 4.1, $\{P_n^i \in A\}$ are $\bigcap_i F^i$-measurable for all $A \in B_{n+1}^I$, all n, all j. This result implies $\tilde{\gamma}_n^{-1}(Y_1 \times A_2)$ is $\bigcap_i F^i$-measurable for all $A_2 \in B_2^I \times ... \times B_n^I$, for all n, i.e., Υ is common knowledge. QED.

Corollary 4.2 states that complete markets imply first-order beliefs are common knowledge. Completeness guarantees that traded securities isolate the person specific knowledge in pure bets, i.e., $\mathbf{1}_{\tilde{A}} \in M$ where $\tilde{A} = \{\omega \in \Omega: P_n^i \in A\}$ for all $A \in B_{n+1}^I$. Common knowledge prices for $\mathbf{1}_{\tilde{A}}$ across all events $\tilde{A}$, therefore, will reveal P_n^i.

If markets are incomplete (i.e., $D \neq \sigma(M) = \mathscr{F}$), first-order beliefs over extrinsic uncertainty need not be common knowledge. In fact in the extreme case, prices reveal no information about intrinsic uncertainty at all. The following class of models, which is often used in financial economics, see Jarrow (1988; Chapters 9, 15), illustrates this case.

We say that *only extrinsic uncertainty governs cash flows* if $m(\omega) \subseteq \xi$ for all $m \in M$. Cash flows would depend only on extrinsic factors if time 1 cash flows had no capital gains component or capital gains were independent of investor beliefs. Under either of these conditions, $\sigma(M) \subset \xi$, because the other market participants effectively have been shut out of determing prices. Since the events $\sigma(M)$ govern arbitrage pricing, intrinsic uncertainty has no influence in this (unrealistic) theory. Indeed, the next proposition restates this point more formally.

Proposition 5 (Extrinsicly-Determined Cash Flows):

If $\sigma(M) \subset \xi$, then given $A_1 \subset \sigma(M)$, $P^i(A_1|F^i)(\omega_0) = P_1^i(\tilde{\gamma}_1(A_1))$ with P^i probability one.

Proof: Fix a $C \in F^i$, then

$$\int_C P_1^i(\tilde{\gamma}_1(A_1))\, dP^i(\omega) = P_1^i(\tilde{\gamma}_1(A_1))P^i(C), \quad \text{since } A_1 \in \xi = \tilde{\gamma}_1^{-1}(B_1)$$

implies $\tilde{\gamma}_1(A_1) \in B_1$,

$$= P^i\big(\tilde{\gamma}_1^{-1}(\tilde{\gamma}_1(A_1))\big)P^i(C)$$

$$= P^i(A_1)\; P^i(C)$$

$$= P^i(A_1 \cap C) \text{ by Assumption 4. QED.}$$

This proposition shows that in models where intrinsic uncertainty doesn't influence future prices, information about higher-order beliefs has no influence on arbitrage pricing. Generating probability statements requires only first-order beliefs. Indeed, D contains no event in the intrinsic uncertainty set Υ. Hence, prices reveal no information about higher-order beliefs. To recap, only *first-order beliefs* are required to generate all probability statements and these probability statements alone, through Assumption 2, generate the arbitrage pricing theory.

6.4 Application to Option Pricing Theory

This section applies the previous analysis to standard option pricing theory as analyzed in Harrison and Pliska (1981) and Duffie and Huang (1985). Option pricing theory takes as given a continuous trading economy and a stochastic process for asset price movements. Although option pricing theory takes place in a dynamic setting, the use of self-financing trading strategies enables one to transform the multiperiod model into the single period economy. Under this transformation, the terminal value of all self-financing trading strategies represent the traded assets $m \in M$. In this setting, to obtain preference-free valuation formulas (like the Black-Scholes model), one needs to assume that the asset markets are complete in the sense of Green and Jarrow (1987). This assumption is required to invoke the martingale representation theorem, which provides 'valuation formulas' for any arbitrarily determined random variable ($m \in M$). In this setting, $D = \sigma(M) \equiv \mathcal{F}$ because trading strategies yielding \$1 under any event $A \equiv \sigma(M) \equiv \mathcal{F}$ and zero otherwise, are needed to construct all contingent claims.

There are two ways to interpret these option pricing models. First, the probability space underlying the asset price dynamics is based solely on extrinsic uncertainty. By construction, this broad class of option pricing models precludes speculative trading based on anticipated gains from changing investor beliefs. Second, let the probability space underlying the asset price process represent both extrinsic and intrinsic uncertainty, as in Section 6.3. However, to develop preference-free valuation formulas, one imposes market completeness ($D = \sigma(M) \equiv \mathcal{F}$). Corollary 4.1 implies that first-order beliefs are common knowledge, and then Corollary 3.1 implies that only extrinsic uncertainty matters. Here again, by implication rather than by construction, these option pricing models exclude speculation based on higher-order beliefs. This implication reveals a strong assumption, which is not likely to be satisfied in practice, of models attempting to provide valuation formulas for any arbitrarily determined random variable.

But what if option pricing models yield fair values for, not any arbitrarily determined random variable but, a proper subset of random variables? The work of Harrison and Pliska (1981) concerns finite-variance random variables, yet this section's analysis still applies. Other option pricing models may not rely on market completeness or martingale representation theorems, in which case our results may need to be qualified accordingly. However, few works, if any, in the option pricing literature extant have even acknowledged the existence of intrinsic uncertainty in financial markets, let alone incorporate it as a trading motive.

One of the more interesting questions in contingent claims models with asymmetric information is how to transform multiperiod models with heterogeneous beliefs into single period models à la Duffie and Huang (1985). Prices in these intertemporal models with information events do more than just clear markets; prices convey information. Changes in (heterogeneous) beliefs, speculative considerations, and the capital gains motive should drive trading in these models. Thus prices should not be exogenously specified as part of the state of the world. However, if prices are not specified as part of the state of the world, then traders might rationally speculate over what prices will prevail in future spot markets.

These complex issues and related ones about mechanisms for revealing prior belief information can create multiple equilibria for prices, rather than a unique solution. In an intertemporal investment model with no information events, only one round of trading is required to act on the information available to traders. Without the arrival of new information and changes in beliefs, these multiperiod models can be transformed into single period models with little difficulty.

Differences in construction between the various models in the contingent claims literature prevent a full discussion of how to transform multiperiod models here. We can comment on these issues within the context of our model. The model in Section 6.2 avoids the issue of intertemporal equilibrium with changing investor beliefs by assuming prices — for whatever unspecified reason — are determined by forces outside the control of the market traders. No information events trigger belief updating and intertemporal trading. The model contains only one trading round by assumption, but it could just as easily depict a transformation of a multiperiod model.

In Section 6.3, we adopt a framework in which both extrinsic and intrinsic uncertainty can affect prices. Obviously, prices in this subsequent framework are going to reveal something about both external factors and the market's internal perception of these factors. We do not address how this more complex economy, where traders may have heterogeneous beliefs about the rest of the market, can be transformed into a single period.

For the model in Section 6.3, it turns out that if a trader has some private information about the beliefs of others, his purchase of contingent claims that payoff according these higher-order beliefs communicates information to the market. His purchase makes common knowledge what this rational individual believes about higher-order beliefs. Interestingly, Proposition 4 indicates this information on higher-order beliefs will be revealed *if* the individual chooses to bet; if he fails to transact, his private information will not be revealed. Our second finding (Proposition 5) states that if you can identify an asset — even in an intertemporal framework — that does not depend on intrinsic uncertainty, then prices will reveal no information about higher-order beliefs for that asset. In fact, the intrinsic uncertainty is irrelevant.

Thus, our model sheds some light on particular transactions in which common knowledge beliefs must not be assumed for the absence of arbitrage. We are aware that not all multiperiod, heterogeneous beliefs models can be transformed into a single period model. The transformation relies on a deeper understanding of the relationship between multiperiod economies with heterogeneous beliefs and those where beliefs may be homogeneous but not common knowledge.

6.5 Summary

The structure of an asset's cash flows determines the necessity for imposing common knowledge priors in arbitrage pricing models. This structure (represented by M) is exogenously specified for arbitrage pricing theory. If market participants determine prices endogenously so that price changes and capital gains depend on higher-order beliefs, then those events that generate potential arbitrage opportunities, (the set D), reveal information about higher-order beliefs and imply necessary conditions on common knowledge priors (Proposition 4). If markets are complete (the set D is large), then priors are common knowledge. Conversely, if the cash flows and capital gains do not depend on higher-order beliefs, then prices reveal no information about higher-order beliefs. Applying these insights, we have shown that standard option pricing theory implicitly assumes common knowledge priors. If one relaxes this restriction, then the intrinsic uncertainty in the model can form the basis for securities trading apart from uncertainty over extrinsic events.

Our results offer then both good news and bad news to financial theorists. Those financial theorists, who suspected arbitrage pricing models implicitly incorporate common knowledge belief assumptions, will be relieved to learn that a large class of these models requires only the weaker homogeneous or common priors assumption. Problems associated with asymmetric information do not crop up in the canonical arbitrage pricing model, even though individual traders do not know how other market participants assign probabilities. These findings are the good news.

The bad news is that if cash flows depend only on extrinsic factors, which seems reasonable for real earnings but not for price movements, then any capital gains component of cash flows must not exist or must be independent of investor beliefs. It is hardly surprising that information about other market participants then has no impact on arbitrage pricing (Proposition 5). However, the ease with which this assumption has worked its way into, and now permeates, arbitrage pricing models is surprising. Most outside reviewers would find this assumption unrealistic and severely limiting the robustness of these models. We recommend that a more plausible treatment of the capital gains motive, speculative considerations, and the impact of uncertain or changing beliefs feature prominently in new theories on arbitrage pricing.

Notes

1. This chapter was co-authored with Robert A. Jarrow, S.C. Johnson Graduate School of Management, Cornell University.

2. Even with heterogeneous and common knowledge priors, no trades will execute, because each individual would know with certainty whether someone's willingness to trade was motivated by his having superior information.

3. *Lemma*. If there exists $m \in M$ such that $m \in \bigcap_i (M^+)^i(\omega_0)$ then Assumption 2(a) implies Assumption 2(b).

   Proof: Suppose $m^* \in (M^0)^j(\omega_0)$ for some trader j. Let $\pi(m^*) > 0$ (without loss of generality). Consider the $m \in \bigcap_i (M^+)^i(\omega_0)$. By Assumption 1(a), $\pi(m) > 0$. But, $-\pi(m)m^*/\pi(m^*) + m \in M$ where $P^j[-\pi(m)m^*(\omega)/\pi(m^*) + m(\omega) \geq 0 \,|F^j](\omega_0) = 1$ since $P^j[m^*(\omega) = 0|F^j](\omega_0) = 1$ and $P^j[m(\omega) \geq 0 \,|F^j](\omega) = 1$. Now $P^j[-\pi^*m)m^*(\omega)/\pi(m^*) + m(\omega) > 0|F^j](\omega_0) > 0$ since $P^j[m(\omega) > 0|F^j](\omega_0) > 0$; and $\pi(-\pi(m)m^*/\pi(m^*) + m) = 0$. This result shows $\pi(m)m^*/\pi(m^*) + m \in (M+)^j(\omega_0)$ with zero price, contradicting Assumption 2(a). Hence, $\pi(m^*) = 0$. QED.

4. Common knowledge beliefs are defined later in Section 6.3, immediately prior to Proposition 4.

5. Mertens and Zamir (1985), by contrast, define trader i's second-order belief as P_2^i: $Y_1 \times B_2^I \rightarrow [0,1]$. They always define higher-order beliefs over the cross product with the original space.

6. Assuming first-order beliefs are common knowledge is identically equivalent to assuming all higher-order beliefs are common knowledge.

7. Market traders do not engage in strategic trading to 'hide' their beliefs. This honest revelation of beliefs comes from arbitrage pricing's assumption of price taking behavior, so the trader does not believe his trades influence prices.

References

Aumann, R., (1976), 'Agreeing to Disagree,' *The Annals of Statistics*, Vol. 4, pp. 1236-1239.

Aumann, R., (1987), 'Correlated Equilibrium as an Expression of Bayesian Rationality,' *Econometrica*, Vol. 55:1, pp. 1-18.

Babbs, S. and M. Selby, (1992), 'Contingent Claims Analysis,' in *The Palgrave Dictionary of Finance*, London.

Brandenburger, A. and E. Dekel, (1987), 'Common Knowledge with Probability 1,' *Journal of Mathematical Economics*, Vol. 16, pp. 237-245.

Breiman, L., (1968), *Probability*, Addison-Wesley: Reading, Massachusetts.

Cass, D. and K. Shell, (1983), 'Do Sunspots Matter?,' *Journal of Political Economy*, Vol. 91:2, pp. 193-227.

Duffie, D. and C. Huang, (1985), 'Implementing Arrow-Debreu Equilibria by Continuous Trading of Few Long-Lived Securities,' *Econometrica*, Vol. 54, pp. 1161-1184.

Geanakoplos, J. and H. Polemarchakis, (1982), 'We Can't Disagree Forever,' *Journal of Economic Theory*, Vol. 28, pp. 192-200.

Green, R. and R. Jarrow, (1987), 'Spanning and Completeness in Markets with Contingent Claims,' *Journal of Economic Theory*, Vol. 41:1, pp. 202-210.

Guth, M.A.S., (1989), 'Intrinsic Uncertainty and Common Knowledge Priors in Financial Economics,' *Journal of Financial Research*, Vol. 22:4, pp. 269-283.

Harrison, J.M. and S. Pliska, (1981), 'Martingales and Stochastic Integrals in the Theory of Continuous Trading,' *Stochastic Processes and Their Applications*, Vol. 11, pp. 215-260.

Jarrow, R., (1987), 'Beliefs and Arbitrage Pricing,' *Economics Letters*, Vol. 24:2, pp. 165-169.

Jarrow, R., (1988), *Finance Theory*, Prentice-Hall, Inc.: Englewood Cliffs, New Jersey.

Loeve, M., (1977), *Probability Theory 1*, 4th Edition, Springer-Verlag Inc.: New York.

Mertens, J.F. and S. Zamir, (1985), 'Formulation of Bayesian Analysis for Games with Incomplete Information,' *International Journal of Game Theory*, Vol. 14:1, pp. 1-29.

Milgrom, P., (1981), 'An Axiomatic Characterization of Common Knowledge,' *Econometrica*, Vol. 49:1, pp. 219-222.

Milgrom, P. and N. Stokey, (1982), 'Information, Trade, and Common Knowledge,' *Journal of Economic Theory*, Vol. 26, pp. 17-27.

Nau, R., (1992), 'Joint Coherence in Games of Incomplete Information,' *Management Science*, Vol. 38:3, pp. 374-387.

Nau, R. and K. McCardle, (1990), 'Cooperative Behavior in Noncooperative Games,' *Journal of Economic Theory*, Vol. 50, pp. 424-444.

Nielsen, L., (1984), 'Common Knowledge, Communication, and Convergence of Beliefs,' *Mathematical Social Sciences*, Vol. 8, pp. 1-14.

Parthasarathy, K., (1967), *Probability Measures on Metric Spaces*, Academic Press: New York.

Royden, H., (1968), *Real Analysis*, 2nd Edition, MacMillan Publishing Co.: New York.

Sebenius, J. and J. Geanakoplos, (1983), 'Don't Bet On It: Contingent Agreements with Asymmetric Information,' *Journal of the American Statistical Association*, Vol. 78, pp. 424-426.

Tan, T.C. and S.R.C. Werlang, (1988), 'The Bayesian Foundations of Solution Concepts of Games, *Journal of Economic Theory*, Vol. 45, pp. 370-391.

Tirole, J., (1983), 'On the Possibility of Speculation Under Rational Expectations,' *Econometrica*, Vol. 50, pp. 1163-1181.

Comment

This chapter derives important results concerning the role of common knowledge and prior probabilities in asset pricing models: it develops a framework for studying the relevance of higher-order beliefs and identifies conditions under which no-arbitrage requires common prior beliefs to be common knowledge. The agents in this analysis are assumed to be risk neutral, as in much of the asset pricing literature and also in the cited papers by Nau and McCardle (1990) and Nau (1992), which use no-arbitrage arguments to derive the existence of a common prior in game theoretic models.

In commenting on this chapter, I would merely like to suggest a direction for generalization — namely, heterogeneous risk preference — which leads to a rather different perspective on common knowledge and common priors. If agents are risk averse, it becomes appropriate to assume that probabilities are neither common property nor common knowledge, and the various agreeing-to-disagree and no-trade theorems and game-theoretic solution concepts acquire new interpretations.

An arbitrage opportunity is basically a publicly observed inconsistency in prices. Under risk neutrality, competitive security prices reflect the agents' true expectations for payoffs, and in particular their (normalized) prices for Arrow-Debreu securities must be their true state probabilities. Hence, the true probabilities of risk neutral agents would naturally be common knowledge in a complete, competitive market, and these probabilities would then have to be identical in order to avoid arbitrage. (Conversely, as the chapter shows, if the market is complete and there are no arbitrage opportunities and priors are commonly held, then the latter must also be common knowledge.) However, it is hard to tell a convincing story about how exact agreement on prior probabilities would arise in nature, and the model has an uncomfortable knife-edge quality: small departures from common beliefs would produce unlimited volumes of trade in contingent claims.

If agents are assumed to be risk averse and heterogeneous in their risk tolerances as well as probabilities, we can tell a more plausible story: they should trade contingent claims and exploit arbitrage opportunities until they reach a competitive equilibrium in which differences in probabilities are compensated by differences in marginal utilities for money. In such an equilibrium, the state prices are still commonly known and commonly held, but they are no longer the agents' true probabilities. Rather, they are products of true probabilities and relative marginal utilities (Drèze 1970). This product is, of course, the 'risk neutral probability distribution' of the representative agent in theories of asset pricing by arbitrage (e.g., Cox and Ross 1976), but it represents the probabilities of real agents only in the aggregate.

This story explains how, in equilibrium, agent can fail to agree on probabilities: they never credibly observe each others' true probabilities. Instead, they observe only prices, in which probabilities and utilities are combined differently for every agent. This illustrates a phenomenon which has been studied in the literature of statistical decision theory, namely that observations of material gambling or trading behavior may be insufficient to separate an agent's probabilities from her utilities, particularly when her utilities are state-dependent and/or her prior endowment of state-contingent wealth is unknown (Kadane and Winkler 1988; Schervish, Seidenfeld, and Kadane 1990; Nau 1994a).

Thus, it can be argued that risk neutral probabilities, rather than true probabilities, are the natural objects of common knowledge and common prior assumptions in information economics. In this manner, a great deal of literature on game theory, decision theory, and finance can be unified under the umbrella of no-arbitrage (Nau and McCardle 1991). For example, if the common priors in Aumann's (1976) and Sebenius and Geanakoplos' (1983) agreeing-to-disagree models are reinterpreted as risk neutral distributions, the results take on a simple no-arbitrage characterization (Nau 1994b). The same reinterpretation of the common prior in game theoretic models leads to a refined form of subjective correlated equilibrium, rather than Nash or objective correlated equilibrium, as the natural solution concept, and the outcome-contingent allocation of wealth is guaranteed to be efficient. (A little-noted property of Nash and objective correlated equilibria is that they can produce inefficient *ex ante* wealth allocations in strictly competitive games among risk averse players: the players may be left with incentives to share risks by making side gambles.) Milgrom and Stokey's (1982) no-trade model already assumes common prior risk neutral probabilities on the entire state space, through the assumptions of an *ex ante* Pareto optimal wealth distribution over payoff-relevant events and concordant conditional probabilities for informational events. The conclusion that there will be no subsequent trade contingent on common knowledge events is therefore tautological: the assumed initial conditions are precisely that all incentives to trade contingent claims have already been exhausted.

Of course, this more realistic view of common knowledge priors still refers only to a static characterization of equilibrium. It does not *per se* address issues of market dynamics such as speculative behavior of the effects of price history on beliefs. The authors have rightly called attention to the importance and difficulty of incorporating these concerns into future extensions of arbitrage pricing models. In a world of heterogeneous beliefs and risk preferences, it would of course be even more difficult to model higher-order beliefs explicitly. As a simpler alternative, we could seek to directly model beliefs about future prices and how these beliefs respond to price trajectories, perhaps through simulation as well as analysis.

Robert F. Nau
Fuqua School of Business
Duke University

References

Cox, J. and S. Ross, (1976), 'The Valuation of Options for Alternative Stochastic Processes,' *Journal of Financial Economics*, Vol. 3, pp. 145-166.

Drèze, Jacques, (1970), 'Market Allocation Under Uncertainty,' *European Economic Review*, Vol. 2, pp. 133-165.

Kadane, J. B., and R. L. Winkler, (1988), 'Separating Probability Elicitation from Utilities,' *Journal of the American Statistical Association*, Vol. 83, pp. 357-363.

Nau, Robert F., (1992), 'Joint Coherence in Games of Incomplete Information,' *Management Science*, Vol. 38:3, pp. 374-387.

Nau, Robert F., (1994a), 'Coherent Decision Analysis With Inseparable Probabilities and Utilities,' forthcoming in *Journal of Risk and Uncertainty*.

Nau, Robert F., (1994b), 'The Incoherence of Agreeing to Disagree,' forthcoming in *Theory and Decision*.

Nau, Robert F. and Kevin F. McCardle, (1991), 'Arbitrage, Rationality, and Equilibrium,' *Theory and Decision*, Vol. 31, pp. 199-240.

Schervish, M. J., T. Seidenfeld, and J. B. Kadane, (1990), 'State-Dependent Utilities,' *Journal of the American Statistical Association*, Vol. 85:411, pp. 840-847.

7 Feedback effects and speculative bubbles in informational price theory

7.1 Introduction

Informational price theory (IPT) has become the main paradigm to explain how prices reveal information. In the older efficient markets literature, prevailing market prices were thought to impound all available information. Thus a price change could indicate that an asset was previously under or overpriced but not that it is currently mispriced.[1] In contrast, IPT implies that prices not only clear markets but signal future movements. Prices convey information about expectations for future earnings, so that a rise today may be confirmed by subsequent rises tomorrow - as more and more people learn the private information.

If prices fully reflect information, then no one has any incentive to buy information. Everyone can simply infer information from prices for free. But if no one purchases information, then market prices will reflect no information. Hence everyone will have an incentive to buy information. The obvious solution to this conundrum is that prices only partially reflect information. Grossman and Stiglitz (1976) developed a model that formalizes this logic.

In equilibrium, some fraction of the market pays to become informed and the remaining fraction chooses to infer information from noisy prices.[2] Prices reflect some, but not all, of the private information which the informed traders have purchased. The competitive advantage of knowing the private information compensates the informed for their acquisition cost. At the margin, prices aggregate just enough information such that the last individual to buy information is indifferent between paying for information or attempting to infer it from prices.

The sequence of events in the Grossman and Stiglitz model looks something like this. Informed traders receive good news about some asset, buy the asset in mass, and thereby raise its price. Uninformed traders witness the increase in price, infer that the informed must have received favorable news, and subsequently buy as well. A similar logic applies when the informed receive unfavorable news and sell some asset. The uninformed follow suit. In both instances, purchases or sales by the informed cause a feedback effect by the uninformed.

One example where the uninformed might benefit from mimicking the actions of the informed, without introducing a feedback effect, would be in selecting a restaurant in an unfamiliar city. Visitors (the uninformed) might patronize a restaurant that seemed crowded. They would reason that local residents (the informed) know the prices and quality of food at that restaurant and have chosen to eat there. In this restaurant selection example, the informed derive no benefit from the actions by the uninformed. But in financial markets, capital gains will usually depend on the purchasing activities of other market participants.

The literature on information and prices has identified three basic speculative problems with the IPT approach.[3] First, in judging the quality of goods or services by price, consumers face uncertainty over whether high prices actually indicate superior quality or merely an attempt by the seller to attract consumers. If a consultant charges a high hourly fee, is it because he is superior to other professionals with a lower fee, or merely a speculative attempt to persuade clients into thinking he must be good if he charges that high fee? Only in strictly competitive supply markets would price-taking behavior by sellers limit the opportunities of low quality vendors to fool new consumers with high prices.

Second, attempts at market timing may limit the extent to which the informed act on their information. If someone receives a favorable signal on a stock, should he rush out and buy it? How can he know whether the current price already impounds his private signal? If other traders are planning to sell the stock and realize short term capital gains, he might gain from waiting until the price has fallen with their sales. Hence, no feature of IPT guarantees the informed will immediately act upon their signal.

Third, feedback effects have been thought to unravel the foundations of IPT, as investors then have incentives

> to acquire (and in some cases disseminate) information on the purchasing proclivities of the market as well as on the 'real' factors of earnings, dividends and so forth. What we end up with is a model of a market in which even when favorable information on earnings is available to insiders or informed traders, there is uncertainty as to whether this will be acted

upon; in which 'tulip bulb mania' factors can be important so that rises in prices might reflect only a belief that the market will value the stock higher next period, independent of earnings; and in which the chances of actually ferreting out any information on earnings prospects from observed prices is miniscule (sic). (Burness, Cummings, and Quirk (1980), p.75)

At first glance, this line of criticism would seem to eradicate any application of IPT to financial markets. However, in moving from words to formal models, we find that generating speculative profits off the feedback effect is actually more difficult then it sounds. Uninformed traders are watching prices. In order to realize their speculative profits, informed traders must buy and *resell*, yet their subsequent sales must not dissuade the uninformed from buying as a feedback.

This criticism of IPT also involves questions about strategic interactions usually applied in noncompetitive environments. Grossman and Stiglitz developed their IPT model with perfect competition: traders take prices as given. If purchases by informed traders cause prices to rise, then prices are indeed a strategic variable under the control of the informed agents - even in the original theory. In financial markets, informed traders could then profit from manipulating the market price in order to fool the uninformed into buying or selling as feedback effects. The question then arises as to what modeling tool best captures the essence of IPT and the possibility for this strategic interaction.

One might envision casting the informed agents as Stackelberg leaders with the uninformed agents acting as followers in a game theory model. However, a Stackelberg equilibrium approach would entail some lack of intelligence or rationality on the part of one or more players.[4] The usual IPT dichotomy of intelligence holds that the uninformed traders 'are smart enough'[5] to know the correlation between market price levels and news. Yet the informed traders are *not* smart enough to realize their purchases (sales) induce a feedback effect.[6] In a Stackelberg equilibrium approach, the leader (the informed) would be smart enough to realize his purchases trigger a feedback effect, but the follower (the uninformed fraction) does not consider the leader's strategy in deciding whether to buy. We need a model in which all players act intelligently.

The first solution developed in this chapter is a Bayesian Nash Equilibrium in a game of incomplete information. Informed traders play opposite uninformed traders, each taking the other's strategy as given. The informed group, having incurred the cost of acquiring private information, moves first. The informed group may try to fool the uninformed into believing that asset returns are better than they actually are. Sometimes the deception succeeds. A bubble results, and after the crash is over and the dust has cleared, the informed group turns out to have gained at the expense of the uninformed. Sometimes the deception fails, and the informed traders wind up losing more money than if they had followed a conventional, fundamental-based strategy.

The equilibria of this game, contained in Sections 7.3 through 7.6, indicate the probability that the informed traders acting as a group will collude (i.e., buy when they have received a low signal) as well as the probability that the uninformed, acting as a group, will buy as a feedback effect. To assure that some informed traders do not deviate from the group strategy, and thereby tip off the uninformed, we employ a self-enforcing[7] Nash equilibrium approach. By restricting individual behavior this way, we are limited to a two-player model, which cannot adequately describe the operation of densely populated, competitive markets.

To generalize the model beyond the two-group, two-player model of informational price theory, we examine subjective correlated equilibria in the final sections of this chapter. In this framework, the informed traders receive correlated - though not identical - signals, and all players act as individuals, rather than as members of an orchestrated group. The equilibrium characterizes the *quantity* of the risky asset that each individual selects, rather than the *probability* of purchasing.

Game theoretic analysis rarely applies to competitive markets. 'Anonymous games' are one class of 'competitive' models where the outcome depends on the actions of each agent only through the proportion of agents that acts in a certain way. Like anonymous games, the pure strategy equilibria in this chapter might be interpreted as the frequency of each population that chooses to engage in this strategic play. Under this interpretation, we must consider each informed trader as having, e.g., firm-specific information. Thus one informed trader's private information and strategic use of that information will not affect another informed trader's strategy, because their strategies are focused upon different stocks. However, since no one individual's purchases should affect prices in a competitive market, this interpretation seems unrealistic at best. Thus we have reason to question the competitive market foundation of IPT regardless of the equilibrium concept chosen.

The significance of the results in this chapter are (1) the derivation of speculative bubbles from fully rational, payoff-maximizing behavior on the part of all market participants;[8] (2) the highlighting of an important feature of IPT: the two-player model; (3) a demonstration of the stringent conditions required for the informed traders to derive speculative profits off the feedback effect, thereby attenuating this criticism of IPT; and (4) utilization of some mathematical results by Nikaidô and Isodo that can be used in proofs of the existence of (subjective correlated) equilibria.

Section 7.2 compares our work to related articles in the speculative bubble and asymmetric information literatures. The players and extensive form game are presented in Section 7.3, the payoffs in Section 7.4, and the pure and mixed strategy equilibria in Section 7.5. A negative bubble is illustrated in Section 7.6. Section 7.7 offers an intelligent critique of the Bayesian Nash Equilibrium speculative bubble models. Section 7.8 generalizes the two-player, high-low demand model of the first six sections to allow for multiple strategies and multiple signals like Kyle (1989), and each player acting as an individual. Section 7.9 presents the conclusions and a discussion of the noncompetitive assumptions of the model. Table 7.1 in Section 7.3 conveniently lists the notation used in the Bayesian Nash Equilibria sections of this chapter.

7.2. The Speculative Bubble and Asymmetric Information Literatures

The traditional view of speculative bubbles maintains that they result from irrational behavior by some or all of the market participants [Kindleberger (1989)]. Our model is distinguished from many previous derivations of speculative bubbles in that *all* the market participants are fully intelligent and rational. Blanchard and Watson (1982) and Leach (1991) illustrate bubble formation in which traders will refrain from participating unless they can rationally determine that the last (n^{th}) trader will execute his trade, the n-1st trader will execute his trade, and so on. In these two articles, players may be induced to buy into the speculative bubble by the fact that the bubble may continue to grow indefinitely. Every 'bubble' in our work, by contrast, bursts with probability 1 as the state of the world is revealed.

DeLong et al. (1990) have demonstrated convincingly that perfectly rational speculators can jump on the feedback effect bandwagon and not buck the trend. Speculators in the DeLong et al. model do not worry that some (n^{th}) trader may get stuck holding the overvalued asset. From an expected profit-maximizing viewpoint, they would be foolish to be overly concerned with some distant collapse point, as long as they expect to realize their capital gains while the bubble still exists. Wang (1993) looks at the same basic model as DeLong et al.; however, 'noise trading' is replaced by 'supply shocks.' He finds the existence of investors with imperfect information increases the risk premia on stocks, and investors with different information will adopt different investment strategies.

Friedman and Aoki (1986, 1989) provide parametric examples of bubble formation when investors are oriented towards long-term gains and expectations; traders in their model ignore short-term capital gains and the potential ability to manipulate prices. Friedman and Aoki (1989) have illustrated a negative bubble arising from momentum in price trajectories over time. The Friedman and Aoki bubbles can result from overshooting, which tends to be self-correcting as the game is played over time and the players become more familiar with price escalations.

O'Flaherty (1987) looks at bubbles as nonconstant correlated equilibria in coordination games with asymmetrically informed agents. He finds a bias towards myopic investment and against public revelation of private signals. Similarly, Fishman and Hagerty (1992) show full disclosure of privately held information would lead insider traders to have zero profits. In the absence of a mandatory disclosure rule, security prices will generally not be efficient in transmitting information between informed and uninformed investors.

Fishman and Hagerty's work extends Kyle's (1985) noisy rational expectations model to study the impact of insider trading on price efficiency. In Kyle's model, informed traders strategically choose their transactions knowing their strategies will affect prices. The resulting Nash equilibrium quantity orders show that informed traders optimally choose to withhold some of their information. Kyle never satisfactorily explained why 'noise traders' come into the market and routinely lose their wealth. Nevertheless, numerous authors have adopted Kyle's Walrasian auctioneer and noise trader framework to examine market issues such as intraday patterns in volume and price variability (Admati and Pleiderer 1988), diversification by the uninformed (Bhushan 1991), transaction costs to the uninformed (Subrahmanyam 1991b), and market liquidity and price efficiency (Subrahmanyam 1991a).

Smith, Suchanek, and Williams (1988) and King, Smith, Williams, and Van Boening (1993) have found evidence for bubble creation in experimental markets from 'homegrown capital gains expectations,' which collapse when dividend and fundamental value information becomes common knowledge. Bubble creation in these experimental markets arise more from myopia than from an attempted manipulation of the uninformed based on feedback effects.

Allen and Gorton (1993) consider bubble creation resulting from incentive contracts paid to portfolio managers. The managers in their model receive no income if their portfolios have non-positive returns. However, they get to keep a portion of any positive return they achieve.

This principal-agent contract leads portfolio managers to prefer taking risks and buying assets above their fundamental value on the chance that they will continue to rise.

Portfolio managers and institutional investors are often said to behave like herds. Banerjee (1992) has studied decision rules that depend on the investment strategies of previous decision makers. He shows that the resulting equilibrium is inefficient. People tend to be guided too much by other people's investments, even to the extent of ignoring their own private information. In Banerjee's Bayesian Nash Equilibrium, the order of play is important. The first few players' decisions have a much greater impact on subsequent investment patterns than those of players entering later in the game.

Our paper is most similar to work simultaneously derived by Gorton and Pennacchi (1989), who also develop a game theoretic model of strategic play between informed and uninformed traders. In the Gorton and Pennacchi model, the informed always try to manipulate and the uninformed always buy, whereas in our model this behavior would tend to drive the uninformed traders out of the market.[9] Gorton and Pennacchi focus on the rise of new securities that split the cash flows of underlying assets and on government intervention to protect the uninformed. Our paper focuses more on the differences between this strategic game and the predictions of informational price theory, as well an analysis of the competitive market assumptions.

7.3. Principals and Extensive Form Game

Consider a market containing two assets, one safe and one risky. Let the return, r, to the risky asset depend on a random variable, η, which can be observed at some cost, and another random variable, ϵ, that cannot be observed:

$$r = \eta + \epsilon, \tag{7.1}$$

where η and ϵ are independent, normally distributed random variables. The informed individuals pay to learn the value of η. Some exogenous risk remains from ϵ, but the informed traders have purchased private information that reduces the risk on the asset's return.

Figure 7.1 shows the extensive form game tree. Chance moves *first* by selecting the value of η. To simplify the game tree, we consider only high or low signals: η_H or η_L.

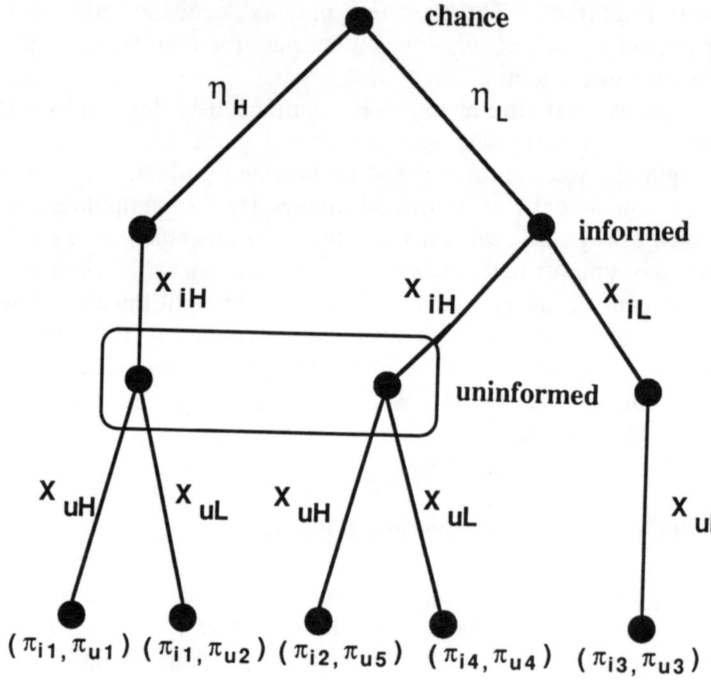

Figure 7.1. Bayes Game of Information Inference Through Prices

The informed traders move *second*. They know the value of η and must select a purchasing strategy for the risky asset. If they receive the signal η_H, we assume the informed traders will have high demand (X_{iH}) for the risky asset to collect the real earnings, just as in IPT. Section 7.6 relaxes this assumption and shows how 'negative bubbles' can be formed. When the earnings signal is η_L, the informed traders must choose whether to exploit the feedback effect. Their expected profits depend on the purchasing proclivities of the uninformed.

The uninformed traders move *third* by choosing a high or low quantity purchase. They observe the price level after the informed traders have moved but not the private signal selected by chance. The uninformed traders can always infer η_L when the informed traders bid low demand (X_{iL}). Consequently, the uninformed will respond with low demand in this scenario. Typically, the uninformed will infer the informed traders have chosen high demand and wonder if they should do likewise.

In Figure 7.1, an information set surrounds two nodes that are indistinguishable to the uninformed.[10] The uninformed traders use Bayes' Rule to infer the real (correct) versus purely speculative (incorrect) prospects for the asset's earnings. Informed traders who have purchased solely to exploit capital gains off the feedback effect will sell off their speculative holdings at the same time that the uninformed are buying. The uninformed cannot observe the informed traders' sales, because traders can only see market clearing prices not the limit orders submitted in advance to the market. Following these moves the game ends. Traders realize payoffs according to the strategies they adopt.

Per capita demand, $X_i(\eta,P,\beta)$, for the risky asset by the informed will vary inversely with the price, P, of the risky asset: $\partial X_i / \partial P < 0$. However, unlike in IPT, we cannot say that $\partial X_i / \partial \eta > 0$. The informed traders may submit either a high or a low demand schedule upon receiving a low signal. Informed trader demand will also depend on β, which is the probability that the uninformed will buy as a feedback effect. Let α denote the probability that the informed will buy the risky asset even though they have learned η_L. For the reader's convenience, Table 7.1 lists the notation used in the next three sections of this chapter.

Demand must equal supply each period in equilibrium:

$$\lambda \ X_i(\eta,P,\beta) + (1-\lambda) \ X_u(P,\alpha) = X^s, \tag{2}$$

where λ is the fraction of the traders who are informed, X_u is the per

Table 7.1. Bayes Game Notation

Symbol	Definition
ρ_L	(objective) prior probability of a low signal, η_L.
ρ_H	(objective) prior probability of a high signal, η_H.
X_{iH}	high demand for the risky asset by the informed traders.
X_{iL}	low demand for the risky asset by the informed traders.
X_{uH}	high demand for the risky asset by the uninformed traders.
X_{uL}	low demand for the risky asset by the uninformed traders.
α	the probability that the informed traders will buy when they have received a low signal, $\Pr(X_{iH} \mid \eta_L)$.
α^*	the value of α that leaves the uninformed traders indifferent between their strategies of purchasing the risky asset upon witnessing the informed traders have purchased (and have high demand).
β	the probability that the uninformed traders will purchase when they infer the informed traders have bought the risky asset, $\Pr(X_{uH} \mid X_{iH})$.
β^*	the value of β that leaves the informed individuals indifferent between their strategies (of various probabilities α) of trying to manipulate the uninformed traders.
z	the value of ρ_L which sets $\alpha^* = 1$.
Section 7.6: Negative Bubble	
γ	the probability the informed traders will show low demand when they have received a high signal, $\Pr(X_{iL} \mid \eta_H)$.
δ	the probability that the uninformed traders will have low demand when they infer the informed traders had low demand, $\Pr(X_{uL} \mid X_{iL})$.

capita demand by the uninformed, and X^s is the per capita supply of the asset.

Before deriving the Bayesian Nash Equilibrium of this game of incomplete information, we can intuitively conclude that if β were sufficiently large, it would always pay for the informed traders to try to take advantage of the uninformed. If β were sufficiently small, so that the feedback effect was small, then the informed traders would seldom gain from attempting to manipulate the uninformed. Consequently, if β were known to be small, then α would be small.

By specifying a range for the exogenous parameters in the model, we will initially focus on the interior solution where both $0 < \alpha < 1$ and $0 < \beta < 1$. The latter condition implies that the uninformed still expect to profit from sometimes buying when they infer the informed have bought.

A speculative bubble is defined as an increase in an asset's price above its fundamental value, based on the information available in the market. The interior solution illustrates one of many speculative bubble equilibria in our model. Speculative bubbles arise here from *fully rational*, payoff-maximizing behavior by all players. These price bubbles stem from informed traders buying the risky asset when they know the earnings signal is η_L, and the uninformed individuals choosing a high demand in response, which drives the price of the risky asset above its fundamental value (conditioned on η_L).

7.4. Payoffs from Alternative Strategies

The payoffs are shown in parentheses at the bottom of the extensive form game tree, Figure 7.1. The first element in the parentheses gives the informed traders' payoff, and the second element is the uninformed traders' payoff. The following assumptions state the relative magnitudes of the payoffs.

Assumption 1: $\pi_{ij} > 0$ and $\pi_{uk} > 0$ for all $j \in \{1,2,3,4\}$, $k \in \{1,2,3,4,5\}$.

Assumption 2: $\pi_{i1} > \pi_{i2} > \pi_{i3} > \pi_{i4}$.

Assumption 3: $\pi_{u1} > \pi_{u2} > \pi_{u3} > \pi_{u4} > \pi_{u5}$.

Assumption 1 states that, in any event, both informed and uninformed traders earn positive profits. This assumption explains why uninformed traders are willing to play the game. The key part of Assumption 2 states informed traders with low signals receive a higher payoff (π_{i2}) if they can successfully fool the uninformed than if they follow the IPT strategy of honestly revealing their signal with low demand purchases (π_{i3}). Without this payoff structure, the informed traders would have no reason to try to capitalize on the feedback effect.

The key to Assumption 3 is that the uninformed receive a higher payoff when they buy high (π_{u1}) and the signal is η_H than when they buy low and the signal is η_L: π_{u3}. If this relationship did not hold, the uninformed traders would always be better off choosing low demand. The fact that they sometimes receive higher payoffs from choosing high demand and collecting real returns actually induces the uninformed to play this speculative feedback game.

The informed receive their second highest payoff (π_{i2}) when the signal is η_L, and they show high demand for the risky asset (X_{iH}), and succeed in fooling the uninformed. This payoff derives from the capital gains realized when the uninformed traders drive up the risky asset price with their high demand.

Obviously, for the informed traders to realize a capital gain, the aggregate demand for the risky asset - both informed selling and uninformed buying - must move outward. Either the uninformed must significantly outnumber the informed, or the informed hold a smaller percentage of the purchasing power in the market.

The informed traders receive the third highest payoff (π_{i3}) when they respond with low demand to the signal η_L. The risky asset then has a low return, but the informed have cut their exposure. If they attempt to take advantage of the feedback effect and fail, then the informed receive (π_{i4}), which is their lowest payoff in the game. In this worst case scenario for the informed, they get a low price for the risky asset which they hold in large quantities.

The uninformed traders receive their two highest payoffs when the risky asset has high earnings (η_H). The worst payoff for the uninformed, (π_{u5}), comes when the informed successfully fool them into bidding high (X_{uH}) even though the signal is η_L.

Definition 1: The *expected payoff* to the informed traders when they receive a low signal, η_L, is $V^i(\alpha;\beta) = \alpha\ [\ \beta\ \pi_{i2} + (1 - \beta)\ \pi_{i4}\ ] + (1 - \alpha)\ \pi_{i3}$. The expected payoff to uninformed traders who witness high prices is $V^u(\beta;\alpha,X_{iH}) = \beta\ [Pr\ (\eta_L|X_{iH})\ \pi_{u5} + Pr\ (\eta_H|X_{iH})\ \pi_{u1}\ ] + (1 - \beta)[Pr\ (\eta_L|X_{iH})\ \pi_{u4} + Pr(\eta_H|X_{iH})\ \pi_{u2}\ ]$.

Notice that both $V^i(\alpha;\beta)$ and $V^u(\beta;\alpha,X_{iH})$ are continuous in their respective choice arguments, α and β, over the interval [0,1]. We can therefore invoke Brower's Fixed Point Theorem to prove the following preliminary lemma on the existence of an equilibrium.

Lemma 1: There exists unique $\alpha' \in [0,1]$ and $\beta' \in [0,1]$ which maximize $V^i(\alpha;\beta)$ and $V^u(\beta;\alpha,X_{iH})$, respectively.

From the Kuhn-Tucker conditions for maximums occurring at the limits of a range, α' is defined by

$$\alpha' = 0 \text{ and } \quad \beta\,\pi_{i2} + (1-\beta)\,\pi_{i4} - \pi_{i3} < 0, \tag{7.5}$$

$$\text{or} \quad \alpha' = 1 \text{ and } \quad \beta\,\pi_{i2} + (1-\beta)\,\pi_{i4} - \pi_{i3} > 0, \tag{7.6}$$

$$\text{or} \quad \alpha' \in [0,1] \text{ and } \quad \beta\,\pi_{i2} + (1-\beta)\,\pi_{i4} - \pi_{i3} = 0, \tag{7.7}$$

Similarly, the Kuhn-Tucker conditions for β' are given by

$$\beta' = 0 \quad \text{and}$$

$$Pr(\eta_L\,|X_{iH})(\pi_{u5} - \pi_{u4}) + Pr(\eta_H\,|X_{iH})(\pi_{u1} - \pi_{u2}) < 0, \tag{7.8}$$

$$\text{or} \quad \beta' = 1 \quad \text{and}$$

$$Pr(\eta_L\,|X_{iH})(\pi_{u5} - \pi_{u4}) + Pr(\eta_H\,|X_{iH})(\pi_{u1} - \pi_{u2}) > 0, \tag{7.9}$$

$$\text{or} \quad \beta' \in [0,1] \quad \text{and}$$

$$Pr(\eta_L\,|X_{iH})(\pi_{u5} - \pi_{u4}) + Pr(\eta_H\,|X_{iH})(\pi_{u1} - \pi_{u2}) = 0. \tag{7.10}$$

Conditions (7.5) through (7.7) state that informed traders who receive low signals will always bid low demand for the risky asset ($\alpha' = 0$), always try to exploit the feedback effect ($\alpha' = 1$), or be indifferent between these strategies ($\alpha' \in [0,1]$) depending on whether the profit from bidding low, π_{i3}, exceeds the expected profit from attempting to exploit the feedback effect, $\beta\,\pi_{i2} + (1-\beta)\,\pi_{i4}$.

Conditions (7.8) through (7.10) state that uninformed traders inferring high demand by the informed traders from prices will always mimic their purchases ($\beta' = 1$), always bid low demand ($\beta' = 0$), or be indifferent between these strategies ($\beta' \in [0,1]$) depending on the expected profits from bidding high.

7.5. Bayesian Nash Equilibrium in Pure Strategies

The problem set out in Section 7.3 (that of determining an optimal investment strategy in light of the feedback effect generated by informed traders' purchases), with payoffs defined in Section 7.4, can be modeled and solved using game theory. The solution for games with incomplete information is the Bayesian Nash Equilibrium introduced by Harsanyi (1967).

Definition 2: The *strategy space* for trading group j is $S_j = [0,1]$. A pure strategy for the informed (i) traders is a scalar $\alpha \in S_i$, and for the uninformed (u) traders is a scaler $\beta \in S_u$.[11]

Definition 3: The *set of best responses* for the informed traders to β is $\phi_i(\beta) = \{\alpha \in S_i \mid V^i(\alpha;\beta) \geq V^i(\alpha';\beta) \;\; \forall\, \alpha' \in S_i\}$. The set of best responses for the uninformed traders to α is $\phi_u(\alpha) = \{\beta \in S_u \mid V^u(\beta;\alpha,X_{iH}) \geq V^u(\beta';\alpha,X_{iH}) \;\; \forall\; \beta' \in S_u\}$.

The functions $\phi_i : S_u \to S_i$ and $\phi_u : S_i \to S_u$ are the best response correspondence for the informed and uninformed traders, respectively.

Assumption 4: The uninformed traders use Bayes' Rule to compute $Pr\,(\eta_L|X_{iH})$ and $Pr\,(\eta_H|X_{iH})$.

Definition 4: The informed traders behave as a *self-enforcing Nash coalition* if in either state η_H or η_L, any subset of the informed traders chooses to abide by the per capita demand assigned by the whole informed group.

Assumption 5: The informed traders act as a self-enforcing Nash coalition in choosing their strategy $\alpha \in S_i$.

Assumption 5 guarantees that no individual informed trader, or any subset of them, will deviate from the group's strategy and thereby tip off the uninformed traders. For the case of η_H, no informed individual would benefit from choosing low demand instead, because he would end up with a smaller quantity of the risky asset when its earnings will be high. The uninformed traders know what the risky asset's price will be when all the informed traders exhibit high demand. If any individual informed trader deviates from the high bid collusion when the signal is η_L, he would spoil the potential feedback profits not only for the rest of the informed group but for himself. In Section 7.7, we will return to the limitations imposed by this assumption.

Definition 5: A strategy pair (α^*,β^*) is a *Nash Equilibrium* for the game $G = (V^i, V^u, S_i, S_u)$ if

(a) $\alpha^* \in S_i$ and $\beta^* \in S_u$;

(b) $V^i(\alpha^*;\beta^*) \geq V^i(\alpha;\beta^*) \quad \forall \quad \alpha \in S_i$; and

(c) $V^u(\beta^*;\alpha^*,X_{iH}) \geq V^u(\beta;\alpha^*,X_{iH}) \quad \forall \quad \beta \in S_u$.

Alternatively, the pair (α^*,β^*) is a *Nash Equilibrium* if $\alpha^* \in \phi_i(\beta^*)$ and $\beta^* \in \phi_u(\alpha^*)$: each strategy is a best response to the other.

Let ρ_L denote the prior $Pr(\eta_L)$.

Theorem 1: Under Assumptions 1 through 4, there exists a Bayesian Nash equilibrium in pure strategies given by

$$(\alpha^*,\beta^*) = \left[\left(\frac{\pi_{u2} - \pi_{u1}}{\pi_{u5} - \pi_{u4}}\right)\left(\frac{1 - \rho_L}{\rho_L}\right), \frac{\pi_{i3} - \pi_{i4}}{\pi_{i2} - \pi_{i4}} \right].$$

Proof: From condition (7.7) we know that for an interior solution for α,

$$\beta \, \pi_{i2} + (1 - \beta) \, \pi_{i4} - \pi_{i3} = 0. \qquad \textbf{(7.11)}$$

Define β^* as that probability that leaves the informed traders who receive a low signal indifferent between attempting to exploit the feedback effect or not. Then solving (7.11) for β^* yields

$$\beta^* = \frac{\pi_{i3} - \pi_{i4}}{\pi_{i2} - \pi_{i4}}. \qquad \textbf{(7.12)}$$

To obtain an interior solution for β, it is necessary but not sufficient from condition (7.10) that $\beta \in [0,1]$ and $Pr(\eta_L|S_{iH})(\pi_{u5} - \pi_{u4}) + Pr(\eta_H|X_{iH})(\pi_{u1} - \pi_{u2}) = 0$. Given $\rho_L + \rho_H = 1$ and Assumption 4, $Pr(\eta_L|X_{iH}) = \dfrac{\alpha\ \rho_L}{\alpha\ \rho_L + 1\ \rho_H} = \dfrac{\alpha\ \rho_L}{\alpha\ \rho_L + (1 - \rho_L)}$. Substituting this latter expression for $Pr(\eta_L|X_{iH})$ in equation (7.10), and recognizing $Pr(\eta_L|X_{iH}) + Pr(\eta_H|X_{iH}) = 1$, yields

$$\begin{aligned}&\alpha\rho_L(\pi_{u5} - \pi_{u4} - \pi_{u1} + \pi_{u2})\\&- (\pi_{u2} - \pi_{u1})[\alpha\rho_L + (1 - \rho_L)] = 0.\end{aligned} \tag{7.13}$$

Solving (7.13) for that value of α that leaves uninformed traders facing a high demand by the informed traders indifferent between choosing high demand or not, we obtain

$$\alpha^* = \left(\frac{\pi_{u2} - \pi_{u1}}{\pi_{u5} - \pi_{u4}}\right)\left(\frac{1 - \rho_L}{\rho_L}\right). \tag{7.14}$$

By definition of the Kuhn-Tucker conditions (7.7) and (7.10), $V^i(\alpha^*;\beta^*) = V^i(\alpha;\beta^*)\ \forall\ \alpha \in [0,1]$, and $V^u(\beta^*;\alpha^*,X_{iH}) = V^u(\beta;\alpha^*,X_{iH})\ \forall\ \beta \in [0,1]$. Therefore, $V^i(\alpha^*;\beta^*) \geq V^i(\alpha;\beta^*)$ and $V^u(\beta^*;\alpha^*,X_{iH}) \geq V^u(\beta;\alpha^*,X_{iH})$ so that (α^*,β^*) is a Nash equilibrium with α^* computed using Bayesian inference. ‖

Equation (7.12) is the informed traders' reaction function when they have received a low signal, η_L. If $\beta > \beta^*$, informed traders would always try to take advantage of the feedback effect. The informed traders do not behave this way because they are inherently bad people. Rather, this strategy simply maximizes their objective function. If the uninformed traders chose X_{uH} with probability $\beta < \beta^*$, the informed traders would never expect to gain from attempting to fool the uninformed; consequently, in these circumstances $\alpha = 0$.

The value of equation (7.14), the uninformed traders' reaction function, depends on the magnitude of ρ_L. In particular, the right-hand side of (7.14) is greater than or equal to 0. However, it may also exceed unity. In this case $\alpha \leq 1 < \alpha^*$, and optimality condition (7.9) would apply so that $\beta = 1$, which is a boundary solution. Figure 7.2 illustrates the interior solution for $\alpha^* < 1$. The informed and uninformed traders' reaction functions intersect at the Bayesian Nash equilibrium, (α^*,β^*).

In Figure 7.2, when $\alpha < \alpha^*$, the uninformed traders will always choose high demand ($\beta = 1$) after inferring X_{iH}, because α is sufficiently small. When $\alpha = \alpha^*$, all of the uninformed traders' strategies, or mixtures of them, result in the same expected payoff. Thus the optimal uninformed traders' reaction function at $\alpha = \alpha^*$ is the entire interval $\beta \in [0,1]$. Finally, when $\alpha > \alpha^*$ the uninformed traders never choose high demand ($\beta = 0$). These facts give the uninformed traders' reaction function a stepwise appearance.

Since the right-hand side of (7.14) depends on ρ_L, the following set of propositions clarify the Bayesian Nash equilibria under varying prior probability specifications. First observe that for some value of ρ_L the equilibrium value of α^* is set equal to 1. Let $\rho_L = z$ denote this value, then

$$z = \frac{\pi_{u2} - \pi_{u1}}{\pi_{u5} - \pi_{u4} + \pi_{u2} - \pi_{u1}} .$$

Proposition 1: If $\rho_L = 1$, the Bayesian Nash Equilibrium of the game is $(\alpha^*,\beta^*) = (0,0)$.

Proof: If $\rho_L = 1$, then from (7.14), $\alpha^* = 0$ and

$$Pr(\eta_L|X_{iH}) = \frac{\alpha\ (1)}{\alpha(1) + 1\ (0)} = 1.$$

Accordingly, $Pr(\eta_L|X_{iH})(\pi_{u5} - \pi_{u4}) + Pr(\eta_H|X_{iH})(\pi_{u1} - \pi_{u2}) = \pi_{u5} - \pi_{u4} < 0$; therefore $\beta = 0$ for all $\alpha \in [0,1]$, which implies $\beta\ \pi_{i2} + (1 - \beta)\pi_{i4} - \pi_{i3} < 0$ and $\alpha = 0$. Thus $0 \in \phi_i(0)$ and $0 \in \phi_u(0)$ so that each strategy is a best response to the other.

The equilibrium of Proposition 1 is shown in Figure 7.3. Proposition 1 states that when $\rho_L = 1$, the uninformed traders know with certainty that high demand by the informed (X_{iH}) is merely an attempt to speculate off the feedback effect. Consequently, the uninformed traders would never choose high demand ($\beta = 0$), which in turn leads to $\alpha = 0$.

Note that in both Figure 7.2 and Figure 7.3, the shape of the informed traders' reaction function remains the same; only the uninformed traders'

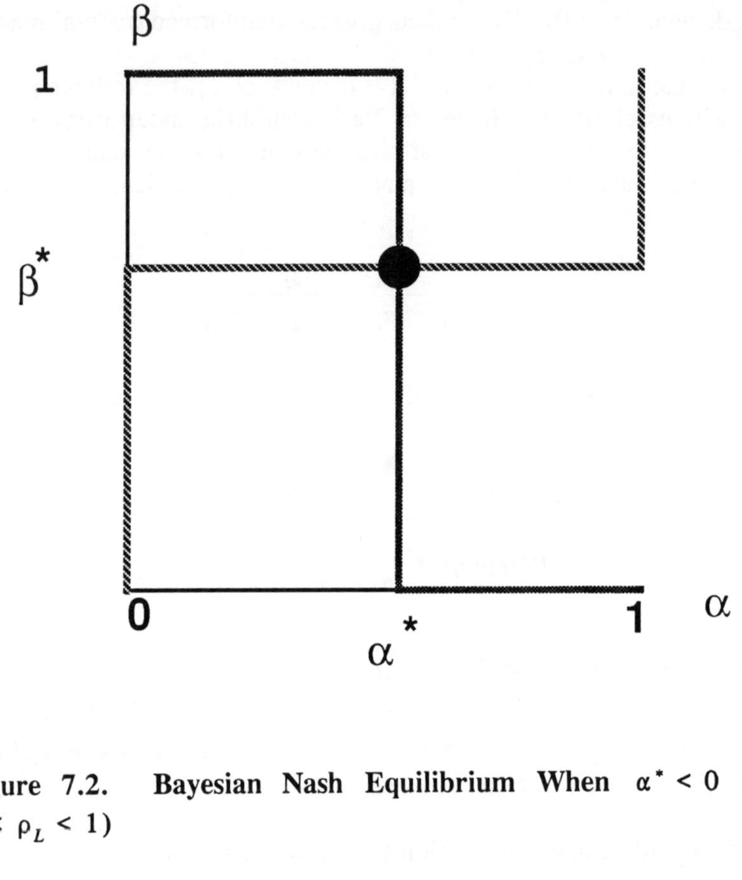

Figure 7.2. Bayesian Nash Equilibrium When $\alpha^* < 0$ (and $z < \rho_L < 1$)

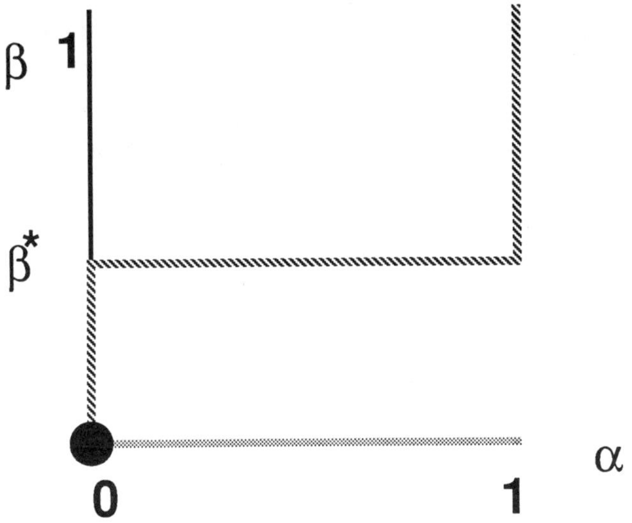

Figure 7.3. Bayesian Nash Equilibrium When $\rho_L = 1$

reaction function has changed. It now lies along the ordinate axis in the unit quadrant. This position signifies that $\beta = 0$ for all values of $\alpha \in [0,1]$. The following proposition merely restates the condition for $\alpha^* < 1$, which yields the equilibrium previously shown in Figure 7.2.

Proposition 2: If $z < \rho_L < 1$, then (α^*, β^*) are defined in Theorem 1.

Proof: The condition $z < \rho_L < 1$ is necessary and sufficient to ensure $0 < \alpha^* < 1$ from (7.14). It then follows that $0 < \beta^* < 1$ by equation (7.12) and Assumption 2.

Proposition 3: If $\rho_L = z$, the Bayesian Nash equilibria are given by $\alpha = 1$ and $\beta \in [\beta^*, 1]$.

Proof: By definition when $\rho_L = z$, $\alpha^* = 1$. This value for α^* implies $V^u(1;\ \alpha<1, X_{iH}) \geq V^u(\beta;\ \alpha<1, X_{iH})$ and $V^u(\beta; 1, X_{iH}) = V^u(\beta'; 1, X_{iH})$ for all $\beta, \beta' \in S_u$, from the uninformed traders' perspective. For the informed traders taking β as given and for all $\beta' \geq \beta^*$, $V^i(1; \beta') \geq$

$V^i(\alpha;\beta')$ for all $\alpha \in S_i$, and in particular $V^i(1;\beta^*) = V^i(\alpha;\beta^*)$ for $\alpha \neq 1$. For all $\beta' < \beta^*$, $\beta' \pi_{i2} + (1 - \beta) \pi_{i4} - \pi_{i3} < 0$, and $\alpha = 0$. Therefore, the mixed strategy Bayesian Nash equilibria will be given by $\alpha = 1$ together with any value of β in the interval $[\beta^*, 1]$.

Proposition 3 shows that when $\alpha^* = 1$, the uninformed traders will be indifferent between any of their strategies ($\beta \in [0,1]$) at the value of $\alpha = 1$. For any value of $\alpha < 1$, the response $\beta = 1$ will be the uninformed traders' dominant strategy. Thus the uninformed traders' optimal reaction function comprises the upper border ($\beta = 1$) and the right border ($\beta \in [0,1]$) of the unit quadrant. The informed traders optimally react with $\alpha = 1$ to values of β on the interval $[\beta^*, 1]$. Again, the informed traders' stepwise reaction function remains the same shape in Figure 7.4 as in the two previous figures. The multiple equilibria, at the intersection of the informed and uninformed traders' reaction functions, are shown in Figure 7.4 by a darkened line connecting endpoints (1,1) and $(1,\beta^*)$.

Proposition 4: If $0 \leq \rho_L < z$, then the Bayesian Nash equilibrium of the game is $(\alpha,\beta) = (1,1)$.

Proof: The condition $0 \leq \rho_L < z$ implies $\alpha^* > 1$ from (7.14). Thus the uninformed traders will always choose $\beta = 1$, which in turn induces the informed traders to set $\alpha = 1$ as a best response. Since each strategy in the pair $(\alpha,\beta) = (1,1)$ is a best response to the other strategy, (1,1) is a Bayesian Nash equilibrium.

Figure 7.5 shows the equilibrium of Proposition 4. When the (objective) prior probability of a low signal is sufficiently small ($\rho_L < z$), the uninformed traders always choose high demand: $\beta = 1$, which is why the uninformed traders' reaction function appears as a straight line on the upper border of the unit quadrant. The informed traders, taking $\beta = 1$ as given, will always profit from exploiting the feedback effect ($\alpha = 1$).

The informational asymmetry and the feedback effect permit the informed to exploit speculative bubble profits off uninformed traders in every scenario except $\rho_L = 1$. Propositions 1 through 4 developed

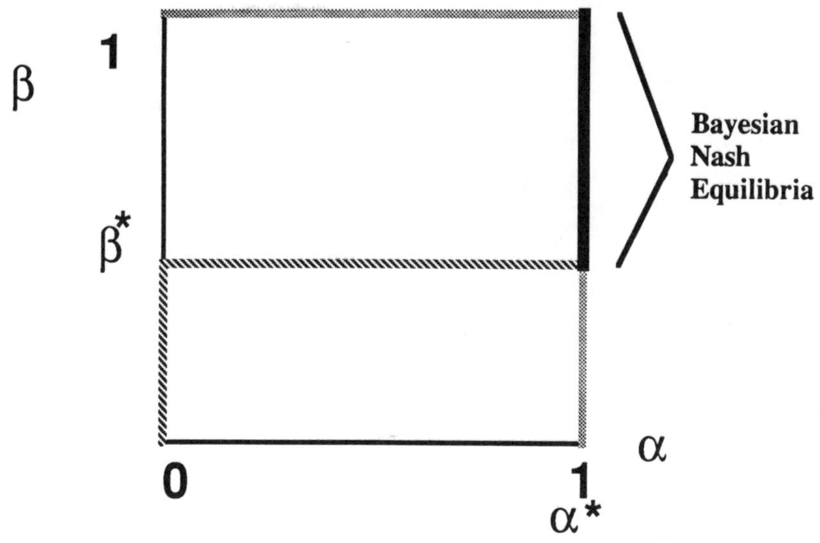

Figure 7.4. Bayesian Nash Equilibria When $\rho_L = z$

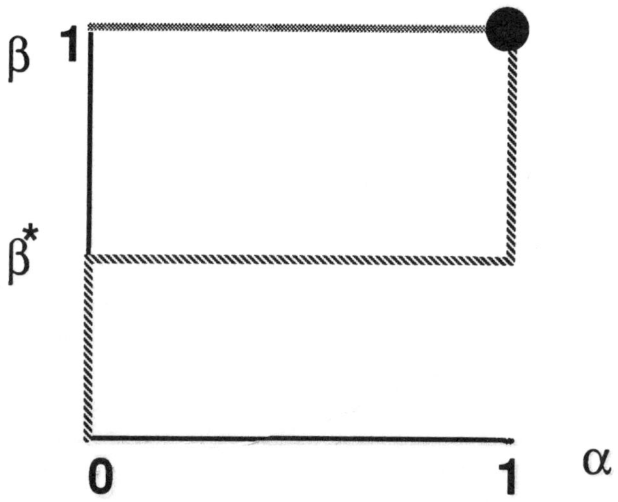

Figure 7.5. Bayesian Nash Equilibria When $0 \leq \rho_L < z$

comparative statics for changes in ρ_L. Corollary 1 summarizes what happens when payoffs change.

Corollary 1: (a) $\dfrac{\partial\alpha^*}{\partial(\pi_{u2} - \pi_{u1})} > 0;$ (b) $\dfrac{\partial\alpha^*}{\partial(\pi_{u5} - \pi_{u4})} < 0;$

(c) $\dfrac{\partial\beta^*}{\partial(\pi_{i3} - \pi_{i4})} > 0;$ and (d) $\dfrac{\partial\beta^*}{\partial(\pi_{i2} - \pi_{i4})} < 0.$

Corollary 1 shows that the spread in potential profits to one group influences the other group's decision to purchase. For example, part (a) indicates that as the profit margin widens for uninformed traders to gain from feedback buying; the informed traders, who are aware of this incentive, respond by increasing α.

We will conclude this section by commenting on two special kinds of Nash equilibria. Since the information set surrounding the informed traders' high demand nodes occurs with positive probability, the Nash equilibrium of this Bayes game will also be Trembling-Hand Perfect [Selten (1975) and Simon (1987)]. Furthermore, because the information set connects all the tree branches, this Bayes game has no subgame short of the entire tree itself. Therefore, the concept of a Subgame Perfect Equilibrium [Hellwig and Leininger (1987)] does not apply to our model.

7.6. Negative Bubbles: The Symmetric Game

Feedback effects can also induce speculative selling. When the signal comes up favorable, (η_H), the informed traders might try to fool the uninformed into thinking earnings are low. If sales by the informed traders trigger subsequent sales by the uninformed, the informed might be able to repurchase these assets at a lower price than they sold them.

Figure 7.6 illustrates an extensive form game, which is symmetrical to the game form in Figure 7.1. Whereas previously the feedback effects created a positive bubble, the symmetric game depicts a negative bubble: a deviation of the price of the risky asset *below* its fundamental value conditioned on the information available to the market.

A closed-end investment trust illustrates an asset with a negative bubble. Despite numerous attempts to explain the mispricing, it remains an unsolved puzzle in finance theory even today. These trusts almost always have a market value less than their liquidation value. See

Thompson (1978) and Weiss, Lehn, and Malmquist (1989). As a general rule, closed-end funds with unrealized capital gains as well as those with capital appreciation objectives tend to have higher mispricing discounts. Closed-end funds that seek to maximize current income sell for comparatively smaller discounts over their liquidation value. Finally, the generally lackluster performance of the New York stock market in the 1970s may represent a macroeconomic negative bubble on stocks vis-à-vis the bond and money markets.

Figure 7.6 shows that informed traders who speculate after receiving a high signal can obtain a higher profit (π_{i1}) than if they followed the safer strategy of choosing high demand, which leads to profits of π_{i2}. Of course, the higher profits come at the expense of greater risk of failure. If the uninformed knew the earnings signal was low (η_L), they would show low demand. Thus the uninformed in this game do not have a dominant strategy in always choosing high demand, X_{uH}.

Together, these two payoff structures pose the following decision problem to informed traders who have received a high signal: should they pretend the signal is low by exhibiting low demand? Let γ denote the probability $Pr(X_{iL}|\eta_H)$. Uninformed traders drawing Bayesian inferences from prices face a related question of whether to choose low demand simply because the informed have. Let δ denote this probability of choosing low demand as a feedback effect.

Theorem 2: There exists a Bayesian Nash Equilibrium in pure strategies given by

$$(\gamma^*,\delta^*) = \left[\left(\frac{\pi_{u1} - \pi_{u3}}{\pi_{u4} - \pi_{u5}} \right) \left(\frac{1 - \rho_H}{\rho_H} \right), \frac{\pi_{i2} - \pi_{i3}}{\pi_{i1} - \pi_{i3}} \right].$$

Proof: Follows analogous steps to the proof of Theorem 1 by maximizing with respect to γ the expected payoff

$$V^i(\gamma;\delta) = \gamma \; [\; \delta\pi_{i1} + (1-\delta)\pi_{i3} \,] + (1-\gamma) \; \pi_{i2};$$

maximizing with respect to δ the expected payoff

$$V^u(\delta;\gamma,X_{iL}) = \delta \left[Pr(\eta_L|X_{iL}) \; \pi_{u4} + Pr(\eta_H|S_{iL}) \; \pi_{u3} \right]$$

$$+ (1-\delta) \left[Pr(\eta_L|X_{iL}) \; \pi_{u5} + Pr(\eta_H|X_{iL})\pi_{u1} \right];$$

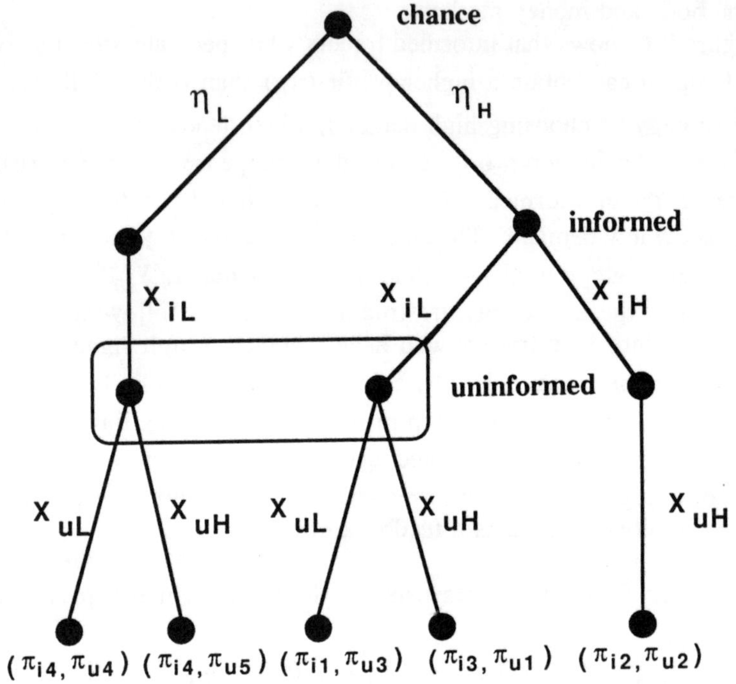

Figure 7.6. Extensive Form Game for Negative Bubbles

and solving for an interior solution. The applicable form of Bayes' Rule for this game will be

$$Pr(\eta_L | X_{iL}) = \frac{\gamma \rho_H}{\gamma \rho_H + 1 \rho_L} = \frac{\gamma \rho_H}{\gamma \rho_H + (1 - \rho_H)} .$$

Theorem 2 shows the creation of a negative bubble from general equilibrium, payoff-maximizing behavior. With some equilibrium probability $\gamma^* > 0$, the informed traders will attempt to exploit capital gains off the uninformed traders' feedback effect when the informed signal is high. With equilibrium probability $\delta^* > 0$, the uninformed are induced into choosing low demand as a strategy upon witnessing low demand by the informed. The combined low demand drives the price of the risky asset below its market fundamental conditioned on η_H.

7.7 Critique of the Bayesian Nash Equilibrium Approach[12]

Some critics of IPT have characterized it as having an 'air of unreality.' However, the orchestrated manipulations by the informed traders, which were covered in Sections 7.3 through 7.6, strike us as even more unrealistic. In trying to use this analysis to understand securities markets, it may be helpful to list some of the obstacles we have confronted.

Payoffs. We specified the payoffs *a priori*, so that each player could determine not only his optimal strategy but also his opponent's optimal strategy under the varying states of the world. These payoffs are the π_i and π_u vectors. In a numerical example, we could fix the various quantities required for market clearing as well as an initial equilibrium price. High demand by the informed traders would lead to excess demand at the current price. The market would clear only with an increase in price. We could then record the cost basis and, eventually, the capital gains for all traders' transactions.

In principle, these payoffs should be independent of the pure and mixed strategies chosen by the two groups. Although the payoff vectors could be transformed into real numbers once we specify the other model parameters, we have left them as ranked variables. One of the rankings provides that the informed traders with a low earnings signal receive a higher payoff if they successfully fool the uninformed than if they simply follow the IPT strategy of exhibiting low demand: $\pi_{i2} > \pi_{i3}$. As previously mentioned, this relationship could only hold if the informed traders realize their capital gains. To do this, the informed must be able to sell their speculative purchases without being detected. However, the uninformed must infer (detect) when the informed have bought.

We rely on the sequence of play to mask the sales order: uninformed traders do not realize the informed have sold until they see the next market clearing price. Then it is too late. Thus for completeness, the two extensive form game trees (Figures 7.1 and 7.6) should contain an additional, simultaneous move by the informed (at the same time as the uninformed move) on the one branch of the tree where the informed try to fool the uninformed.

The need for specified payoffs at the bottom of the tree severely limits the Nash equilibrium approach. In financial markets, payoffs from investments can rarely be written in advance. For that reason, I remain disillusioned with game theory, in general, as a useful tool for explaining how financial markets operate. Consider, for example, what happens if we combine Figures 7.1 and 7.6, so that the informed traders can attempt to create a speculative bubble regardless of the signal. Figure 7.7 shows the generalized game tree with two information sets. Note the tree contains no payoffs at the bottom. Depending on how we choose to specify payoffs, we can either replicate the positive and negative bubble equilibria or we can eliminate the bubble paths (branches of the tree) from consideration. Thus the bubble results are very sensitive to how we specify the payoffs.

Two-Player, High-Low Limitations. The mathematics of the formal model as well as Figures 7.1 through 7.6 all apply to two-player games. However, the informal comments in this chapter describe many traders who belong to one of two groups: the informed and the uninformed. This two-player environment corresponds precisely with Informational Price Theory. Instead of criticizing the relevance of the two-player framework for populated markets, we can consider ways to generalize the model.

Each of the traders should have a continuum of strategies, not just high or low demand. Individual informed traders should receive correlated but not uniform information signals. The solution for such an economy could then be either a separating or a pooling equilibrium. The separating equilibrium would be a victory for the efficient markets hypothesis. The pooling equilibrium, in which one or more informed traders sells his information to one or more of the uninformed, would not be efficient. It would also not lead to speculative bubbles, since the informed traders share news about the low signal.

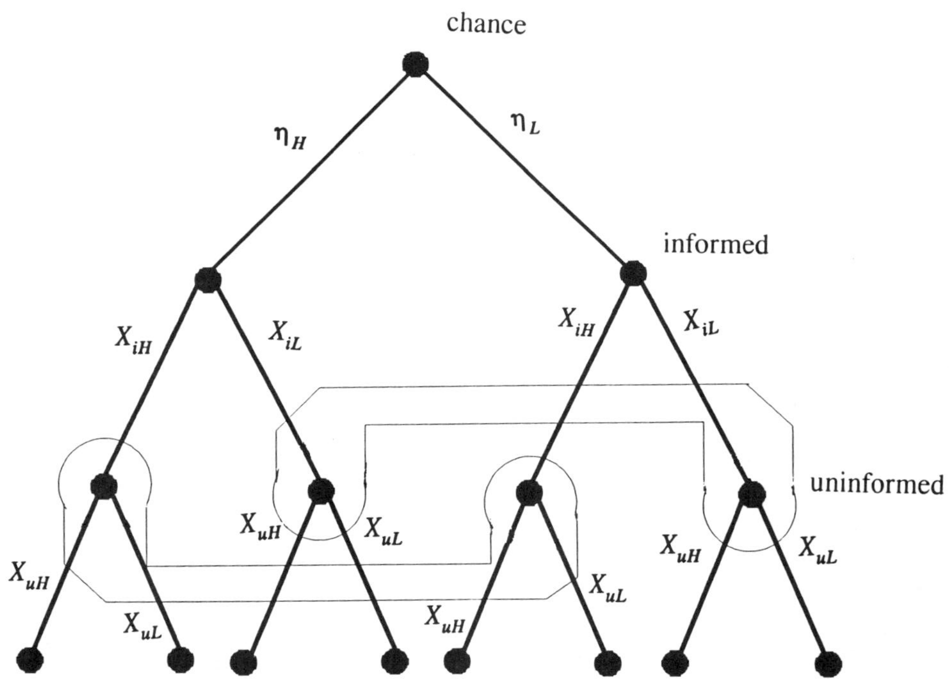

Figure 7.7. Generalized Bayes Game in Extensive Form With Unspecified Payoffs

Our bubble results thus appear to rely on the underlying discrete (high or low) purchase decisions. We initially viewed the high-low quantity choice as a minor simplification; now it turns out to be more crucial than expected. Favorable news does not equate with a unique price level in either (1) a model in which informed traders can choose from a continuum of quantities to purchase, or (2) one with discreet quantity purchases but where the informed traders mix their strategies independently. Hence, even if informed traders wanted to send a false signal, they have no price target to aim for with their purchases. Computational problems can also restrict the traders' knowledge about a price target: traders may not have access to all the information they need to compute future market-clearing prices.

By allowing each trader to act as an individual, in the next section, we can expand the decision range to include no action. Some of the informed may feel prices already impound their private signals; some may feel they should wait for a better price before purchasing. This generalized model should accommodate the market timing criticism of IPT.

Noncompetitive Behavior. If no individual informed trader can move prices with his purchases, but all the informed traders as a group can influence prices, do we still have a competitive market? Grossman and Stiglitz clearly feel they do; the critics of IPT would disagree. To the extent either trading group can form a self-enforcing coalition, then clearly they exert monopolistic influences on market prices. However, our analysis has shown just how difficult it may be for such a coalition to exist and succeed in extracting speculative bubble profits.

Gorton and Pennacchi (1989) describe 'imperfectly competitive rational expectations equilibrium prices' that are 'fully revealing in only two of the four states.' In contrast, no prices in the Grossman and Stiglitz (1976) model are fully revealing; the difference between noisy prices and fully revealing prices compensates the informed for their cost of acquiring information. Yet Grossman and Stiglitz state they are modeling competitive markets with asymmetric information. Gorton and Pennacchi trace the source of their price inefficiency to insider collusion.

In the model of Sections 7.3 through 7.5, the informed traders receive payoff π_{i3} if they choose low demand upon receiving a low signal. They receive payoff π_{i4} if they take part in the attempted manipulation and fail. Since $\pi_{i3} > \pi_{i4}$, each informed trader faces an incentive to deviate from the coalition. The size of the incentive varies inversely with the probability that the uninformed will buy as a feedback effect. If the uninformed are likely to mimic purchases by the informed, then individual informed traders would prefer to adhere to the coalition's strategy. When they expect the coalition will fail, because the probability of feedback buying is too low, individual informed investors would rationally choose to abandon the coalition's strategy. But if $\beta < \beta^*$, then Kuhn-Tucker condition (7.5) applies. Thus the informed traders as a group choose to bid low demand without any collusion.

If we changed the payoff structure so that $\pi_{i3} < \pi_{i4}$, then individual informed traders would have no reason to depart from the group's manipulation strategy. Assumption 5 under the condition $\pi_{i3} < \pi_{i4}$ would be superfluous. Individual informed investors would adhere to the coalition strategy by construction. As the game now stands, the speculative bubble strategy might crumble without Assumption 5.

7.8. Existence of Subjective Correlated Equilibria

If the informed and uninformed traders decide what quantity of the risky asset to purchase, rather than the probability of purchasing a fixed quantity, then Brower's Fixed Point Theorem can no longer be used to establish the existence of an equilibrium. This section shows that by imposing appropriate concavity and continuity assumptions on the payoffs in a generalized game form, we can prove the existence of a correlated equilibrium in pure strategies. Assumption 6 converts our n-player game of incomplete information into a convex game.

Assumption 6: The noncooperative n-person game satisfies the following conditions:

(a) The ith player's strategy space is a compact convex set S_i of a topological linear space E_i.

(b) The ith player's payoff $V_i(s_1,\ldots s_i,\ldots.s_n)$ is concave with respect to his own strategy variable $s_1 \in S_i$.

(c) The sum of payoffs $\sum_{i=1}^{n} V_i(s_1,\ldots,s_i,\ldots s_n)$ is continuous over the Cartesian product space $S = S_1 \otimes S_2 \otimes \cdots \otimes S_n$.

(d) For each fixed s_i, $V_i(s_1,\ldots,s_i,\ldots s_n)$ is a continuous function of the $(n\text{-}1)$-tuple $(s_1,\ldots, s_{i-1}, s_{i+1},\ldots s_n) \in S_1 \otimes \cdots \otimes S_{i-1} \otimes S_{i+1} \cdots \otimes S_n$, respectively.

For constant sum games, 6(c) is automatically fulfilled. If all the payoffs are continuous over $S_1 \otimes \cdots \otimes S_n$, then 6(c) and 6(d) are also fulfilled. Kakutani's fixed-point theorem cannot be applied to convex games since conditions 6(a) through 6(d) do not guarantee the required upper semi-continuity.

Definition 5: A *Nash equilibrium point* is an n-tuple $(\hat{s}_1,\hat{s}_2,...,\hat{s}_n) \in S$ that maximizes the s_i-function $V_i(\hat{s}_1,\hat{s}_2,...,\hat{s}_{i-1}, s_i, \hat{s}_{i+1},...,\hat{s}_n)$, at $s_i = \hat{s}_i$ for $i = 1, 2, \ldots n$.

This generalized game contains *n* players constituting both informed and uninformed traders: each individual is a player. If the informed traders mix their strategies independently, then the economy will attain a correlated equilibrium not a Nash equilibrium. Each player *i* has a subjective prior P^i, which is a probability measure on the space Ω with $\omega \in \Omega$, and an information signal σ_i about the risky asset's return $r = \eta + \epsilon$. The σ_i are correlated with η, though not the actual value.

Definition 6: A *subjective correlated equilibrium* is an *n*-tuple $(s_1,..., s_n) \in S$ such that for every individual *i*

$$\sum_{\omega\in\Omega} P^i(\omega)\ V_i[s_i(\omega),\ s_{-i}(\omega)] \geq \sum_{\omega} P^i(\omega)\ V_i[\hat{s}_i(\omega),\ s_{-i}(\omega)], \qquad (7.15)$$

for all $\hat{s}_i \in S_i$.

Note that the correlated equilibrium is only a condition on individual rationality rather than market clearing. The difference between an objective and a subjective correlated equilibrium is based on assumptions about the P^i. If the traders' priors are equal and common knowledge, as with the value of ρ_L in Sections 7.3 through 7.6, then we would have an objective correlated equilibrium. Definition 6 generalizes the agreed common knowledge prior concept to include possible heterogeneous priors.

Recall from Chapter 2 the distinction between *ex ante* optimal and *ex post* optimal allocations. The subjective correlated equilibrium only requires the traders' strategies be optimal *ex ante* to receiving their private signals. For the strategies to be optimal even after the traders have received their signals, Brandenberger and Dekel-Tabak (1987) define an *a posteriori equilibrium*, which looks like (7.15) but with the substitution $P^i(\omega\,|\,\sigma_i)$ for the prior, and presumably $s_i(\omega) \equiv s_i(\omega\,|\,\sigma_i)$ and $s_{-i}(\omega) \equiv s_{-i}(\omega\,|\,\sigma_{-i})$ for the strategies. 'Uninformed' traders receive a signal that gives them no information: actual earnings belong to the state space Ω.

Before proving the existence of a subjective correlated equilibrium for our generalized game, we must first introduce a summed expected payoff function:

$$\Phi(\hat{s}_i,s_{-i}) = \sum_{i=1}^{n} \sum_{\omega\in\Omega} P^{i}(\omega)\; V_i(s_1,s_2, \ldots, s_{i-1}, \hat{s}_i, s_{i+1}, \ldots, s_n),$$

which is also concave with respect to the n-tuple $(s_1, s_2,\ldots, s_n) \in S$.

Theorem 3: Under Assumptions 6(a) - 6(d), there exists at least one subjective correlated equilibrium point.

Proof: [Adapted from Nikaidô and Isodo (1955), p.809-10] The concavity of V_i (by Assumption 6(b)) with respect to the choice variable $\hat{s}_i$ implies $\Phi(\hat{s}_i,s_{-i})$ is concave with respect to $\hat{s}_i$. From Definition 6 and the concavity of $\Phi(\hat{s}_i,s_{-i})$, a point $s = (s_1,\ldots..s_n)$ is a subjective correlated equilibrium point if $\Phi(\hat{s}_i,s_{-i})$ is maximized at $\hat{s}_i = s_i$. We must now prove the existence of a point $s \in S$ such that $\Phi(s_i,s_{-i}) \geq \Phi(\hat{s}_i,s_{-i})$ for any $\hat{s}_i \in S_i$. Suppose to the contrary that for each $s \in S$, there exists some $\hat{s}$ such that

$$\Phi(s) = \Phi(s_i,s_{-i}) < \Phi(\hat{s}_i,s_{-i}) \qquad \textbf{(7.16)}$$

Define $G_{\hat{s}} = \{ s\!: \;\Phi(s) < \Phi(\hat{s}_i,s_{-i})\}$. Then $G_{\hat{s}}$ is open by Assumptions 6(c) and 6(d) and $S \subset \bigcup_{\hat{s}\in S} G_{\hat{s}}$ from (7.16). The compactness of S by assumption 6(a) enables us to define a set $A = \{a_1, a_2,\ldots, a_n\} \subset S$ such that $S \subset \bigcup_{i=1}^{n} G_{a_i}$. This condition implies $\Phi(s) < \underset{i}{MAX}\; \Phi(a_i,s_{-i})$ for any $s \in S$. Let $f_i(s) = MAX\; [\Phi(a_i,s_{-i}) - \Phi(s), 0]$ with $i = 1, 2,\ldots..n$. These n functions are continuous under Assumptions 6(c) and 6(d) and satisfy $f_i(s) \geq 0$ and $\sum_{i=1}^{n} f_i(s) > 0$ for any $s \in S$. The continuous mapping

$$s \rightarrow \sum_{i=1}^{n} f_i(s)\, a_i \,/\, \sum_{i=1}^{n} f_i(s)$$

maps S into the convex hull of A, $C(A)$, and therefore maps $C(A)$ into itself. Since $C(A)$ is homeomorphic to a compact convex set in an Euclidean space, Brower's Fixed Point Theorem establishes the existence of a fixed point. Let $\tilde{s}$ denote one such fixed point. Then

$$\tilde{s} = \sum_{i=1}^{n} f_i(\tilde{s}) a_i \,/\, \sum_{i=1}^{n} f_i(\tilde{s}) \in C(A) \subset S.$$

For such an i that $f_i(s) > 0$, then $\Phi(a_i, \tilde{s}_{-i}) > \Phi(\tilde{s}_i, \tilde{s}_{-i})$. Since $\Phi(s_i, s_{-i})$ is concave in s_i, it follows that $\Phi(\tilde{s}_i, \tilde{s}_{-i}) > \Phi(\tilde{s}_i, \tilde{s}_{-i})$, which is a contradiction. *Q.E.D.*

The subjective correlated equilibria of this game of incomplete information depend on how we transform the general model into particular situations. Suppose the informed traders receive (correlated) low signals along with a separate signal that says 'fleece the uninformed' α percent of the time. Essentially, we give chance three signals from which to choose: high, low and fleece, and low and don't fleece. We do not need to specify whether the uninformed correlate their random strategies.

The obvious question is whether such a correlated equilibrium exists: is it optimal for individual informed traders to obey the signal? The answer is yes; such a model could fit within the parameters of Theorem 3. Once the 'fleece the uninformed' signal is given, every informed trader is rational to obey it under particular specifications of the model's parameters. Public goods theory may have free rider problems, but apparently public pillaging models have no free raiders. Of course, we still face the knotty problem of how the pillaging informed traders realize their capital gains without tipping off the uninformed.

We will conclude this section by seeing how far we can go to model a (separating) correlated equilibrium without invoking the same pitfalls of the Bayesian Nash equilibrium approach: specifying the payoffs *a priori*, two-player model, discrete strategies, etc. Grossman and Stiglitz let λ denote the fraction of the population who choose to become informed. With n players in the model, then λn is the number of informed traders; players $\lambda n + 1$ to n are uninformed.

Assume that the informed players cooperate in attempts to speculate off the feedback effect. Suppose all the traders play m original Bayes games of incomplete information simultaneously according to some special rules. Denote these m games as $G_1, G_2, \ldots, G_m$, respectively. In game G_j, the informed and uninformed traders select respective strategies of

$$\tilde{s} = \begin{bmatrix} \tilde{s}_{1,1}, & \tilde{s}_{1,2}, & \ldots, & \tilde{s}_{1,m} \\ & \cdot & & \\ & \cdot & & \\ \tilde{s}_{\lambda n,1}, & \tilde{s}_{\lambda n,2}, & \ldots, & \tilde{s}_{\lambda n,m} \end{bmatrix} \quad \text{and} \quad s = \begin{bmatrix} s_{\lambda n+1,1}, & s_{\lambda n+1,2}, & \ldots, & s_{\lambda n+1,m} \\ & \cdot & & \\ & \cdot & & \\ s_{n,1}, & s_{n,2}, & \ldots, & s_{n,m} \end{bmatrix}.$$

The individual informed traders may choose different quantities to purchase, i.e., the $\tilde{s}$ and s notation is not meant to indicate the individuals grouped in a matrix adopt the same strategy. As outside theorists, we can fix different quantities across the individuals and label a matrix of these strategies as $\tilde{s}$ or $\bar{s}$ or whatever.

The special rules[13] then for this game are that when the informed traders choose the $\tilde{s}$ strategy and the uninformed traders choose s, the uninformed traders pay each of the λn informed traders their respective expected payoff $P^i(\omega)\, V_i[\tilde{s}_i(\omega), s_{-i}(\omega)]$, where $i = 1, 2 \ldots, \lambda n$, and $-i = \lambda n+1, \lambda n+2, \ldots\, n$, as the outcome of G_j. The informed traders pay the uninformed traders the amount

$$\sum_{j=1}^{m} V_j(s_1, s_2, \ldots, s_n) \tag{7.17}$$

as the premium for participating in these speculative feedback games. Each uninformed trader receives that portion of the amount in (7.17) that represents his own individual summed payoffs across the m games. Condensing notation, the informed traders receive a gain of $\Phi(\tilde{s},s) - \Phi(s,s)$, while the uninformed receive $\Phi(s,s) - \Phi(\tilde{s},s)$.

In our Bayesian Nash equilibrium model, we assumed $\pi_i, \pi_u > 0$, so that the uninformed have a reason to play the game. Expression (7.17) gives a statement of the premium the uninformed traders expect for agreeing to play the game. The uninformed know the informed cooperate (share their correlated signals) to maximize their own payoff. Although we have not proved it here, we suspect that the amount in (7.17) and the s strategies are tied to competitive (fair) play in informational price theory: informed buying only when the signal is good and selling only when the signal is bad. If the given n-person game is constant sum, a criterion for the existence of an equilibrium would be

$$\underset{s \in S}{MIN} \ \underset{\tilde{s} \in S}{MAX} \ \Phi(\tilde{s}, s) = C,$$

where C is the constant sum.

7.8. Conclusions and Issues for Future Research

This chapter identified three areas of concern with informational price theory (IPT): low quality vendors using high prices to lure customers, market timing decisions, and the feedback effect. Our Bayesian Nash equilibrium model of speculative behavior focused on the feedback effect generated by uninformed traders purchasing when they learn informed traders have bought.

In the process of analyzing these feedback effects, we have introduced a game theoretic analysis of speculative bubbles, which are created from fully rational, payoff-maximizing behavior on the part of all market participants. Various assumptions about the external prior probability for low earnings can eliminate the bubble equilibria, show bubbles will form with probability equal to one, or lead to occasional bubble formation. Further study of feedback effects, particularly in speculative markets, could provide rich new models that can explain factors ranging from stock market overshooting and excess volatility to dividend signals sent by firm managers.

The traditional IPT literature has not addressed individual departures from group behavior. Individual informed traders in those markets could set up side deals to sell news directly to one or more of the uninformed. The stability of the Grossman-Stiglitz equilibrium, for example, depends on achieving the optimal percentage of informed traders so that the marginal informed trader is just compensated for the cost of his information. If other traders convey this same information to the uninformed at a lower cost, then the entire information gathering mechanism will unravel or continually be in a state of disequilibrium.

In addition to deviations from group behavior, we have identified three other broad objections to the Bayesian Nash equilibrium approach to speculative bubbles. First, payoffs for investment strategies must be specified at the bottom of the extensive form game tree. Without these payoffs, players could not compute their optimal strategies, which are best responses to the other player's strategy. We also assumed that when the informed traders succeed in manipulating the uninformed, they are able to realize their capital gains (sell the asset) without their sales affecting the uninformed traders' strategy.

The two-player, high-low demand framework severely limits a realistic portrayal of financial markets. Our work has highlighted the two-player focus of the mathematics of even traditional IPT, which might go unrecognized due to the informal comments about large numbers of informed and uninformed traders. Speculative bubbles arise in the Bayesian Nash equilibrium model due to the high-low quantity constraint. Without this constraint, no unique price target exists to signal high earnings. Uninformed traders may observe a price increase and wonder if it really reflects high earnings news.

Finally, the informed traders - acting as a collusive group - influence prices. This fact tends to negate claims that IPT or the Bayes game model portrays how competitive markets operate under uncertainty. In neither model will prices fully reflect the information available in the market. The more competitive the market, the more individual informed traders face incentives to deviate from group behavior and sell their private information to the uninformed.

These combined factors mean that the feedback effect does not create significant problems for the validity of IPT. The informed traders face more difficultly in capitalizing on this feedback effect than the critics of IPT have admitted. Market timing decisions and attempts to lure customers with high prices still limit the amount of information reflected in prices.

In the generalized model of Section 7.8 with many players of each type, the resulting individual rationality condition is correlated equilibria rather than a Nash equilibrium. The multiple correlated equilibria, under specified exogenous conditions, will either be separating or pooling equilibria. The separating equilibria are in the Grossman-Stiglitz tradition of homogeneous groups. The pooling equilibrium eliminates the kind of speculative bubbles studied in this chapter.

The presence of witless noise traders in many asymmetric information models represent a principal shortcoming in the literature. We have quantified in Section 7.8 a premium that uninformed traders expect to receive for playing a game in which others collude and occasionally take advantage of them. The means by which the uninformed collect this premium comes from buying when they infer the informed have bought and earnings are actually high: no manipulation occurs.

The separating correlated equilibrium, which leads to speculative bubbles, is not unique. In fact, the equilibrium appears suspect due to the informational gymnastics required by the informed traders: they must participate in a giant, carefully-orchestrated conspiracy. It is good to know that such equilibria exist as polar cases, but other more relevant and interesting ones deserve our attention. Financial theorists should continue to look for them.

Notes

1. The *weak form* of the efficient markets hypothesis (EMH) states all information on past price movements is fully reflected in current market prices. The *semi-strong form* of the EMH states all publicly available information is impounded in prices, and the *strong form* of the EMH states all information - both publicly and privately held - is reflected in market prices.

2. Additional works in the informational price theory literature include Grossman (1976) and (1978), Kyle (1985), Grinblatt and Ross (1987), and the writings of Shiller (1990), among others.

3. See Burness, Cummings, and Quirk (1980) and Shleifer and Summers (1990).

4. Shleifer and Summers (1990), Kyle (1985), Kindleberger (1989) and others have no reluctance to introduce irrational investors into their models. Economists have traditionally objected to irrationality arguments, because they abandon the discipline's expected utility maximizing hypothesis and permit the explanation of just about any phenomenon.

5. Burness, Cummings, and Quirk (1980), p.74.

6. How ironic that the 'informed' traders are the stupid players in informational price theory. In most feedback models, uninformed traders act as witless noise traders, who continually let the informed traders exploit them.

7. Bernheim, Peleg, and Whinston (1987).

8. This chapter comes from my draft dissertation that I wrote and first presented at a workshop at the University of California, Los Angeles, back in 1984. At the time, it was the *first* game theoretic analysis of speculative bubbles and the *first* derivation of bubbles from purely rational behavior.

9. For specific values of the external parameters of the model, we can derive as a special case an equilibrium in which the informed traders always try to exploit the uninformed traders, and the uninformed may be willing to buy if the objective prior probability

of unfavorable news is sufficiently small. See Proposition 4.

10. Simply from observing an increase in the risky asset's price, uninformed traders can no longer on average infer η. A high price can now mean either a high signal (η_H), or a low signal (η_L) together with an attempted manipulation.

11. The Bayesian Nash Equilibrium in this section yields a probability that the informed will choose high demand. In one sense, this probability can be considered as a mixed strategy between high and low demand. However, since we have defined the strategy space in this section over probabilities and not over quantities demanded, a single value for the probability represents a pure strategy.

12. This section benefitted greatly from discussions I have had with Brendan O'Flaherty. He also identified the work by Nikaidô and Isodo to me. However, he bears no responsibility for any errors contained in my analysis.

13. The special rules and alternative definition of the minimax theorem are adapted from an example by Nikaidô and Isodo (1955), p.811.

References

Admati, Anat R., and Paul Pfleiderer, 'A Theory of Intraday Patterns: Volume and Price Variability,' *Review of Financial Studies*, Vol. 1:1, pp. 3-40.

Allen, Franklin, and Gary Gorton, (1993), 'Churning Bubbles,' *Review of Economic Studies*, Vol. 60, pp. 813-836.

Aumann, Robert, (1987), 'Correlated Equilibrium as an Expression of Bayesian Rationality,' *Econometrica*, Vol. 55:1, pp. 1-18.

Banerjee, Abhijit V., (1992), 'A Simple Model of Herd Behavior,' *Quarterly Journal of Economics*, Vol. 107:3, pp. 797-817.

Bernheim, B. Douglas, Bezalel Peleg, and Michael D. Whinston, (1987), 'Coalition-Proof Nash Equilibria I. Concepts,' *Journal of Economic Theory*, Vol. 42, pp. 1-12.

Blanchard, Olivier J., and Mark W. Watson, (1982), 'Bubbles, Rational Expectations, and Financial Markets,' in *Crises in the Economic and Financial Structure*, ed. by P. Wachtel, (Lexington, Mass.: Lexington Books).

Brandenburger, Adam, and Eddie Dekel-Tabak, (1987), 'Rationalizability and Correlated Equilibria,' *Econometrica*, Vol. 55:6, pp. 1391-1402.

Burness, Stuart, Ronald Cummings, and James Quirk, (1980), 'Speculative Behavior and the Operation of Competitive Markets Under Uncertainty: A Survey Article,' Staff Paper 80-11, Department of Economics, Montana State University, Bozeman.

Cutler, David M., James M. Poterba, and Lawrence H. Summers, (1989), 'What Moves Stock Prices?,' *Journal of Portfolio Management*, Vol. 15, pp. 4-12.

De Long, J. Bradford, Andrei Schleifer, Lawrence H. Summers, and Robert J. Waldmann, (1990), 'Positive Feedback Investment Strategies and Destabilizing Rational Speculation,' *Journal of Finance*, Vol. 45:2, pp. 379-395.

Fishman, Michael J., and Kathleen M. Hagerty, (1992), 'Insider

Trading and the Efficiency of Stock Prices,' *Rand Journal of Economics*, Vol. 23:1, pp. 106-122.

Friedman, Daniel, and Masanao Aoki, (1986), 'Asset Price Bubbles from Poorly Aggregated Information: A Parametric Example,' *Economic Letters*, Vol. 21, pp. 49-52.

Friedman, Daniel, and Masanao Aoki, (1992), 'Inefficient Information Aggregation as a Source of Asset Price Bubbles,' *Bulletin of Economic Research*, Vol. 44:4, pp. 251-279.

Gilles, Christian, and Stephen E. Leroy, (1990), 'Bubbles and Charges,' unpublished manuscript.

Gorton, Gary and George Pennacchi, 'Financial Intermediaries and Liquidity Creation,' *Journal of Finance*, (March 1989).

Grinblatt, Mark S. and Stephen A. Ross, (1985), 'Market Power in a Securities Market with Endogenous Information,' *Quarterly Journal of Economics*, Vol. 100, pp. 1143-1167.

Grossman, Sanford J., (1976), 'On the Efficiency of Competitive Stock Markets Where Traders Have Diverse Information,' *Journal of Finance*, Vol. 31:2, pp. 573-585.

Grossman, Sanford J., (1978), 'Further Results on the Informational Efficiency of Competitive Stock Markets,' *Journal of Economic Theory*, Vol. 18:1, pp. 81-101.

Grossman, Sanford J., (1981), 'An Introduction to the Theory of Rational Expectations Under Asymmetric Information,' *Review of Economic Studies*, Vol. 48, pp. 541-559.

Grossman, Sanford J., and Joseph E. Stiglitz, (1976), 'Informational and Competitive Price Systems,' *American Economic Review*, Vol. 66, pp. 246-254.

Harsanyi, John C., (1967), 'Games with Incomplete Information Played by Bayesian Players, Parts I-III,' *Management Science*, Vol. 14, pp. 159-189, 320-33, 486-502.

Hellwig, Martin, and Wolfgang Leininger, (1987), 'On the Existence of

Subgame-Perfect Equilibrium in Infinite-Action Games of Perfect Information,' *Journal of Economic Theory*, Vol. 43, pp. 55-75.

Kindleberger, Charles P., (1989), *Manias, Panics, and Crashes*, (New York: Basic Books).

King, Ronald R., Vernon L. Smith, and Arlington W. Williams, and Mark Van Boening (1993),'The Robustness of Bubbles and Crashes in Experimental Stock Markets,' in *Nonlinear Dynamics and Evolutionary Economics*, ed. by R. Day and P. Chen (Oxford: Oxford University Press).

Kyle, Albert S., (1985), 'Continuous Auctions and Insider Trading,' *Econometrica*, Vol. 53, pp. 1315-1335.

Kyle, Albert S., (1989), 'Informed Speculation with Imperfect Competition,' *Review of Economic Studies*, Vol. 56, pp. 317-356.

Leach, John, 'Rational Speculation,' (1991), *Journal of Political Economy*, Vol. 99:1, pp. 131-144.

Lehman, Bruce, (1990), 'Fads, Martingales, and Market Efficiency,' *Quarterly Journal of Economics*, Vol. 55:1, pp. 1-28.

Nikaidô, Hukukane, and Kazuo Isodo, (1955), 'Note on Noncooperative Convex Games,' *Pacific Journal of Mathematics*, pp. 807-815,

O'Flaherty, Brendan, (1987), 'Guessing Better than the Crowd How the Crowd Will Behave: Conventions, Beauty Contests, and Bubbles,' Discussion Paper #347, Department of Economics, Columbia University, New York.

Selten, Robert, (1975), 'Reexamination of the Perfectness Concept for Equilibrium Points in Extensive Games,' *International Journal of Game Theory*, Vol. 4, pp. 25-55.

Shiller, Robert J., (1989), *Market Volatility*, (Cambridge: MIT Press).

Shleifer, Andrei, and Lawrence H. Summers, (1990), 'The Noise Trader Approach,' *Journal of Economic Perspectives*, Vol. 4:2, pp. 19-33.

Simon, Leo K., (1987), 'Local Perfection,' *Journal of Economic Theory*,

Vol. 43, pp. 134-156.

Smith, Vernon L., Gerry L. Suchanek, and Arlington W. Williams, (1988), 'Bubbles, Crashes, and Endogenous Expectations in Experimental Spot Asset Markets,' *Econometrica*, Vol. 56:5, pp. 1119-1151.

Subrahmanyam, Avanidhar, (1991a), 'Risk Aversion, Market Liquidity, and Price Efficiency,' *Review of Financial Studies*, Vol. 4:3, pp. 417-441.

Subrahmanyam, Avanidhar, (1991b), 'A Theory of Trading in Stock Index Futures,' *Review of Financial Studies*, Vol. 4, pp. 17-51.

Thompson, Rex, (1978), 'The Information Content of Discounts and Premiums on Closed-End Fund Shares,' *Journal of Financial Economics*, Vol. 6, pp. 151-186.

Wang, Jiang, (1993), 'A Model of Intertemporal Asset Prices Under Asymmetric Information,' *Review of Economic Studies*, Vol. 60, pp. 249-282.

Weiss, Kathleen, Kenneth Lehn, and David Malmquist, (1989), 'The Post-Offering Price Performance of Closed-End Funds,' Office of Economic Analysis working paper, Securities and Exchange Commission, 450 Fifth Street NW, Washington, D.C., 20549.

Comment

This chapter explores one of the many different ways of arguing that security prices are based on something other than fundamentals. The chief conclusion is that this particular attempt doesn't work very well, but that doesn't imply that no method is capable of showing that serious deviations from fundamentals can occur.

The question is important. Adam Smith's claim about the capitalist system was that it allocated capital well: the claim had nothing to do with the static Pareto optimality that dominates modern welfare theorems. Even today, claims of the superiority of capitalism over socialism are, for 99% of the world, claims about growth, not claims about static efficiency. Growth depend on allocating capital. The system isn't called capitalism incorrectly. Investigations of bubbles and speculative behavior challenge the most fundamental and deep-rooted claims for any kind of superiority of the capitalist system.

One of the most pervasive difficulties in developing models where speculation matters are multiple equilibria. Typically, game theoretic models of security markets end up with several equilibria, one of which is the fundamental equilibrium and one (or more) of which is a speculative equilibrium. My 1987 paper is a good example of this sort of result, as are the subjective correlated equilibria in the latter part of the chapter. One of the great strengths of the first model in this chapter is that the speculative equilibrium is unique. In the study of speculative equilibria, too much attention has been paid to existence, and not enough to uniqueness.

What's so important about uniqueness? As Jagdish Bhagwati argues in a slightly different context, multiple equilibria say something about modelling not the world; they are signs of incomplete modelling, not of an undetermined world. In reality only one thing happens. From the existence of multiple equilibria one can draw inferences about the logical structure of a model; one cannot draw inferences about the reality the model is trying to capture. Having a calculator that doesn't take square roots does not entitle you to assert that the square root of seven is five or that it is indeterminate.

An example with a model not usually thought of as having multiple equilibria can make the point clearer. The theory of human capital is compatible with the president of General Motors wearing a red tie and also compatible with his wearing a blue tie; so there are (at least) two equilibria. We conclude from the existence of these multiple equilibria that the theory of human capital is not very useful if we are interested in tie color — but no one ever claimed it was. We do not conclude that the president's tie color is indeterminate or that it is purple because nothing in the theory of human capital, a very good theory, rules that out. We conclude only that to answer tie color questions another model should be used. The same conclusion should be reached whenever multiple equilibria are encountered.

Brendan O'Flaherty
Department of Economics
Columbia University